BOTH SIDES

Both Sides

THE STORY OF REVELATION

by

GABRIEL MORAN

PAULIST PRESS
New York/Mahwah, N.J.

Library of Congress Cataloging-in-Publication Data

Moran, Gabriel.
    Both sides : the story of Revelation / by Gabriel Moran.
        p. cm.
    Includes bibliographical references and index.
    ISBN 0-8091-4105-1
    1. Revelation. I. Title.
    BT127.3 .M67 2002
    231.7'4—dc21

                                                2002004481

Published by Paulist Press
997 Macarthur Boulevard
Mahwah, New Jersey 07430

www.paulistpress.com

Printed and bound in the
United States of America

Contents

Preface

THE QUESTION OF REVELATION has interested me for almost forty years. When I began writing on this topic, many people seemed to assume that it belonged within Protestant theology. The Second Vatican Council, however, gave revelation a prominent place in Roman Catholic discussions. During the late 1960s, revelation was a much-discussed topic among Catholic educators, missionaries, and social activists, as well as theologians. With the waning of the "spirit of Vatican II," the dynamic charge given to the discussion of revelation also waned. Protestant and Catholic theology had moved closer together, particularly because of collaborative study of the Bible. Revelation was a concept implied in biblical studies, but there seemed not much else to say on the matter.

Between 1963 and 1972 I published four books on the issue of revelation. At that point I thought I had written whatever I had to say on the matter. And yet I have constantly been brought back to the topic from a peculiar range of sources. Whether I was studying mysticism, epistemology, seventeenth-century science, modern educational theory, or international ethics, I found myself bothered by the unresolved question of revelation as an intelligible and defensible idea. I found myself pulled back into exploring a theme that I had intended to leave behind.

There is no method ready-at-hand for studying revelation. It is a concept that Christianity needs but that Christian theology cannot directly study. When I published a book called *Theology of Revelation*, I was aware that the title was illogical. What is presupposed by theology cannot be a part of theology. Despite the layout of the book, my actual starting place was education. My question was what the term revelation must mean if the experience of Christians and the work of education are to make sense. That approach may seem strange, but it seems to me a way to begin exploring the wide range of sources needed for this topic.

In recent years the question of revelation seems to have been relegated to a small band of philosophers. The general lack of interest in the issue could be indicative of a belief that there is no longer a problem. Or it could mean there is a big problem that Christian writers and church officials would prefer not to talk about. In either case, I think the meaning of revelation remains central to the present shape of church life and to conflicts within the churches.

At the beginning of the twenty-first century the problem of method for studying this question is more complex than ever. In the first five chapters of this book I have put together the findings of many historians and other scholars whose work is directly or indirectly related to the issue of revelation. My findings there allow and to some extent support what I think is the most intelligible and practical meaning of revelation. My approach is to follow the strange history of "revelation"—that is, the word itself. Or more exactly, I follow what happened when the single Greek word was translated by two Latin words that come into English as "revelation" and "apocalypse." As often happens in translation, two words that presumably have the same meaning at the start can develop very different connotations. My intention is to find a meaning of the term revelation that incorporates the meaning of apocalypse.

In the last three chapters and the conclusion, I develop the implications of a meaning of revelation that is supported by the historical survey. Although I do not constantly refer to revelation throughout these three chapters, each chapter is articulated as a practical embodiment of the meaning of revelation. In the first of these chapters, I treat responsibility as the ethical translation of revelation. In the last chapter, I take the relation of teaching–learning as the model for the relation of divine revelation and human response. And the middle chapter entitled "The Logic of Revelation" is a direct attempt to rethink the basis of Christianity in relation both to Jewish religion and modern secular thought.

The Christian church will never have a consistent and comprehensive meaning of revelation until Christians have an extensive conversation on the topic with Jews and Muslims. I would have liked to include more than I have on Jewish and Muslim views of revelation. But any serious attention to either Jewish or Muslim histories would require at least another book. Nonetheless, because Christianity arose from ancient Jewish religion and has retained a relation to Judaism throughout the centuries, I have made occasional references to Jewish history and Jewish religion. One of the main conclusions of this book is the need for Jewish–Christian conversation beyond what has happened in the twentieth century. As soon as possible the conversation should include Muslim voices. In a few places, there is already a dialogue, but the world's conversation is still at the beginning stage.

Another main theme of this book concerns the metaphor for knowing that is implied by the term revelation. I question whether the Christian church made a wise choice in importing a visual metaphor for human knowledge of the divine. That is, revelation as a claim that the truth has been unveiled, that what was once in darkness is now in the light, seems to skew Christian life toward the speculative and toward the claim to possess secrets about God. But whether or not another term might have been more appropriate, I take "revelation" to be an important and permanent part of the Christian story.

I think the mystical strand of Christian, Jewish, and Muslim religions has always sensed a problem with the fact that revelation is a visual metaphor. For the mystic, "revelation" is a minimal claim, the denial that darkness is final. But the mystical alternative to darkness is not clarity of sight; it is the claim that we are to search for God and be open to God with all of our bodily senses. Albert Schweitzer thought that the world was in need of either an ethical mysticism or a mystical ethic. I think much of the twentieth century's attempt to go "beyond enlightenment" illustrates Schweitzer's point. But lest that search end in the darkness of despair, we need to consider the strengths and the limitations of revelation as a metaphor for human knowledge of the divine. How did that idea evolve and where does it stand today?

PART ONE

1

Is There a Problem?

C AN ANYTHING NEW be said about revelation? More important, is there any widespread interest in discussing the topic at all? My answer to the first question is that it is probably impossible to say anything entirely new on the topic of revelation, and this book does not claim to do so. Our own time, however, may be ripe for retrieving some old ideas, eliminating some unhelpful modern terms, and proposing a few well-placed distinctions.

The answer to the second question—Is anyone interested?—is yes, although much of the interest may seem peculiar. That is, if one goes to the Internet web sites on revelation or to a bookstore's section on revelation, the vast majority of entries refer to one thing: the book of Revelation. In contrast, if one looks up the entry "revelation" in encyclopedias of religion or in theological dictionaries, the book of Revelation receives, at most, a passing reference.

The question of interest in this topic, therefore, cannot be answered before clarifying whether the term revelation refers to a single topic. A question always presupposes the context of a community of speakers for whom the question makes sense. The answer to a question will vary depending on the community in which the respondent is located. A person in today's secular society might not have any specific reference for the term revelation and consequently little interest in its meaning. A Jew or a Muslim will likely be familiar with "revelation" and perhaps with a range of meanings within Jewish or Muslim traditions. But if a Christian is asked about the meaning of "revelation," the answer will likely presuppose one of two disparate histories. While I do not wish to exclude secular, Jewish, and Muslim answers to the question of revelation, the split within Christian history is the complex story that will be the main focus of this book.

On one side of this story, Christian theologians presuppose a meaning of revelation as the basis of their theology. The typical entry in a theological dictionary defines revelation as "the corpus of truth about

3

Himself which God discloses. . . ."[1] Surprisingly, the literature that analyzes this meaning of "revelation" is not very extensive. It seems to be assumed that the question of revelation was settled some centuries ago. If that is the case, then another book on the topic would be superfluous.

On the other side of this story, the book of Revelation, also known as the Apocalypse, has spawned an avalanche of writing. This book, which concludes the Christian New Testament, is favorite reading for people who are given to prophesying the future, especially dire events in the future. Because the symbol of a thousand years is central to the book of Revelation, interest in revelation/apocalypse has been especially intense at the beginning of the new millennium. One commentator notes that "we are arguably in the throes of the most intense period of apocalyptic activity in recent history."[2] Numerous popular books and many scholarly studies have recounted the history of millennial movements, the meaning of the book of Revelation, and the expected end of the world.[3] If there is prolific writing on this meaning of revelation, then here again another book seems superfluous.

What would not be superfluous is a book that fills the gap between these two literatures. The two sides of revelation's history are seldom related because they are not seen to be part of the same story. The split is embodied in the two words "revelation" and "apocalypse." Both terms translate the same Greek term *apokalypsis,* but the two English words have very different connotations. Our English words continue a split that was present in Latin between *revelatio* and *apocalypsis.* Starting in the second century, these two words went their separate ways. An understanding of why this split occurred and why it remains a dangerous division is crucial for Christianity's health and for its neighbors' safety.

This twofold topic is especially important for the United States, which was founded on an uneasy alliance between rationalistic thinkers who subscribed to an eighteenth-century version of revelation and evangelical Christians who had a strongly apocalyptic orientation. Liberal Christian theology with its assumed meaning of revelation has generally had a good working relation with secular culture's science and technology. Some people would say that the relation is too cozy. In contrast, the apocalyptic element has had an uneasy relation to secular culture. Periodically, apocalyptic tendencies burst to the surface when groups such as the Branch Davidians or Heaven's Gate engage in activities that grab the attention of the country. Less obvious but more important is the apocalyptic element just below the surface of domestic and international policies of the United States. A constant flow of books have titles that begin with *The End of . . . , Last Chance for . . . , A Whole New . . . .* The roots of an apocalyptic attitude run deep in the United States. Scholars seldom note this fact when they puzzle over outbursts of violence and a continuing strain of irrationality which has not been eliminated by more science. Rational enlightenment and apocalyptic impulse continue to form an uneasy alliance in the United States.

"Revelation" is a common word that can be found in the daily newspaper's discussions of art, business, or politics ("In a new revelation from the White House today . . ."). It nearly always means that some dark secret has suddenly come to light. The veil has been removed; what had been hidden is now open to public scrutiny. The word revelation is used both for the act of revealing and for what is revealed. Once the revealer has revealed the secret, the revelation (the what) becomes fixed in the past.

Christian theologians are generally uneasy about examining revelation, if they examine it at all. Since the idea is assumed to be a premise of Christian theology, rather than a part of theology proper, the hope is that philosophy is taking care of it. Philosophers in recent times, however, with few exceptions, have wanted no part of such an inquiry. If the term revelation had disappeared entirely from Christian theology, that might not have been a problem. But Christian writing still assumes that the term is meaningful so that it pops out at crucial moments. Thus, when Christians argue about homosexuality, women's ordination, or wifely submission by citing text against text, the parties assume that somewhere, somehow there is something called (Christian) revelation.

"Apocalypse" is a less commonly used word, but its contemporary meaning is widely understood. It refers to a catastrophe of cosmic proportions, a fiery destruction beyond all measure. Hollywood has had a hand in popularizing the word, especially in movies of the last two decades. Today the term apocalyptic is casually used for all kinds of threatening or disastrous events.

The study of apocalyptic/apocalypticism constitutes a large body of scholarship. In fact, there are really three discrete areas in the study of apocalypticism: (1) the term can refer to a genre of Jewish and Christian literature: several dozen works are identified as apocalypses, the most famous example of them being the book of Revelation; (2) the term apocalyptic is used within Christian theology, most often as an adjective before eschatology (the study of last things); and (3) the term is also used by historians and social scientists to describe a wide range of rebellious social movements that have religious motivation.[4]

In referring to apocalypse/apocalyptic I am, on the one hand, obviously dependent on the scholarship of all three of these areas. On the other hand, I do not wish to locate this study within any one of the three areas. I am interested in how "apocalyptic" took on literary, theological, and social-science meanings. Part of the ambiguity in today's use of "apocalyptic" is that it is cut off from "revelation." That is, what eventually became the main story line of apocalypse/apocalyptic in Christian history is not recognized as being in the story at all.

The split in the meaning of revelation/apocalypse holds the key to several paradoxes in Christianity. How can the same term be used for the whole Bible and at the same time for one book, the concluding book, of the Bible? Why does liberal Christian theology have almost nothing to say about the book of Revelation, while the right wing of Christianity is devoted to almost nothing else? How did "apocalypse" come to mean a destruction of everything? I think there are answers for these questions, but a search for them requires stepping back from the well-worn paths of modern Christian theology.

In this book my aim is to open the possibility of a new conversation, one that does not banish either left or right of Christianity but is also not limited to that range of views. What I offer are a few simple changes of language that would make possible a different discussion. I describe the approach in this book as an educational one. I draw on history, philosophy, theology, and any other source that might lead to an understanding of revelation/apocalypse. The last chapter of this book is explicitly on education. It deals with teaching–learning as a metaphor for revelation and with several writers in history who took an educational approach to the religious meaning of revelation.

Each of the eight chapters of this book is an educational journey in which I try to puzzle out the meaning of revelation. I do not begin with radical doubt and a rejection of the past. On the contrary, I begin with respect for the past, especially the deep past of our most important vocabulary. Like a child first encountering the buzz of human language, I am interested in why the words mean what they do. Who says this is what "revelation" means? Why and how has the word changed its meaning? What about inconsistencies in its usage? Suppose we play with the word in another way?

REFLECTING ON LANGUAGE

Some initial reflection on the general topic of language may be helpful here; it is a topic I return to repeatedly. I am interested in the meaning of words. I am not much interested in definition, that is, someone's decision about the right or proper meaning of a term. In trying to get a new conversation, one in which previously excluded voices can be heard, one's initial stance has to be antidefinitional. It is easy to define a word, that is, set limits to its meaning. It takes more effort to resist definitions.

Any small dictionary provides the wonderful illusion that each word has a correct meaning. In contrast, the *Oxford English Dictionary* provides a long list of meanings, showing how the word has been used over the centuries. If you are looking for the definition of a word, the *OED* is likely to be overwhelming and unhelpful. But in looking for the wide range of a word's meanings, including meaning seemingly forgotten, the *OED* is invaluable.

If someone wants to know the *correct* meaning of a word, there may be no answer, at least apart from a particular context. Two points, however, should be kept in mind. First, one meaning of a word may be better than another, and some meanings are simply incorrect. We do correct a child or a non-native speaker if he or she has misunderstood a word. Beyond the basic, acceptable meaning of terms, an educator tries to bring out a more richly textured meaning to the words. Theoretically, anyone can advocate that any word can mean anything. But practically speaking, if one is all alone in the meaning that is given to a word, one will be judged wrong. Suppose I get two friends or two dozen friends to agree with me about the meaning of a term. Do I now have a correct meaning? Possibly I am on the way to that position, but I would need some connection with the history of the term's usage.

That brings me to the second point. A word's etymology, its original coinage, is always helpful in deciding how to use a term. The etymology is usually not conclusive but always has to be respected. The philosopher J. L. Austin wrote that "a word never—well, hardly ever—shakes off its etymology."[5] I think Austin could have left out his qualifying phrase. Even when etymology seems to have been "shaken off," the original meaning still lurks in the wings waiting to be brought to center stage by poet, storyteller, or philosopher.

The meanings of a word thus have to be explored through the history of its usage. That history leads up to a geography of meanings, the range of current uses that are dependent on the past. When the poet, storyteller, or philosopher seems to be coining a new meaning, he or she is usually digging down into the past. Otherwise, the poem, story, or philosophy is strangled by its own jargon or triviality.[6]

On the basis of the history and geography of "revelation," I will propose an adequate meaning for today. But a speaker or writer cannot bring about change in just one word. Each word is embedded in patterns from the past and a pattern in the present. Touching one important word reverberates outward to surrounding language.[7] While I am concentrating on the single word revelation, I am not unmindful of its connection to the rest of language. I can only suggest the larger patterns of change implied in a shift of meaning for revelation. The chapters in the second half of this book (chapters six to eight) exemplify some of the patterns needed to sustain the proposed use of "revelation."

The biggest problem in writing a book on such a large topic is that most of the meaning is excluded before the exploration begins. That happens not because the author *intends* to exclude the meaning but simply because ordinary usage has fixed patterns that, if writer and reader do not notice, limit the term to only part of its meaning. I am trying to address the whole question of "revelation" without any modifiers (for example,"Christian") being assumed.

I call attention to two major dialogues that accompany anyone's choice to explore "revelation": (1) the interrelation of the major religions that have used the term; and (2) the relation of religious and secular uses.

By choosing the term revelation I have located this study between the two most commonly assumed genres of religious writing. The usual choice for writers on religion is either to encompass all of religion by an ambitious survey of humanity or else to write within a clearly defined territory, such as Christian theology, Talmudic commentary, or Islamic law. "Revelation" offers an interesting alternative: It implies a conversation among three great religions. This conversation should not be closed to others, but the three religions that trace themselves to Abraham have given a centrality to the term that is not evident elsewhere.

A Christian (Jew, Muslim) has no right to discuss revelation as if the term were entirely under the control of Christian (Muslim, Jewish) sources. Of course, one can write a polemic, denouncing the other two religions as false. But few writers today wish to do that. Instead, they simply neglect to consider the historical fact that "revelation" belongs to three religious traditions. Although an explicit dialogue is not always possible, dialogue has to be feasible in the language used. For example, if Christian writers say, as they often do, that Jews and Christians have the same view of revelation—except for Christ—any serious dialogue is abruptly terminated before the range of similarities and differences have begun to be explored.

The second major dialogue entailed by choosing to explore "revelation" is the relation of religious and secular meanings. One is faced with trying to comprehend the geography of nonreligious uses that can be found every day on television, in newspapers, or walking down the street.

The term revelation had a philosophical and religious history before Christianity adopted it. That original meaning did not get eliminated by Christianity's attempt to control the meaning. The religious use of a term has an inbuilt tension. A religious use tries to bring out a more than ordinary meaning while not completely obscuring the ordinary uses. A word that has nothing but religious meaning cannot resonate through a person's thinking, behavior, and whole way of life.

In Christianity, words such as redemption, salvation, sacrament, grace may have only a tenuous connection to the daily vocabulary of the Christian. The christianizing of these terms may have been overly successful. Every technical term, however, need not be immediately translatable into casual everyday exchanges. Some terms at the root of theology—revelation has been one of those—need a nonreligious or secular meaning to be operative. The issue is not one of limiting the religious meaning by what is assumed to be a secular meaning. Instead, the religious meaning can be enlivened and enriched by exploring the secular meaning(s). Recognizing the strengths and limitations in the secular meaning of the term might suggest strategies for the religious use of the term and for supplementary terms to support its use.

At present, we seem to be on the threshold of a new conversation between religion and science. The term revelation can be a large stumbling block to any such conversation. But a history of the secular and religious meanings of the term might remove much of the obstruction. It is even possible that "revelation" could be a bridge of understanding between science and religion. To sustain this last claim would require an exploration beyond what I can undertake here. I am only trying to overcome an obstacle to the beginning of the conversation.

The title of this book, *Both Sides: The Story of Revelation*, indicates the range of exploration. My aim is to provide a basic grammar, that is, I wish to show that some ways of speaking are better than others and that there are ways of speaking that do not work because they are too narrow, inconsistent, or lack sufficient support from history. Because I am trying to tell a twofold story, the subtitle could be "the story of revelation/apocalypse." While at the beginning of the story it often makes sense to refer to revelation/apocalypse, my aim is to show an integration of these two terms. In referring to the story of revelation, I am always mindful that the connotations of "apocalypse" have to be included in philosophical and theological discussions of the meaning of revelation.

I considered using the title *Religious Revelation*, indicating my intent to explore mainly, but not exclusively, the religious dimensions of the term. While there are hundreds of books with the titles of *Revelation*,

Divine Revelation, or *Christian Revelation,* the title *Religious Revelation* is almost unknown. I decided against referring to religious revelation in the title because one of the theses in this book is that every adjective before "revelation" is suspect. I do not claim that an adjective can never be validly used, but in a religious use of the term every adjective is to be challenged. If in Christian, Jewish, and Muslim speech revelation is a relation between divine and human, then reduction of that ultimacy to an object or thing needs resisting. Any adjective pushes in the direction of setting up an object separate from other objects. My use of the adjective religious would have been intended to indicate a dimension of the term's meaning, but that usage could instead convey that I was referring to one kind of thing called "religious revelation" in contrast to other things that are "secular revelations."

A similar problem exists with the phrase "divine revelation." Does the phrase mean a revelation is from God (as opposed to those that are not)? Or does it mean that the divine is attained or available through revelation? I do not wish to exclude either that God is the agent of revelation or that God is met within revelation. But employing the adjective "divine" before beginning the inquiry into revelation can be presumptuous and segregating.

I concentrate on the Christian interpretation of "revelation," leaving to others more competent than I to discuss Jewish and Muslim interpretations. Even with this restriction, the topic of revelation/apocalypse is unmanageable in a single volume. There are scholarly studies of revelation/apocalypse in the second century B.C.E., in Jewish mysticism, in the Christian Middle Ages, or in seventeenth-century England. Such studies depend on understanding individual authors: John of Patmos, Augustine of Hippo, John Calvin, Nicholas Cusanus, John Locke, Gotthold Lessing, or hundreds of other prominent names. Is there a place for a book that proposes to study the whole topic? Only if the author can modestly claim to have located a couple of key spots that might make the topic come alive for a general reader. I lay claim only to setting an overall context, an enterprise that does not substitute for carefully limited historical research but might connect some of that scholarship to personal lives and religious organizations today.

REVELATION AS PRESENT

The historical split that I describe in the following chapters is between a "revelation" that is oriented to the past and an "apocalypse" that looks to the future. A healing of that split would require a revelation/apocalypse firmly set within the present. Such a use of language would require considerable change in Christian writing, but it would not be a complete novelty. The mystical strand of Christianity affirms the principle that the One who is beyond all names has to be listened for today.[8] The "word of God" is always spoken in the present. This principle would include the demand that a Christian interpretation of revelation be always aware of Jewish and Muslim interpretations of the same revelation.

This principle—revelation is present—far from rejecting the past can affirm the whole Christian tradition. A conservative Christianity should not be a defense of isolated statements from the first, fourth, or sixteenth centuries. This book is conservative toward all two thousand years of Christian tradition, the visual and the nonvisual parts, the verbal and the nonverbal. The statement that revelation is present has been made numerous times, but the statement is nearly always contradicted by surrounding statements. My aim is to show that there is some historical basis for revelation as a present reality and to develop language required for speaking in a way consistent with that use.

The statement that revelation as a religious term should only be used to refer to the present may seem to some people to be a well-worn piety. Do not the Christian liturgy and numerous books of prayer and meditation say that God speaks through the daily events of one's life and the church's proclaiming of scripture? For other readers, however, the formula that God speaks only in the present may seem to be a blatant rejection of biblical revelation, Christian doctrine, church authority, and the unsurpassable importance of Jesus of Nazareth. The theme of *present*, if it is to be more than a pietistic formula, does have to challenge many of the customary ways that Christian theology has referred to Bible, doctrine, authority, and Jesus.

The most contentious word in the above statement is not *present* but *only*. If one were to say that God is revealed *also* in the present, there would be little objection. Christian theology developed ways to handle that claim, for example, the distinction between public and private revelations. Within that distinction, the claim to a present (and, therefore, private) revelation, must always be tested against the public revelation in the past. Within Catholic Christianity that public revelation is preserved and safeguarded by the bishops' authority. In Protestant Christianity the present, private revelation is always to be judged by biblical revelation.

In our dominant image of time, the present is a point that divides past from future. The past is a series of points to the left of the present; the future is a series of points to the right. In the image of time that I wish to employ, the present is not a point, nor does the present exclude the past. The temporal present arises out of the presence of persons to each other. The past can be discovered within that meaning of the present. To say that revelation is always in the present is to say that the present can include the past but not vice-versa.

If my thesis requires transforming our standard image of time, then is not the whole attempt quixotic? Can we possibly reappropriate and live by some poetic or primitive notion of time? In response to that objection, I would note two qualifications concerning our ordinary picture of time. First, nearly everyone at some time notices that our standard image of time involves self-contradictions. The past does not really disappear behind us; the past remains as a powerful influence in the present. And the future does not come forward to confront us; the future does not yet exist.

Second, when people grapple with great historical happenings or personal crises, they instinctively reach for other images and metaphors of time than a line with points to the left and to the right of the present. We might, for example, speak of time slowing down, speeding up, or standing still.[9] Mostly these are unsuccessful attempts to escape from an image of time that fails in practice. One may seriously wonder whether it is possible to get satisfactory images and metaphors of time; nevertheless, Christian, Jewish, and Muslim religions require such a search.

Puzzling over the nature of time is not just a modern preoccupation. Augustine is often cited as the first thinker to grapple with the nature of time and to have worked out a philosophy of history. But the issue is already prominent in the writings of the New Testament. Paul, Luke, John, and the author of the letter to the Hebrews sought to relate their story of divine activity to the temporal flow of life. Each writer was aware that what came to be called "revelation" could be neither an atemporal object nor a mere selection of temporal occurrences. How could past, present, and future be affirmed together? Paul was the most consciously aware of the problem. He debated on two fronts those who would locate a revelation exclusively in the past and those who would collapse a difference between present and future. Paul's reflection on Jesus' resurrection in 1 Corinthians 15 reflects that tension, affirming a continuity of the past within the present, while not short-circuiting a relation to the future.

The question of time is related to a simple but crucial question: What "kind of thing" is revelation? I have referred to revelation as present, but as a present what? One response is to say that it is not any kind of thing, that the term revelation points to a breakthrough beyond human kinds of things.[10] That is, revelation refers to divine activity and our language obviously fails when we try to describe God. Some term, however, will inevitably be used to convey the kind of thing suggested by the word revelation. Even if one says that revelation is "divine activity," there is a question of which activity in human experience is analogous to it. As soon as one says "revelation is ____," one has attributed a limitation to God; such is the nature of human language. The task is not to find the one right term that expresses what revelation is; rather, it is to find a term that is both comprehensive and also open to further enrichment of understanding.

THEOLOGICAL STANDOFF

A few comments on twentieth-century Christian theology will illustrate the inherent difficulty of finding an adequate way to address this question. An example of language that is regularly attacked as too limiting is "propositional revelation." The phrase seems to suggest that revelation is a set of statements or propositions. Although this view is sometimes attributed to ancient and medieval Christianity, the phrase "propositional revelation" was born of the nineteenth-century defense of the Bible. Earlier periods of Christianity spoke of "revealed truths," but that phrase allowed some maneuverability in relating divine truths and human language.

Propositional revelation, in contrast, seems to lead straight to what the twentieth century named "fundamentalism," a belief that a certain set of statements has been deposited into history by miraculous, divine intervention. For nearly everyone who accepts the tools of modern scholarship, this belief has seemed indefensible. But while "propositional revelation" has been an easy target to attack, opposition to that idea has not produced a consistent and comprehensive alternative.

The favorite alternative in twentieth-century theology seems to be that God reveals God, that is, instead of God revealing propositions, God reveals himself.[11] That claim is seemingly invulnerable to attack. Who among Christian writers can reject the claim that it is God who is revealed by God. But posited as an alternative to propositions, God's self as the only object of "reveal" says both too much and too little. It says too much in that God's "self" as the object of "reveal" has little basis in the Old Testament, the New Testament, and the church fathers. One could claim that the *idea* of self-revelation is implied in these writings; a good case can be made for this implication. But then self-revelation says too little; it says nothing about how the self is revealed, which is the nub of the problem. By opposing self-revelation to propositional revelation, the clearest thing affirmed is that propositions are *excluded*. But might the abandonment of propositions be itself a severe limitation?

An underlying problem here and a main issue throughout this book is that "revelation" may not have been the wisest choice of a term with which to point to this ultimacy in human life. In ordinary usage, "revelation" has a quite narrow meaning. We do not use it as a general description for the communicating of knowledge. We use it when there is a secret hidden from one or all. An agent dis-closes or unveils a secret. Ordinarily, "revelation" is used when there is a revealer, a secret revealed, and a receiver. The agent can be said to reveal something about himself or herself in the revealing, but any self-revelation, whether profound or superficial, takes place through, in, and with the action of revealing something.[12]

Much of what Christian theology tries to do with "revelation" goes counter to this ordinary usage. In opposing self-revelation to propositional revelation and in grappling with the question of time, Christian writers confront dilemmas inherent in the metaphor of revelation. Revelation has a strongly visual meaning, not only in first-century Greek but in twenty-first-century English, French, or German. One cannot simply decide that in religious uses of the term the nonvisual aspects of truth and being will also be included. One can issue decrees or stipulations, but metaphors do not change accordingly.

The attempt to subsume oral/aural aspects of Christianity under the term revelation has never succeeded, a failure that is perhaps fortunate. Although speaking is usually involved in the revelation of human secrets, revelation involves elements other than speech and in some instances can be perfectly speechless (as, for example, a smile or a frown). Conversely, speech has dozens of purposes and forms that have nothing to do with the ordinary meaning of revelation. If one assumes that speaking is only a form of revelation or a means of revelation, most of the possibilities of language are collapsed into one narrow format. That was the problem with the use of "propositional revelation." It assumed that God could only speak in one way. The reactions against propositional revelation, instead of exploring other forms of speaking, have often been wary of the idea of God speaking at all. The idea that God speaks is audacious, but it is at the heart of the Christian, as well as the Jewish and Muslim religions.[13]

By choosing "self-revelation" in contrast to "propositional revelation," Christian theologians tried to emphasize God's activity instead of a fixed object. But the result was still mainly visual. The "mighty acts" of God's self-revelation occurred in the distant past. What exists in the present are biblical and doctrinal statements by which these acts are known. Thus, talking about "revelation through history" as the dynamic solution to the question of revelation only led into complicated debates about the meaning of "history."[14]

In back of most of the twentieth-century debates about revelation is the towering figure of Karl Barth (1868–1968). Barth is famous for his use of "Word of God" and also for the centrality of revelation.[15] I suggested above that far from being synonymous, these two ideas are in considerable tension. Barth's way of resolving the tension is to apply both of them to Jesus Christ, who is Word of God and revelation of God. From that focus, the "word of God" is derivatively applied to the Bible and church proclamation. The prophets and apostles are said to be the direct witnesses of revelation, but their writings are derivatively the word of God. It seems to me that this way of speaking subordinates word of God to the visual connotations of revelation. The divine has been *shown* in one strip of space and time: "God's revelation is Jesus Christ, the Son of God."[16] Although this revelation is the self-revelation of God, "our relationship to the revelation of God is indirect. The Word waits for us in the words of the prophets and apostles."[17]

Although Barth distinguished his position from that of fundamentalism, he refers to revelation being contained "in the book." I think either he is inconsistent or else he unwittingly gives away the kind of thing revelation is by saying that "what we have come to know as revelation in the Christian sense is to be found in a book, in the book of the Old and New Testaments."[18] Revelation here becomes an object from the past; the only direct witnesses to revelation are in the distant past. As with Luther and Calvin, the word of God in Barth is to come alive in the church's preaching, but his use of revelation weights its meaning toward the past. Revelation was once an event of unveiling; it is now a thing of the past, available today as mediated by words.

<hr>

RESITUATING THE QUESTION

My brief excursion into Christian theology is meant only to indicate that there is no simple resolution of the question. I sympathize with Barth's attempt to straddle the conflicting metaphors of revelation and word of God. I think a revelation, which is anchored in the tradition of the past but brought to bear in preaching, can be a powerful challenge to the contemporary world. Nonetheless, I wish to argue that the focus has to be the present, a richly relational present that can include the actuality of the past and the possibilities of the future.

What kind of thing does revelation have to be to fulfill this task? The meaning of revelation should not exclude statement, event, person, history, or word, but none of these terms embraces all of the needed elements. To bear a religious meaning, revelation has to be a kind of relation. Despite the fact that the term relation (or "relationship") is overused and misused in popular speech, it can still convey the sense of a rich variety of participation and interaction. Relation can include the personal and the impersonal, two people and many people, the spatial and the temporal, the human and the greater than human.

By positing that revelation is relation, I am excluding two reductionistic tendencies in Christian usage, namely, a use of "revelation" to refer to divine activity without adverting to the human recipient, and a use of revelation to refer to the content that has been revealed. Both of these meanings come within the ordinary uses of revelation and, in fact, are the most common uses of the term. But here is where resistance can and should be offered to the ordinary limitations of the term. The visual metaphor at the root of revelation implies that the agent can unveil what has been hidden, whether or not anyone else is there to see it. Likewise, what has been revealed is revealed once; henceforth it is something that once was secret but now is known.

Both of these meanings—revelation as act of the agent alone and revelation as the content of what is revealed—are inappropriate for the religious uses of the term. God could presumably reveal something when there is no human recipient, but humans have no way of knowing that. The only revelation at issue is divine activity that involves human reception. Although Christian writers are careful to protect divine initiative ("prevenience"), it can still be said paradoxically that divine revealing depends on human responding. Revelation only applies when there is a divine–human relation.

This relational context would also exclude using "revelation" for the content of what is revealed, that is, what is exchanged between relational partners. In ordinary uses of "revelation," the content can be abstracted from the relation: the revelation is the secret which passed from A to B. In the religious use of revelation, what is between the divine and the human is never that clear. Even Christianity, probably the most presumptuous of religions, can only lay claim to a key of interpretation. Does the Christian claim to have seen God? Has God been shown to the humans? Not exactly. The New Testament and church doctrine are aware of a future still to come. There is undeniably a strong tendency for the term revelation to turn into a thing, fixed once and for all in the past. But there is also the need for a continuing current of resistance so that the future is not excluded. A tension between past and future is best served by speaking of revelation as a present relation.

Such a relation involves a knowing but a more indirect and murky knowledge than the phrase "God's self-revelation" seems to suggest. The content has to do less with factual information and clear pictures than with a sense of command and obedience, promise and hope.[19] Command or promise are forms of speech (or speech acts) that do not fit comfortably under "revelation." They can, however, keep a lively tension between speaking and showing within the relation that is called revelation. Some speaking is at the service of showing the truth and enlightening the mind. Other speaking reminds us that life is not mainly a matter of gaining information but of living in response to what life offers.

This starting point is intended to include both paths of revelation in Christian history. I call this division within Christian history its upper and lower paths.[20] Along the upper path, the term revelation means the knowledge that God has granted and the church preserves. By the Middle Ages, although revelation was regularly contrasted with reason, it was concerned with the same general area as reason: an ordered and controlled knowledge that is to direct human actions. The speculative gaze of the believer is directed toward revelation as an object in the past.

On the lower path of Christianity, revelation/apocalypse has meant ecstatic visions of the future, which are often brought on by duress. The conflict between a few loyal believers and the threatening outside world is always fraught with danger and the possibility of violence. The term apocalypse came to mean the violent overthrow of the existing order and the victory of the chosen few who foresaw the coming destruction. Here revelation is not just non-rational but antirational. Any attempt to order the world rationally is suspected of being "rationalization" whose purpose is to blur a clear choice between God and evil.

Since both paths have existed from early in Christianity, there is most likely something indispensable along each path. The lower path is sometimes invisible because it can go underground for long periods, but it does not cease to exist. My choice of the terms upper and lower deliberately plays into a central metaphor of Western history. The metaphor of up/down has been regularly used as a judgment of what is good/bad: up is good, down is bad. In our usual ways of speaking, the higher that something is, the better it is. A good person lives according to high-minded motives. God is the most high who dwells in the highest heaven. If one is to imitate God and become a morally good person, one must go up a ladder of virtue from material world to spiritual values. In modern secu-

lar terms the ladder remains, but it is now stages of psychological development that are reached by higher and higher levels of abstraction.

Not unexpectedly, revelation as a logical or epistemological problem
occupies the "better" class of people: philosopher, theologian, scientist,
historian; anyone who tends to think in high-level abstractions. In contrast, revelation as apocalyptic ending has been most often appropriated
by the "lower" class: more women than men, by slaves rather than slave
holders, by the poor and the dispossessed who will have little to lose when
the fire begins.[21]

Any healing of the split in Christianity requires challenging the
image of up and down as the basis for judgments of value. The upper as
well as the lower path should be absorbed into another image. Of course,
the image of up/down is so embedded in our language that total removal
is impossible. But other images can be used that complement up/down.
For example, the image of a sphere can include up and down but is more
concerned with center and periphery, interior and exterior, the integrity
of the whole.

The assumption that higher is better, blended with our standard
image of time as a series of points, leads to a naive belief in progress.
Moral progress for the individual is imagined as going up steps toward a
highest point. But moral and religious development could be imagined as
a more complex movement than forward and upward along a straight
line. The movement could be one in which the past is not left behind,
one in which depth is as valuable as height. The steps in the movement
might be imagined as steps on a dance floor rather than steps going up a
staircase. As it so happens the sense of time in the Hebrew scriptures is
something closer to the rhythm of a dance than to a line going forward
and up.

2

Bible and Revelation

THE REFERENCE AT THE END of chapter 1 to the Hebrew scriptures brings me to the point where the reader might have expected this inquiry to begin. I have proposed the thesis that revelation is a present relation without citing the Bible as my source. Is not the proper Christian (or Jewish) way to determine the meaning of revelation to consult the Bible? That seems to be the method in most Christian books that ask this question.

A hint of uneasiness usually hangs over this way of getting an answer because of the circularity of the method. Why does one go to the Bible to find out what revelation is? Because the Bible is God's revelation. Where does the Bible say that God is revealed? In the Bible. Anyone who defends this method has to acknowledge that the argument is circular, but he or she presumes that there is no other way to get started. The alternative method seems to be to start with reason as judge, subjecting all claims of revelation to a secular criterion.

A degree of circularity may be unavoidable, but the method need not be a single, closed circle. An alternative method is indicated by the metaphor of dialectic, a conversation that has no clear beginning and no necessary conclusion. I readily admit that I would not be asking the question of revelation if there were not a Bible and subsequent history influenced by the Bible. My starting point for a meaning of revelation is a panoramic view of Christianity, including its relation to Judaism and Islam. The initial meaning of "revelation" is subject to change on the basis of biblical and historical materials. I have made no pretense of deducing this meaning from the Bible by citing texts to prove my case. I am mindful, however, that my thesis should be compatible with the Bible and how the Bible has been central to Christian history.

A compatibility with the Bible does not include saying that the Bible is revealed or that the Bible contains revelation. References to "biblical revelation" obstruct a full examination of how the Bible and revelation are related. The casual use of phrases such as "revealed scriptures," "revealed word of God," or "revealed truths in the Bible" ultimately does a disservice to the Bible. Such attributions are illogical and indefensible, not to mention unbiblical. For the last hundred and fifty years, if not much longer, it has been clear that the words in the Bible were not dictated by God but were written, compiled, edited, and translated by human agents.

We have an appropriate term to describe the greatness of the biblical literature. It is a term that goes back to ancient times and is clearly distinguishable from revelation. I refer to the term "inspiration."[1] Christians have a firm basis for saying that the Bible is inspired. In contemporary speech, "inspiration" is used as frequently as is "revelation" and without confusion between the meanings of the two words. It is puzzling that Christian writers so often confuse the two terms when speaking of the Bible. When they presumably mean "inspired" they often inject "revealed."

Great works of art and literature are regularly said to be inspired or to be works of inspiration. A person engaged in an extraordinary activity feels swept up by a great motivating force. The spirit of the moment takes over the artist's work and the result is something that seems to go beyond the ability of the author. Or else, the spirit of a whole era can seem to infuse a particular work. In both cases, the work remains the distinctive product of its author, even though the author might give much of the credit to what inspired her or him.

Many Christians and Jews would bristle at the idea of defining "inspiration" and then locating the Bible within that general category. Just as with the meaning of the term revelation, however, some dialectical interplay is unavoidable. One should not violate the meaning of one or several ancient words that have to be translated for today. But one also has to examine the range of meanings in any contemporary term that is employed to convey that meaning. Thus, a Jew or a Christian will reject a use of "inspiration" that puts the Bible on a par with Shakespeare, Proust, or Seinfeld. But it is doubtful that what James Barr calls "the strict old-fashioned view of inspiration" is what makes sense for Jews or Christians today. In that view "all books within the canon are fully inspired by the Holy Spirit, and no books outside it, however good in other respects, are inspired."[2]

Inspiration was a concept that emerged with the prophets in the Hebrew Bible. The prophetic utterance was thought to be inspired by God. Only gradually did the idea get applied to the New Testament writings.[3] Origen is the first to extend the idea to the whole Bible. "The scriptures were written by the Spirit of God, and have a meaning, not such as is apparent at first sight, but also another which escapes the notice of most."[4] Origen's use of "inspiration" to support his own spiritual exegesis may have been partly responsible for that traditional view that stamped each book and each statement of the Bible as coming directly from God. Especially after the seventeenth century, the "inspired text" and "revealed text" were often interchanged.

There is no possibility of returning to a use of inspiration that preceded Origen. In any case, the contemporary meanings of inspiration can provide a workable context for those who revere the Bible. Even in a thoroughly secular framework, the Bible can be recognized as a work of inspiration. Jews and Christians trace the inspiring to its ultimate source: they speak of the inspirer as the Spirit of God. There is no inherent contradiction here; divinely inspired does not have to replace humanly inspired. And divinely inspired literature is not equivalent to a set of divinely revealed truths.[5]

Within the Christian and Jewish traditions, the affirmation of the scriptures as divinely inspired places them at the center of life. The Christian or Jew reads or hears the scripture not as what was once revealed but as what can be revelatory in the present. The idea of revelation as present speaking-listening is not a new idea. It is found in both Jewish and Christian traditions. It is especially present in the mystical side of each tradition but by no means exclusively there. Jewish midrash asks: "When was the Torah given?" The answer: "It is given whenever a person receives it."[6]

The key to notice here is the receiver. The human recipient is an indispensable element for the meaning of revelation. Words on a piece of paper are not revelation; only words spoken and heard reveal. The written words of Amos or Isaiah were presumably an element in revelation as experienced by Amos or Isaiah. Those same words today are not revelation. They are revealing of the divine only if someone is open to hearing and responding. Revelation is not an object that can be put on a shelf; it is a present, personal, living interaction.

Modern liberal theology went astray in speaking of revelation as unfolding, developing, or progressing from ancient times.[7] It tried to *add* a present revelation to the past. Such theology has been attacked for demeaning the biblical revelation. But, paradoxically, the problem with a progressive revelation was its attempt to hold on to a biblical revelation, instead of uncoupling the words biblical and revelation. Since theorists assumed that the Bible is revelation, they had to try to stretch something from the distant past to the present.

A "continuing revelation," tied to modern theories of progress, implied that the present era is superior to the biblical era. My own thesis of revelation as present relation is not a claim of development beyond the wisdom of the Bible nor is it tied to any belief in historical progress. I make no claim to know whether or not we are morally and religiously superior to people of one, two, or three thousand years ago.

Christians and Jews share a large body of inspired and revered literature. There are some discrepancies over the inclusion of a few books in what Christians call their Old Testament and Jews call Tanakh. The main difference between the religions, however, is the order of the books and how the resulting book of books is read.[8] The Christian Old Testament ends with the prophetic books that lead into the New Testament's claim of prophetic fulfillment. The apocalyptic element plays a central role, related as it is to the messianic promise. For Christian readers, Jesus fulfills the prophecies of the Old Testament.[9]

In the Jewish arrangement of these writings in the Tanakh, the prophets are placed in the middle. The prophets recall the community to live up to what they have promised. By 100 B.C.E. it was said that prophecy had come to an end. The author of 1 Maccabees says that prophecy had ended with Judas Maccabee (9:27) and that Simon was appointed "high priest forever until a trustworthy prophet should arise" (14:41). The Tanakh therefore ends with the Writings on everyday life.

Christians and Jews have deep differences, even when they seem to be drawing from the same source. At first, when the Christians said "scripture" they meant the Hebrew scripture. An Old Testament came into existence only with the establishing of a New Testament. Everything in the Christian's Bible was then read differently, the Christians now laying claim to works that the Jews had produced and possessed. The presumptuous attitude is captured in a remark of Justin Martyr late in the second century. Justin, in his exchange with the fictional Jew, Trypho, says, " Are you acquainted with them, Trypho? They are contained in your Scriptures, or rather not yours, but ours."[10] Although I am mainly tracing the Christian story, I try to avoid simply reading the New Testament and Christian doctrine into the Hebrew scripture. Such a reading back into the text is illustrated by Christian writers imputing the idea of revelation to the Old Testament even though no Hebrew word corresponds to it.

The story of "revelation" in the Old Testament can be brief because it is mainly a story of what is not there. Those who propose to establish the meaning of revelation by citing the Bible are somewhat embarrassed by the absence of the word in the Old Testament. That fact, however, does not stop writers from forging ahead with the claim that revelation is in the Old Testament in different terms, such as "word" or "prophecy."

Can people be talking about something if they do not have a word for it? Or from the opposite direction: Is it accurate to impute to people in the past a word they did not use?[11] Sometimes an affirmative answer to both questions seems justified. Certainly, we often engage in this anachronistic reading of history. One could mention here "ethics" or "theology" as other words not in the Bible but discussed as if they were. But at the least we ought to wonder whether we have missed something when we proceed in this way. Perhaps a group of people in the past did not have a word because they had a framework of understanding that is different from ours. If we were to take that suspicion seriously, it might lead us to think about the inadequacy of our own language.

There is no "revelation of God" in the Old Testament. God is not revealed, brought from darkness into the light. There are places, as I note below, where God is said to appear, but no text refers to a "self-revelation" of God.[12] When someone today refers to Old Testament revelation, it can obscure the nature of Hebrew religion and the meaning of the Hebrew scriptures. The absence of "revelation" in ancient Hebrew points to a different metaphor for relating divine activity and human response.

The central metaphor for the Old Testament's claim that God acts in human history, and more specifically in Israel's history, is speech. God speaks and the proper human response is listening and obedience. Especially in the prophets, the claim is, "The Lord said" (Jer. 15:11; Jer. 11:21) or "I heard the voice of the Lord" (Isa. 6:8). Variations on the phrase "word of God" are used about four hundred times in the Old Testament.

At their beginning, "revelation of God" and "word of God" are fundamentally different metaphors. They appeal to different senses and convey different kinds of knowing. In the Old Testament, "word of God" is not a species of revelation, a subset in the generic category of revelations. After two thousand years of Christian history, we may wish to claim that "revelation" has sufficiently changed in meaning to be able to subsume "word of God." Even if we do that, however, we should notice what may have been lost and what may need to be retrieved.

Our contemporary Western world is heir to Hebrew religion and Greek philosophy. Jews, Christians, and Muslims worked out their respective syntheses of these two elements. The Greeks and Hebrews differed sharply in their ideas of space, time, body, community, and everything connected to these basic notions. An overarching contrast can be found in their root metaphors: the Greeks were a strikingly visual people; the Hebrew metaphors are usually oral/aural. The Greeks sought for a vision of the truth. The Hebrews listened to the word of God because listening was at the root of all their knowing. The Greeks saw time unfolding along a mathematical line; the Hebrews heard time as a rhythm, not as past, present, future but as complete or incomplete action. Truth for the Greeks was an object of reflection; truth for the Hebrews was a trust born of action.[13]

By the first century C.E. this sharp contrast between Hebrew and Greek attitudes had become blurred by a process called "Hellenization," which was an amalgamation of Greek culture, language, and religion with other cultures.[14] Jews in great cultural centers, such as Alexandria, were receptive to this hellenizing attitude; Jews in Palestine tended to be more resistant. It was in Alexandria that the Bible was translated into Greek; it is known as the Septuagint translation (referring to the legendary account of seventy-two translators).[15] This version of the Bible had a profound effect on Jewish religion and the spread of biblical ideas beyond the Jews. The translation became a factor in Christian-Jewish disputes; Christian criticism was sometimes based on faulty translations. These conflicts led to new Jewish translations in the second century C.E.[16]

In the original translation into Greek, the term "revelation" was occasionally used to refer to human activities of uncovering. The word also appears about two dozen times where God is the subject of the verb "to reveal." For example, God says, "I will lift up your skirts over your face, and your shame will be seen" (Jer. 13:26; see also Nah. 3:5). The word is not used as a noun for any object called divine revelation. Nor does the use of the term in the Septuagint provide the historical basis for calling a collection of works by the name "apocalypse."[17] The employment of "apocalypse" for that purpose does not arise until the second century C.E.

The introduction of the word *apokalypsis* and the more general pattern of Greek notions of truth affected Jewish religious thinking and subsequently had profound effects on Christianity. The metaphor of vision—the truth is what you see—nearly overwhelmed Western philosophy and religion. If one were confronted with trying to retrieve a primitive or prelogical way of living and knowing, Jewish and Christian religions would have to be handed over to anthropologists. But the tension between the visual and the aural/oral is as alive today as it has ever been. In the modern period, Jews, Christians, and Muslims have had to resist the overwhelming power of "enlightenment" imagery and language.

A surprising twist in the twentieth century was that many philosophers joined in with a criticism of the visual; the aural/oral has reasserted itself.[18] Television and the computer are recent additions to this mixture of metaphors; their effect on thinking and speaking about knowledge will take decades to determine. The implications of the tension between these contrasting metaphors occupy every chapter of this book.

Note that the oral does not exclude the visual. For a full human life such an exclusion would be undesirable and impossible. All the senses should be included in the process of knowing and in speaking about knowing. In the Old Testament, seeing is subservient to hearing. The Bible begins with the image of God dividing the light from the darkness, but preceding this division is God's speaking: "God said, 'Let there be light'" (Gen. 1:4). Similarly, the story of Abraham's journey begins: "Now the Lord said to Abraham . . ." (Gen. 12:1). And although God is said to speak to Moses "face to face," it is the speaking rather than the visual imagery that is emphasized (Exod. 33:11). In fact, immediately following the reference of "face to face," God says: "You cannot see my face for no one shall see me and live" (Exod. 33:20).

The Old Testament does not exclude visual knowing or the importance of what is visible. The visible is a sign of the qualities of the possessor. But one must see below the surface to the heart (1 Sam. 16:7). Especially in the Psalms, light is associated with God's kindness and salvation. "The Lord is my light and salvation; whom shall I fear" (Ps. 27:1) (also Pss. 136:7-9; 138:1-4). The sun and moon provide light and warmth; they thereby *speak* of God night and day: "Their voice goes out through all the earth, and their words to the end of the world" (Ps. 19:4).

There are several verbs in ancient Hebrew that relate knowing and seeing. The most common term is *galah,* which can mean "disclose" or "reveal."[19] The word is not used as a substantive, that is, there is no object that is "the revelation of God." There are early references to God's appearances, especially through an angel or in dreams (Judg. 13:21; 1 Kings 3:5; 1 Sam. 3:21). Usually, what is revealed is some aspect of divine activity. "To whom has the arm of the Lord been revealed?" (Isa. 53:1). "Surely the Lord does nothing without revealing his secret to his servants the prophets" (Amos 3:7). Above all, the whole earth is full of his glory (Isa. 6:3) and is visible to all (Isa. 40:5; Ps. 97:6).

One might gain some knowledge of God through the appearance of God's law or of vindication. God is known as the one who sent the Israelites into exile and then restores them to the land (Ezek. 39:28) (Isa. 49:26). God can be heard in human speech or a gentle wind, but attempts to picture God in our imaginations or in stone are likely to be corruptive. In Jewish religion the main prayer and belief begins with the word "listen." The Shema, "Hear, O Israel, the Lord thy God is one," is said loudly, not because God needs to be told he is one but because the prayer is said to oneself and to other Jews.[20]

From our Greek ancestry we tend to separate word and action. Many is the politician who has said, "Watch what I do, not what I say," as if a politician's actions were not mainly speech. The contrast of speech and action is enshrined in the first amendment of the United States Constitution. People are allowed to say almost anything, apparently based on the assumption that words are merely words, not actions. Only if speech presents "a clear and present danger" of violence is there a restraint on freedom of speech.[21]

At crucial moments of life, however, we draw on our Hebrew ancestry in which words are deeds. The philosopher J. L. Austin named such speech acts "illocutionary" actions.[22] In a marriage ceremony or other contractual relations, in a court of law or a political address, in saying "I love you" or "I am sorry," the deed is the speaking. For the Hebrews, God's speaking and doing were always one. One term, *dabar*, can mean both word and action. Similarly, the Hebrew or Jew could know God only by doing, both in the movement of the body in prayer and in works of kindness. "To know God, as Jeremias said, is to practice justice and charity."[23]

One can speculate that the dominance of oral/aural metaphors in the Hebrew religion was due to the material having originated before the spread of writing. The human perception of the world changed as literacy spread during a period of several centuries. Some shift toward visual metaphors for knowledge was inevitable. The change is dramatically evident in Greek philosophy after Socrates. Most of the Greek words for knowing go back to the root of seeing. Knowing means having *ideas*, or visual forms. The central term *logos* shifts from meaning "word" to "idea."

The shift to the visual was less striking for the Jews. The introduction of writing did mean a stabilizing of the community and a drift of authority toward those who controlled the documents. At first, the function of the scribe was simply to provide an aid to memory. But writing, as Plato warned, could undermine memory; and indeed it did, although memory of the spoken word was never entirely replaced by writing.[24] Especially in Jewish and Muslim religions, the spoken word and human memory retain a prominent place. In Christianity the written document, and in later times the printed document, exercised greater influence.

One of the great novelties of Jewish history was oral tradition.[25] Religious reformers, instead of attacking the authority of the written word and the literate class who controlled the documents, placed the written word in the context of oral interpretation and commentary. The Pharisees arose as a reform group that laid claim to an authority derived orally from Moses, the same authority claimed for the written material. During more than twenty-three hundred years since then, "tradition" ("handing over") has been a flexible source of reform in Jewish, Christian, and Muslim religions. The term at various times means a source that parallels writing or a commentary that interprets writing or an encompassing of history, including writing.[26]

Eventually, elements of the oral tradition get written down, but neither in Jewish, Christian, or Muslim religions does the oral tradition get completely encapsulated in writing. In modern times, tradition is often assumed to be a reactionary term. That happens because people see only the results of the act of tradition. But reformers usually reach down for something deeper in the past. Tradition as the basis of reform can break out at any time.[27]

In Jewish history, writing about mysticism is contained in the *Kabbala*, which means tradition. Mystics are usually reluctant to put anything in writing. The mystical tradition was often thought to be dangerous, and mystics were often at the center of radical political movements. The mystical tradition mainly relies on communication through oral/aural and tactile means.[28]

Apocalypses

This mystical strand of Jewish tradition is historically related to the literature known as apocalypses, the issue I turn to in this section. By 100 C.E. there were about seventy of these works, but the rabbis did not give a prominent place to them. In the second century C.E. and thereafter, Christian writers showed more interest in preserving and interpreting these apocalypses. That is not surprising because Christianity was itself based on many of the themes in this apocalyptic literature, starting with the idea of a messiah whose presence signals the last days and divine judgment. The secrets that were known to a few chosen recipients would now be shown to all.

The history of Jewish apocalypses is a long and complicated story. The beginning of the story is often traced to the prophets. Amos is the first to announce that "the end has come upon my people" (8:2). Amos is referring to the northern kingdom but in later centuries references to divine judgment and "the end" often pertain to larger patterns of history or all history. John Collins distinguishes three periods of apocalyptic literature: (1) the sixth and fifth centuries B.C.E.; (2) the second century B.C.E.; and (3) the first century C.E. before and after the destruction of the temple.[29]

In the first period, after the return from exile in 539 B.C.E., sections of the Bible reflect a proto-apocalyptic attitude. The book of Isaiah, chapters 24 to 27, recounts that "the Lord is about to lay waste the earth" (24:1) but "on that day this song will be sung in the land of Judah: We have a strong city; he sets up victory like walls and bulwarks" (25:1). The Lord will kill Leviathan the twisting serpent and he will kill the dragon that is in the sea (27:1). On that "day a great trumpet will summon those who were lost in Assyria and those driven out of Egypt, and they will worship at the holy mountain at Jerusalem" (27:12). The immediate historical reference may have been to Xerxes' sack of Babylon in 485. But ancient religious myths were mixed with a vision of divine judgment and restoration of Israel.

Similar themes are found in Ezekiel 37 and 38. The former chapter has the famous passage about the prophet trying to raise the dry bones, which are "the whole house of Israel." In the latter chapter, God overcomes Gog of Magog. "I will display my greatness and my holiness and make myself known in the eyes of many nations. Then they shall know that I am the Lord" (38:23). Similarly in Joel 3:16: "The Lord roars from Zion, and utters his voice from Jerusalem, and the heavens and the earth shake. But the Lord is a refuge for his people."

The second intense period of apocalyptic activity is the second century B.C.E. The book of Enoch (also known as *1 Enoch*) is usually designated the oldest apocalypse. It engages in prophecy after the fact, as was typical of these works. There is a link to the early testimony of prophets, but apocalypse was a new kind of literature. In the section of Enoch called "The Apocalypse of Weeks," history is said to have ten periods, and the literal end of the world is prophesied. The Jewish author seems to have borrowed some of these elements from Persian religion.[30]

The most famous of the apocalypses is the book of Daniel, whose origin can be quite precisely dated to 165 B.C.E. The vision of Daniel in chapter 7 provided the most influential imagery for subsequent apocalypses, including that of John in the New Testament. Daniel sees four great beasts coming up out of the sea. The fourth (perhaps representing the Greek empire) is especially terrifying and strong. But the beast was judged and put to death. Then, "I saw one like a human being coming with the clouds of heaven . . . to him was given dominion and glory and kingship, that all nations, and languages should serve him" (7:13-14). In chapter 9, Gabriel explains to Daniel that there will be desolation for 70 years (interpreted as 70 weeks of years or 490 years). Chapter 12 provides a prediction of when the end will come, but the calculation remains ambiguous.[31]

In the third period of apocalyptic activity from the end of the second century B.C.E. to the end of the first century C.E., apocalyptic ideas are spread widely, but the number of apocalypses declines. From the Dead Sea scrolls we now know more about a community at Qumran that manifested apocalyptic traits. Hope centered on a great teacher of righteousness who would usher in the final days. There is also the book known as *4 Ezra*, which reflects on the destruction of the temple in 70 C.E. The prophet argues with an angel over the nature of justice, in a scene reminiscent of Job. In the end a messianic figure, derived from the book of Daniel, brings about a final judgment. A work with some similar traits is known as *2 Baruch*. It takes *1 Enoch*'s description of the exuberance of nature in the world-to-come and applies it to a land of delights in the days of King Messiah.[32]

All of the works called apocalyptic do not have the same set of characteristics. They do have sufficient family resemblances to merit a common title. There remains today points of debate that can be important in the use of the term apocalyptic to describe later movements. Clearly, the unveiling of secrets is a central element. There is a sense of the unity of history as divinely predetermined. This history is seen as coming to a crisis with divine judgment being imminent. One point of debate is whether there can be an apocalypse of the strong. That is, the literature and the movement are typically associated with a suffering and alienated people. Is it ever appropriate to speak of the apocalyptic when a group is trying to maintain its power?[33] My interest at present is simply to indicate one of the channels by which apocalypse came to occupy a central place in Christianity by the second century.

After the destruction of the temple in 70 C.E., the pharisaic reform evolved into rabbinic Judaism. The rabbis or teachers were the leaders of household and synagogue. The presence of God was centered in the ritual and ethical practices of *halakah* ("to go"). Observance of God's teachings known through Torah, Prophets, and Writings, together with subsequent commentary on these scriptures, roots the Jew in a "spacious present," even when driven from the land of Israel. The requirements of the law are not extrinsic duties imposed by revelation. They are, rather, the response that is integral to the covenant of God's speaking and human answering.[34]

Jewish writing in the form of commentary and wisdom literature continued throughout the period in which Christianity arose.[35] The Jesus or
Christian movement was initially one of several reform movements that
arose within Judaism. The Synoptic Gospels, centered on the extraordinary teachings of Jesus of Nazareth, reflect some of the intra-Jewish differences. But from the earliest compositions that would become the New
Testament, Christianity showed a decided influence of Greek (Hellenistic) thought patterns. That fact is central to the emergence of "revelation."

Jewish religion, as indicated above, had undergone a hellenizing
influence in the two centuries before the common era. While battling for
their autonomy against Greek, Roman, and other regimes, the Jews
absorbed elements of those cultures. Aramaic as the spoken language and
Greek as the written language had become common. One individual can
be cited as symbolic of the shift from Hebrew to Greek metaphors: Philo
of Alexandria.[36] Although also known as Philo the Jew, he is of greater
importance to Christianity than to Judaism. Living in the great intellectual center of Alexandria, Philo embraced Greek philosophical thought.
While professing loyalty to his people and to his Jewish tradition, he
overlaid biblical ways of thinking with Hellenistic philosophy, especially
the Stoicism of his day.[37]

Three contributions of Philo are relevant to the present study. First,
Philo practiced a form of biblical interpretation that became known as
allegory. His Christian successors in Alexandria found this way of reading
the Old Testament to be very fruitful for their theologizing.[38] Allegory
meant for Philo that there was a meaning of a text "in the shadow" of the
literal sense. The Christian church fathers elaborated three, four, or five
meanings of a scriptural text, but the many meanings start from the theory that a text may have a hidden meaning, a meaning perhaps not even
intended by the author. Philo and the church fathers provided the basis
for later theories of textual interpretation, although the allegorizing of the
Bible needed to be reined in by modern scholarship.

Philo's second contribution was to mediate a doctrine of *Logos* from
Greek philosophy into Christian theology. The Fourth Gospel's opening
line is, "In the beginning was the *Logos* and the *Logos* was with God."
One could ask which *Logos* is referred to here: Heraclitus's, Socrates',
Aristotle's, Philo's? The author of the Fourth Gospel probably had not
read any of those authors. But when early Christian writers read Philo,
they saw something close to the nascent doctrines of Incarnation and

Trinity. For Philo, the *Logos* was an intermediary between God and the world, the firstborn among creatures.

These two contributions of Philo to early Christianity are well known and well documented. The third contribution is the one I would highlight. Its influence may be subtler, but it provides the context of the first two contributions and it relates directly to the place of "revelation."

Philo shifted the metaphors of divine–human relation from the oral/aural to the visual. He systematically replaced God's speaking and human listening with the language of seeing. Employing his own peculiar interpretation and etymology, Philo concluded that Israel means "he who sees God." Given what was said above about the Hebrew avoidance of picturing God and having visions of God, this etymology was wildly inaccurate. In contrast, the actual meaning of "Israel" as "he who strives with God" captures the spirit of much of Hebrew and Jewish religion.

Philo posits a movement from hearing to seeing that is embodied in God's changing Jacob's name to Israel (Gen. 9:10). The Jews become heirs to the one who sees God. "Jacob is a name for learning and progress, gifts which depend upon hearing; Israel [is a name] for perfection, for the name expresses the vision of God."[39]

If vision is the chief metaphor for knowing God, Philo's use of metaphors consigns all other descendants of Abraham to an inferior level. "Ishmael means 'hearkening to God.' Hearing takes the second place, yielding the first to sight, and sight is the portion of Israel."[40] Thus, for Philo the relation to God is best captured in *theoria*, reflective contemplation. That premise was more acceptable a few centuries later in Christianity than it ever was in Judaism.

At the very beginning, however, Christianity was not a theory or a vision. It began with a preacher whose stories and sayings were typical of Jewish teachers. The only time Jesus is said to have written anything was on an occasion when he traced letters in the sand (John 8:8). The followers of Jesus committed his teaching to memory. They celebrated his life, death, and resurrection according to his command, "Do this in remembrance of me." The Jewish rituals of baptism and the breaking of bread were transformed into Christian rituals, later called sacraments.

Only after a period of decades did oral remembrances of Jesus get written down and circulated. What the Christians called the "good news" eventually appeared in several written versions. The celebrating of the liturgy engendered many readings that gradually coalesced into the Gospels of the New Testament. Surprisingly, the early church did not try to get its story straight in one approved version of the Gospel.[41]

The need for written material became more evident as time passed,

and the expected end of the world did not occur. Eventually, writing took
a central place. Although the Muslim phrase "people of the book" is regularly applied to Christianity, this was far from true in the first century.
Even when writing took over the task of preserving the material, it was
not in literary Greek that the New Testament was composed but in the
vernacular Greek (*koine*) of the time.[42]

Knowing and seeing are closely connected in the New Testament, not
surprisingly since it was written in Greek. Jesus is presented as an *eikon*
of the invisible God. "He who sees me has seen the Father" (John 14:9).
But neither "reveal" nor "manifest" is used with God as the subject and
God's self as the object.

Synoptic Gospels

The three Synoptic Gospels are the closest record we have of the preaching of Jesus. A discussion of *apokalypsis* in the Synoptic Gospels can refer
to each of the three literatures discussed in the previous section: literary
genre, theological theme, social movement. But there is in addition the
use of the word itself which went beyond the apocalyptic to the more
mainstream use of revelation as the name of any secrets now become
known.

In relation to the literary genre, the Synoptic Gospels as a whole do
not fit that category. There are, however, apocalyptic units within the
Synoptics, passages that have a family resemblance to Enoch, Daniel,
4 Ezra, and other works called apocalypses.[43] A clear example is found in
Luke 17:20-30. Jesus describes the end of days when the Son of Man will
appear. He will be rejected just as in the days of Sodom when "fire and
sulphur rained from heaven and destroyed them all—so will it be on the
day when the Son of Man is revealed" (17:30). Other passages also contain apocalyptic elements. In Mark 13:2-37 Jesus describes the signs leading up to the final judgment and warns his disciples to take heed and
watch.

A passage with similar themes is found in Matthew 24 and 25, which
concludes with the specifics of divine judgment: "You that are accursed,
depart from me into eternal fire . . . for I was hungry and you gave me
no food, I was thirsty and you gave me no drink . . ." (25:40-41). Apocalyptic literature was flourishing in Jesus' time, and he shared the "sense of
imminent transformation."[44]

As to the theological theme, there are apocalyptic units within the
Synoptic Gospels in line with the Gospels as a whole which lead to death,
resurrection, and the promise of divine justice. One of the strongest

theological themes of the past century is that "Jesus' message can fairly be characterized as apocalyptic eschatology."[45] The term eschatology was invented in the middle of the nineteenth century for that part of Christian theology that deals with "last things," including death, judgment, heaven, and hell. In the late nineteenth century, starting with Johannes Weiss's *Jesus' Proclamation of the Kingdom of God*, the Gospels were seen as announcements of the end of history and the imminence of the Kingdom of God.[46] Albert Schweitzer's *The Quest of the Historical Jesus* pushed the theme furthest in his "thoroughgoing eschatology."[47] All of Jesus' teaching has to be interpreted as coming from someone who believed that the end of the world was at hand. When the phrase "apocalyptic eschatology" is used in Christian theology, the noun tends to swallow the adjective. And once the term eschatology moves away from its most literal reference its meaning tends to get murky.

As to the third literature on apocalyptic—the social science name of an uprising—it is not difficult to see how the Gospels did set off a Jesus movement that challenged ordinary society. Those disciples who confronted Jesus' stark choices left home and possessions, preparing themselves for the Kingdom of God.[48] Within a few centuries, this movement settled into a more stable ecclesiastical structure. The explosive, revolutionary character of apocalyptic movements was brought under control. As the following chapters show, the Christian church has never completely suppressed the apocalyptic drive. The church would have to suppress too much of its own foundational documents to eliminate the apocalyptic impulse.[49] The church channeled some of this impulse into religious orders, where monks were said to live according to the "evangelical counsels."

The term *apokalypsis* was not logically or historically tied to eschatology or to the Son of Man arriving on a cloud. The root meaning of the term—to uncover or disclose—did not disappear when the term was appropriated to describe a literary genre, a theological theme, or a social movement. The Gospels and subsequent literature, both Christian and non-Christian, were able to use reveal/revelation simply to refer to secrets.[50] Harold Bloom writes that "prophetic religion becomes apocalyptic when prophecy fails, and apocalyptic religion becomes Gnosticism when apocalypse fails."[51] Christians would not agree with that statement because of the connotations of gnosticism. But if gnosis and gnostic were used as some Greek fathers did—simply as a claim to revelation—then one can perceive a transition in Christianity made possible by the term *apokalypsis,* that is, a movement from Christians expecting an end of history to a claim that the church is in possession of divine knowledge.

Jesus did see himself as a prophet uncovering the secrets of heaven
(Matt. 10:26; Luke 12:2). The occasional use of the verb "reveal" is not
usually in an explicitly eschatological setting. Jesus gives thanks to his
Father "because you have hidden these things from the wise and intelligent and have revealed them to infants" (Matt.11:25; Luke 10:21). The
emphasis here and elsewhere is a knowledge which "flesh and blood has
not revealed" but which has been gained by Jesus' followers (Matt.
16:17). In only one place is God the direct object of reveal: "No one
knows the Son except the Father and no one knows the Father except the
Son and anyone to whom the Son chooses to reveal him" (Matt. 11:27;
see Luke 10:22).

Paul's Letters

The earliest Christian documents we have are letters that Paul sent to various churches. Just as the Synoptic Gospels could be related to the three
main branches of apocalypticism, so also Paul's letters have some relation
to the literary genre, theological theme, and social movement. And even
more than is the case with the Synoptics, Paul's both casual and self-
conscious use of *apokalypsis* became the basis of the church's adoption of
"revelation" as the encompassing way to speak of God being known.[52]

Paul's letters, especially the early ones, contain "little apocalypses." In
1 Thessalonians he encourages his readers that "the Lord himself will
descend from heaven with a cry of command, with the archangel's call,
and with the sound of the trumpet of God. And the dead in Christ will
rise first; then we who are alive, who are left, shall be caught up together
with them in the clouds to meet the Lord in the air" (4:16-17). Clearly
at this point in his life, Paul believed that the end was near and that the
end would have many of the elements that are found in the apocalyptic
literature between second century B.C.E. and second century C.E.

In 2 Thessalonians 2:1-12, Paul is especially concerned with the
"lawless one." The three times that the word "reveal" is used are in that
connection. Paul refreshes the community's memory of his preaching that
"the mystery of lawlessness is already at work; only he who now restrains
it will be so until he is out of the way. And then the lawless one will be
revealed, and the Lord Jesus will slay him with the breath of his mouth
and destroy him by his appearing and his coming" (2:7-8).

Paul's letters have been important to the theological theme of eschatology. His writing is centered on Christ crucified, Christ risen. So much
is this the Pauline concern that the story of Jesus, the preacher from

Nazareth, is almost obscured. Paul does not spend his efforts exegeting Jesus' sermons. He seems to claim a special relation to Christ that bypasses the teacher–disciple relation that the other apostles relied on for their claim to authority in the community. But Paul does not negate history (a move that would have taken him from apocalypticism to gnosticism); he paints with a broad brush from Adam to Moses to David to the Christ. Paul thus has much to say about the last things, based on his reading of God's plan in history.

As for inspiring social uprisings, Paul's passionate pleadings to see this world as antechamber to the next world contributed motivation if not the main imagery to such movements. Paul's radical stance toward law and social institutions could be cited by groups intent on revolutionary change. Communal groups that proclaim the triumph of love over law are at least indirectly related to Paul's view. I noted in the previous section that the religious order was a continuation of the early church's eschatological outlook. A crucial text that monks and nuns found support in was 1 Corinthians 7. Within a larger discussion of marriage, Paul says, "those who marry will have worldly troubles, and I would spare you that. I mean, brethren, the appointed time has grown very short; from now on, let those who have wives live as though they had none. . . . For the form of this world is passing away" (1 Cor. 7:28–29:31).

As to the use of the word "apocalypse" itself, all of the New Testament uses outside the Gospels are found in Paul's writings (with the one exception of the first verse of the book of Revelation). Paul uses the word both as a central category on which to base his belief and also as an ordinary term for some human exchanges.

Paul's ministry as a follower of Christ began with a dramatic moment described in the Acts of the Apostles and the Letter to the Galatians. It is traditionally referred to as his conversion, a term that Krister Stendahl has argued is inappropriate.[53] Paul himself described the event as "a revelation of Jesus Christ" (Gal. 1:12). Morton Smith points out that this choice of a term was not dictated by the root meaning of apocalypse/revelation. In fact, Smith thinks the choice is a curious one, given that the center of Paul's thinking is not a revelation *to* Paul but *in* Paul.[54] The transformation of the interior life is not well captured by this visual metaphor. As recounted in Acts 9, Paul does not get his start by seeing the truth in a heavenly book. On the contrary, he is struck blind and had to be led by hand into Damascus. "God . . . was pleased to reveal his Son to me" (Gal. 1:15), but that seems to have been by sound rather than sight.

For the rest of his life, Paul's teaching revolved about the theme of the believer "in Christ" and "Christ in you." Paul presents himself as a living revelation of God. "Christ is speaking in me" (1 Cor. 13:3). He tells his hearers that Christ is also in them, if they will but realize it (1 Cor. 13:5). The moral life of the Christian wholly depends on this recognition: "But if Christ is in you, although your bodies are dead because of sin, your spirits are alive because of righteousness" (Rom. 8:10). Paul's use of apocalypse/revelation thus links up with the prophetic tradition from which apocalypticism arose. But there is still a strained usage here both because of the root meaning of revelation—uncovering—and the way "apocalypse" would come to be used in the second century.

In his more casual use of apocalypse/revelation, Paul associates the word with prophecy and speaking in tongues. He gives advice to the Corinthians on keeping peace in the community. "If a revelation is made to another sitting by, let the first be silent. For you can prophesy one by one, so that all may learn and all be encouraged" (1 Cor. 14:30-31). Here revelation is a kind of religious experience, but it seems to be behavior that is not far out of the ordinary exchanges in the community.

Throughout his letters, Paul maintains a tension of knowing/unknowing. What is praised by the Greeks as knowing is declared by Paul to be not knowing. He allows that the philosophers have a kind of knowledge, but because it does not lead to obedience and worship it is not genuine knowledge of the one God. "Though they knew God, they did not know him as God or give thanks to him but they became futile in their thinking and their senseless minds were darkened" (Rom. 1:21).

This false wisdom of the world is contrasted with a meaning of wisdom that had been personified in Proverbs, Wisdom of Solomon, and Sirach. For Paul, Jesus not only reveals that wisdom, but he is the wisdom (1 Cor. 1:24). The foolishness of the Christian proves to be true wisdom. Faith, which had been lowest in the Platonic scale of knowing, becomes for Paul the royal road to truth and salvation. "We walk by faith [a kind of hearing] and not by sight" (2 Cor. 5:7). Our knowledge is a seeing "in a mirror dimly," which is the best we can attain in this life (1 Cor. 13:20-23).[55]

In that same passage in 1 Corinthians, Paul uses the words "revealing" and "revelation" for the knowledge that culminates in seeing face to face. This is a second tension in Paul's writing: the past and the future held together in the present. Paul seems to have believed that the end was imminent, that the manifestations of the Spirit were a sign of the new age, as prophesied in Joel 2:28: "I will pour out my spirit on all flesh; your sons and your daughters shall prophesy, your old men shall dream dreams, and your young men shall see visions." The resurrection of Jesus means that the last days are upon us. His rising is the "first fruits" of the new creation (1 Cor. 15:23).

The problem for Paul, and for subsequent generations of Christians, was that the end was here but it was not here. In his Letters to the Thessalonians, as noted above, Paul says that those who are alive will live to see the coming of the Lord. As the years passed, Paul had to readjust his thinking and speak about a future of indefinite length. The present has to keep together the definite past and a message about an expected future (1 Cor. 15:20, 23) "We are being saved," he says several times, but the process will be completed in the future (1 Cor. 1:18; 15:2; 2 Cor. 2:15).[56]

Most of the time, Paul speaks of salvation in the future tense (Rom. 5:9-10; 1 Cor. 3:15). One of the few places where he uses the present tense, "we are saved," it is with the qualification "in hope" (Rom. 8:23). The revelation that is intrinsic to salvation is to be found in the future. To the Corinthians he writes, "so that you are not lacking in any spiritual gift as you wait for the revealing of Our Lord Jesus Christ" (1 Cor. 1:7). To the Romans, Paul writes, "For the creation waits with eager longing for the revealing of the children of God" (Rom. 8:18). The Christians are participants in the death-resurrection of Christ; the term Christ provides both a title attached to Jesus and the name of the judge before whose seat all must stand (2 Cor. 5:10).

Paul links this future-oriented revelation to the knowledge of God's plan for all creation. "Christ" here refers to a fullness of time in the present (Gal. 4:4) that reveals what has been going on throughout the ages. "With all wisdom and insight he has made known to us the mystery of his will, according to his good pleasure that he set forth in Christ as a plan for the fullness of time" (Eph. 1:10). Paul refers in this passage to the "mystery of his will" and in other places to "the mystery that has been hidden throughout the ages" (Gal. 1:26) or "the mystery that was kept secret for long ages but is now disclosed" (Rom. 16:25-26).

The New Testament, and Christian writers thereafter, tried to transform the meaning of "mystery." Revelation directed toward mystery might seem to have an obvious meaning. A mystery is something that is unknown or it is a secret which is known to only a select few. The revealing of a mystery solves the puzzle, provides the right answer, ends the game. The man who went on television and revealed how magicians do their tricks put many magicians out of work: the mystery was revealed, no mystery remains. Most mystery thrillers are not worth reading if someone has revealed to you which character did the deed.

Paul's use of mystery has some of this meaning of a movement from hidden secret to mystery ended. But he also tries to twist the meaning into its near opposite. All mysteries are gathered up into one mystery. Paul—like Mark but unlike Luke—usually uses the word in the singular. If there were to be Christian mysteries they had to relate back to a single mystery. This mystery, although now revealed, is still to be revealed in the future.

The above formula would be self-contradictory if mystery referred to a puzzle that is to be solved; either a puzzle is solved or it is not. But in the peculiar usage of Paul and other Christian writers, the knowledge of the mystery is a knowing/unknowing of something or someone that changes our way of knowing everything else. In the classic Christian formula, mystery is that which can always be understood further.[57] Mystery is that which makes other things clear. This paradox of mystery has not been an easy one to maintain. Generations of catechism teachers in response to difficult questions by children have answered, Take it on faith; it's a mystery.

Paul linked his usage of revelation and mystery to the book of Daniel: "Then the mystery was revealed to Daniel in a vision of the night" (Dan. 2:18). Paul makes revelation a mystery that is fully known only to God. The secret mystery is not a puzzle to be decoded by an arcane instrument. Revelation is a daily living out of the mystery based on faith, hope, and love.

John's Gospel and First Epistle

The Fourth Gospel is in some ways a bridge between the letters of Paul and the Revelation of John. But in its framework for knowing God, it is distinctly different from both. Ancient sources asserted that both the Fourth Gospel and the book of Revelation were written by the apostle John. Modern scholarship is nearly unanimous in concluding that the two documents come from different hands.[58] The real companion to the Gospel attributed to the apostle John is the First Letter of John. The Fourth Gospel was suspect in the second century and was admitted to the New Testament canon only because it was balanced by 1 John.[59]

The Gospel of John is taken up with the conflict between light and darkness. The light represents goodness, while dark is synonymous with evil. Much of apocalyptic literature draws on this cosmic opposition of the forces of light confronted by demonic darkness. The Qumran literature, as noted above, is an example from the period of Christianity's formation where the "sons of light" are in a cosmic battle. In this kind of literature the forces of light await or try to bring on final victory.

Interestingly, John's Gospel does not go in this direction. Others continued to wait for the end, but the author of John's Gospel announces that the end is already here. The Light had come into the world; the darkness had been overcome. "We have seen his glory, the glory of a father's only son, full of grace and truth" (1:14). The end of history comes for anyone who sees the truth in his or her heart.

John uses the verb "reveal" once in 12:38 but only within a quotation from Isaiah 53:1: "Lord, who has believed our message, and to whom has the arm of the Lord been revealed?" He uses two other verbs that can mean show or disclose (1:31, 2:11), most strikingly in 14:9: "Whosoever has seen me has seen the Father." In such passages God seems to be transparently visible, a position that distances the Fourth Gospel from the Jewish flavor of the Synoptics. But in other ways, John's Gospel pushes the Jewish opposition to idols even further. God is spirit, the Gospel says; no thing can represent him, even though the actions of Jesus make present his father.

I said the document that was paired with the Gospel of John was the First Letter of John. The situation that is intimated in the letter is that a community trying to live out the Gospel of John has split into factions over the Gospel's implications.[60] The overarching metaphor in the letter is still the conflict of light and darkness. But in the letter the light has not yet completed the conquest. The darkness is passing away and the light is shining (2:7). We are God's children now, but what we will be has not yet been revealed. What we know is this: "When he is revealed, we will be like him" (3:2-3).

The shift in 1 John to the future tense for "reveal" is very striking. The Gospel of John could be read, and has been read, as announcing the age of the Spirit, which makes institutional restrictions obsolete. The community of 1 John is warned that an old commandment has become a new commandment. Spirit has not replaced law; authority is still needed in the community; the stern judge is still to be revealed, along with our failings. "Abide in him, so that when he is revealed we may have confidence and not be put to shame before him at his coming" (2:28). The letter is a continuous exhortation to love, but lest that be taken sentimentally, the author notes, "For the love of God is this: that we obey his commandments" (5:3).

The Book of Revelation

Friedrich Nietzsche wrote that it was strange that when God decided to write a book he learned Greek, and stranger still that he did not learn it better.[61] His comment was especially meant for the strange book known as the book of Revelation. Nietzsche described this book as "the most rabid outburst of vindictiveness in all recorded history."[62] That is not at all how the book has been perceived by people who, caught in oppressive situations, have found hope and consolation in its pages.

As I suggested in chapter 1, the key to Christianity's continuing problem with "revelation" is shown in the role that this last book of the New Testament has played in Christian history. What I have called the upper path of Christianity dismisses the book by the simple linguistic move of calling it "apocalyptic," a word that bears no resemblance to "revelation" in Latin, French, German, English, and other languages. The title of the book—Revelation—is passed over as an anomaly, a strange coincidence. One would almost be embarrassed to bring up the book of Revelation to scholars who discuss the philosophical meaning of revelation. But among groups along the lower path of Christianity, especially the dispossessed and the revolutionary, the book of Revelation has been a driving force from the second century to the beginning of the third millennium.

The book of Revelation is in continuity with the apocalyptic strand of Jewish thought, most clearly exemplified by the book of Daniel.[63] Those who would say that "apocalyptic is failed prophecy" see the book of Revelation as an attempt to jump over time and usher in the last days. Such a move may involve some kind of wrenching violence, even for those groups that proclaim peace.

Commentators who see the book of Revelation more positively would dispute the characterization of it as failed prophecy. Revelation has its own form of prophetic criticism; it is not mainly about predicting the end but is directed at the oppressive forces in the present. Like the Gospel of John, the book of Revelation speaks *from* the end, not *to* the end. Confronted by the imperial power of the empire, the community of Christ's followers is comforted by the assurance that the main battle has already been won.

The figure of Christ in the book of Revelation gives a unity to an otherwise disparate set of images. This unifying image runs from the opening sentence, "The revelation of Jesus Christ which God gave him to show his servants what must soon take place," to the final warning that "the one who testifies to these things says 'Surely I am coming soon.'" The first sentence, surprisingly, is the only place in the book where "apocalypse/revelation" is used. Perhaps it was clear enough from that opening scene that all of what follows is encompassed by the term apocalypse/revelation. Right-wing preachers today commonly cite the book as Revelations, but, like Paul's use of "revelation," only one revelation is the subject of the book: the mystery of Christ from the beginning of the universe to its end.

More than any other book of the Bible, Revelation uses a profusion of visual metaphors. True, it begins with a voice from heaven, but when John turns toward the voice he has a vision—a vision of "one like the Son of man." And then John is commanded, "Write what you have seen, what is, and what is to take place after this" (1:12-13). For perhaps the first time in the Bible, writing is more than the recording of remembered events. Here writing has a "performative power,"[64] that is, it is integral to revelatory experience. Writing is taken to be a necessary element in revelation being possible.

In one scene we have "eating," which in the Middle Ages is a common metaphor for knowing.[65] But in the book of Revelation what is eaten is a scroll. The action is similar to Ezekiel 33:1-9 and Jeremiah 1:9 where the prophet has to swallow the words on the scroll before he can preach. In the book of Revelation, the command is reminiscent of the eucharistic formula, "Take it, and eat." After eating the scroll, John is told to prophesy again about many peoples and nations and languages and kings (10:9-11).

The book of Revelation culminates in a grand vision of a new heaven and a new earth. A new Jerusalem comes down out of heaven. Thus, the Bible begins in a garden and ends in a city, but it is a strange kind of city. Its relation to the earthly Jerusalem, already more than a thousand years old at the time of the book's writing, is difficult to grasp. The inhabitants of the new Jerusalem do not seem to be in any physical interaction with one another. All eyes are turned to the throne of God. The people "will see his face, and his name will be on their foreheads. And there will be no more night" (22:45). Light will have triumphed and the one remaining sense seems to be vision.

This last book of the New Testament had a long struggle to get full acceptance into the church's canon of divinely inspired writings. Eusebius of Caesarea is the first writer to clearly identify a list of canonical books. He indicates a spirited argument over whether to include the book of Revelation. Eusebius, relying especially on Dionysius of Alexandria in the third century, says that "it seems desirable" to include the Revelation of John.[66] The school at Antioch, attending to the historical and literal rendering of the scriptures, resisted for centuries. Origen in Alexandria applied an allegorical interpretation: the book is a revelation of past Christian truths. Neither rejection nor easy acceptance could do justice to the book. How to read the book remains a matter of dispute.

One might have expected that with such a spotty history the book's effects would be negligible. But its significance has not depended on agreement about its secret or not-so-secret messages. Its twofold importance lies in what it in fact ended and in what it suggests remains open. Both effects pertain to the meaning of the term revelation.

What the book of Revelation closed is the Bible, but this is more than a simple fact of chronological sequence. The book of Revelation had a major part in helping to invent the idea of *the book*, the Bible. That invention could have happened without the book of Revelation, but its sense of ending fit well with the Christian movement. When Christianity began to use writing, its penchant was not for the scroll, which is unrolled and rerolled, but for the codex. In the codex, the pages, which are fastened in the middle and folded over, move from beginning to end.[67]

Every book in its physical appearance suggests a beginning, a middle, and an end, even if many books do not carry out the suggestion. Christianity had its Old Testament as its beginning; it had the Gospels, Acts, and Letters as climactic middle. With the book of Revelation, the Christian Bible found its end. That neatly tied up story line took several centuries, but once the Bible had an ending the meaning of revelation was sealed.[68]

Surely it is not just a coincidence that the name of the last book became a name for the whole book. The unveiling of secret truths at the end threw light on everything that had preceded. A well-written mystery novel makes us reflect back on the plausibility of the plot, the function of subplots, the disposableness of details that proved to be irrelevant. But we are unlikely to reread a mystery novel from beginning to end once we have found out the solution in the final pages. Revelation is what the Bible is said to be about, and the plot that counts is the one that ends with not getting thrown into the lake of fire, but instead joining the 144,000 who are redeemed.

If as a human being one has only a limited time to attend to the Bible's revelation, there is an understandable logic in concentrating on the book of Revelation, where *the book's* final truth is to be found. The book of Revelation bears some responsibility for a Christian obsession with a future world to the neglect of this one. The mundane political life of men, women, and children has sometimes been left behind for the sake of visions, truths, and the claim to possess the key to understanding all of history.

A more positive view of the book of Revelation acknowledges the book's neglect of ordinary politics but sees its alternative to be extraordinary politics. "In a situation where direct political action is not feasible, it is a text that keeps alive the expectation of a better world."[69] Here is the second reason for the importance of the book of Revelation, one that is almost the opposite of the first. The history of apocalyptic/revelatory movements can be read as a continuing protest against the closing of revelation. The divine–human relation is not closed or finished. In Christian terms, Christ is still to come.

Within this framework for the book of Revelation, those who have relegated revelation to a series of truths that are offered to our speculative curiosity have gone down a sterile path. The divine–human story, at the center of the creator–creature relation, is a moral and religious engagement that cannot neglect body, land, community, and history. As "protest," in the common meaning of saying no to something, the book of Revelation has often shown its power. But as "protest" in its etymological meaning of saying yes to something, one must wonder whether the book of Revelation provides the basis for a fuller meaning of revelation, given its emphasis upon vision, writing, and arcane symbols.

The more radical question raised by questioning the book's adequacy as reform instrument is the adequacy of "revelation" itself. The emphasis on the writing down of visions can simply mean the book is about "revelation." But no matter what the quality of the visions or the accuracy and power of the writing, can revelation be the basis for political, religious, and educational reform? Is the typical question to politicians—What is your vision of the future?—a secular remnant of religious versions of revelation, but not a very good test of political skill or dedication?

CONCLUSION

One point that emerges from this brief survey is that "revelation" is not a central term in the Bible. I have acknowledged that one can argue that the *idea* is there (our idea of what "revelation" means), but the scarce use of the term should give us pause. The ascendancy of "revelation" in the early church, the Middle Ages, and modern times may have brought progress in conceptual clarity but at the cost of something lost or obscured. This criticism applies especially to the Old Testament.

Christian scholars try hard these days to get away from a "supersessionist" attitude, the presumption that Christianity fulfills God's promises to the Jews and renders Judaism superfluous. I doubt that the attitude can be avoided while still assuming that an Old Testament revelation leads into a New Testament revelation. Many Christian writers now avoid the term "Old Testament," but the problem is not only Christianity's inherent structure of old/new but with the term "revelation." Of course, Jews themselves have to wonder how the term "revelation" came to prominence in Jewish writing of the medieval and modern periods. That is a story line I cannot pursue. But if Christians and Jews are to have true healing and deep understanding, they have to start by listening to what God says today, instead of from the assumption that revelation is contained in any documents of the past.

Is it possible that after more than a century and a half of brilliant scholarship on the Bible we still cannot let it be what it is: an extremely diverse collection of writings, different genres of literature that deserve appreciative reading as epic or poem, fable or memoir, traditional advice or good news? Can a Christian get free of the assumption that the Bible is the book that contains the revelation? In scholarly as well as popular literature the linguistic distinctions to effect such a change are not evident.

Diana Eck uses as a test case the biblical text favored at football games, John 3:16: "For God so loved the world that he gave his only son so that everyone who believes in him may not perish but may have eternal life."[70] If one takes that statement as a revealed truth, one might infer that everyone who does not believe in him is damned. Suppose, asks Eck, one reads the line as a prayer of thanksgiving rather than as the revelation of a truth. Then it would not be illogical to also praise God for sending the Qur'an into the world.

I would suggest that the logic of a Christian praising God for the Qur'an might be used as a criterion for a Christian understanding of Christ and revelation.[71] The single sentence of John 3:16 cries out for the context of John's Gospel, but the Gospel itself needs situating in time, place, and social conditions. The great work of recent decades on the social situation of each biblical book has enriched our understanding of the Bible while suggesting the need for new dialogues between biblical scholar, historian, and social scientist, as well as Jew, Christian, and Muslim. If the Bible is to be revelatory of God today we have to be receptive to hearing it in its integrity and responding to it with critical understanding, prayerful appreciation, and moral determination.

3

A Split World

THIS CHAPTER ATTEMPTS to trace the history of revelation/apocalypse from the New Testament era to the later Middle Ages. Of course, nothing more than the sketchiest outline, illustrated with a few key figures, is possible. An adequate history of the theme would involve the survey of thousands of books, not to mention nonliterary sources such as iconography. My aim in this chapter is a fairly modest one of establishing a framework for a conversation between two literatures that have been split from the third century to the present.

There is, on the one hand, a literature that traces the idea or the term revelation. The philosophically minded have been interested in the claim of Christianity to possess inside knowledge of divine matters. Starting from the somewhat scanty New Testament material on revelation examined in the previous chapter, Christian theologians work to show a continuity throughout the early centuries of Christianity.

There is, on the other hand, a literature on apocalypticism that has stirred a great interest in recent times. There is no dearth of material discussed under this theme in reference to the first centuries of Christianity or the Middle Ages. The problem, as noted in the previous chapter, is that "apocalyptic" has quite different meanings in different scholarly settings. And the popular meaning of "apocalypse/apocalyptic" today has only a tenuous connection to any scholarly and technical meaning.

EARLY CHURCH FATHERS

If one asks, Were the first two centuries of Christianity apocalyptic? one would have to draw some distinctions before answering. In some sense of the term apocalyptic, the early Christian centuries have an obvious share in the term. But one has to be careful about what the term means today for various audiences. As the name for a literary genre, "apocalyptic" refers most clearly to a body of Jewish writings and one Christian work, the Apocalypse or Revelation of John. Other Christian works in the first two centuries have some but not all of the family characteristics of Jewish apocalypses/Apocalypse of John. Thus, their apocalyptic nature is subject to debate.

A stronger case can be made for apocalyptic as a theological theme in the early church. What is usually implied here are characteristics directly stemming from Jesus' preaching and from reflection on his death and resurrection. There is little doubt that Jesus preached that the kingdom of God is "at hand" and that his own life and death were to usher in the kingdom of God. If the central characteristic of apocalyptic is the urgency to orient one's whole life to the coming judgment of God, then it makes sense to say that the first two centuries of Christianity were apocalyptic. The famous line of Ernst Käsemann that "apocalyptic is the mother of all Christian theology" is not then such a surprising claim.[1]

The question becomes more complicated and confusing when apocalyptic is used as a term to describe social movements among oppressed people who engage in violent uprisings. The most common name for these movements during the last half century has been millenarian or millennialist.[2] The reference here is to a thousand years, one of the elements in apocalyptic writing. Some of the characteristics of millenarian uprisings in medieval and modern times do not apply to the early centuries of Christianity. For example, the early church did not engage in a violent uprising. Admittedly, there are images of military conflict—the forces of light versus the forces of darkness, God and his angels overcoming the antichrist and his followers. Nonetheless, the early church is not accurately described as a millenarian uprising.[3]

A more specific confusion is related to the number "one thousand." In millenarian or millennialist movements "one thousand" can be interpreted literally or symbolically, but belief in a millennium refers to a golden age in which the messiah reigns. Some of the later Jewish apocalypses, especially *2 Baruch* and *4 Ezra,* envision an earthly and temporal kingdom in which the messiah will rule. The Apocalypse of John, written at about the same time as these Jewish apocalypses, used this same imagery. Since Christians, however, believed that Jesus is the messiah and that resurrection had already begun, the imagery would have to be employed differently.[4] As I indicated in the previous chapter, how to read John's Apocalypse—especially chapters 20–22 on the millennium—remains disputed. That also means we are not sure how apocalyptic literature was interpreted in the first few centuries. The evidence, although more extensive because of recent scholarship, will always be fragmentary. In any case, apocalyptic and millenarian should not be used interchangeably in reference to the early church, the Middle Ages, or contemporary discussion of religious sects.

The ambiguity in the use of apocalypse/apocalyptic partially explains how the Greek word split into two Latin words. It is understandable how some historians can find revelation or apocalypse back in the fifth century B.C.E. and then trace the gradual disclosure or uncovering of the divine, culminating in the "revelation of Jesus Christ." Subsequent Christian theology is in this view the reflection on the revelation that was given once for all, at one time, in one place, embodied in one person.

It is also understandable that other historians could trace revelation or apocalypse from its infrequent use in classical Greek to its sudden emergence in the Hellenistic religious literature of the Mediterranean in the first century B.C.E. The expectation of a divine intervention led to the birth of Christianity and the belief that the messiah had come. It also led to a dashing of Jewish hopes with the destruction of the temple in 70 C.E. and the disastrous Bar Cochba revolt in 132–135 C.E. The theme of apocalyptic lived on in Christian sects and in messianic movements for radical change.

Given the split today in the meanings of "apocalypse" and "revelation," there is no way simply to paste them back together. It is nonetheless important to be aware that the two divergent English words are translated from a single Greek word. Part of my argument for attempting to heal this split in Christianity is that the destructive and violent connotations of today's "apocalyptic" need to be ameliorated. I argue that "apocalyptic" has to be brought within "revelation" for the health of both concepts.

The split that occurred in the first two centuries can be most simply seen as a temporal division between past and future. The authors of the Synoptics and Pauline literature tried to maintain a tension of past/future in the present. The Apocalypse of John may have tipped the balance too much toward the future. Whether or not that was the case, the first followers of Jesus lived with an intensity in the present. They believed the present recapitulated the past and was pregnant with imminent divine judgment. As Christianity continued, as the disciples of Jesus were followed by a first, second, and third generation of Christians, the intensity was bound to subside. The church acquired a past. Now the culmination of history in the life, death, and resurrection of Jesus had decades of history that followed. The memory of history's climactic event now had to be preserved as revelation that looked to a past.

On the other side of the past/future tension, the quick end in the future had not occurred. Many of Jesus' disciples had understood him to say that the end would come while they were still alive. In the Easter liturgy they prayed, "Come, Lord Jesus." That liturgical formula continued beyond the first generation but it had to embody a different attitude for Christians of the second century. A decisive shift is symbolized by a liturgical prayer that Tertullian cites. The prayer is "for the Caesars, for their ministers, and for all who are in high position." Most significantly, the prayer concludes with a petition "for the delay of the end."[5] The apocalyptic expectation of a consummation in the near future has clearly begun to recede and revelation as what has come down from the past attains a new prominence. Apocalypse becomes a minority view that concerns itself with the sudden calamity that will finish history.

The sign that the past and future orientations were splitting is the use of two Latin words to translate the one Greek word, *apokalypsis*. The first use of *apocalypsis* as a Latin term is found in Tertullian when he is referring to the Revelation/Apocalypse of John.[6] Whether or not Tertullian wished to separate revelation in the Letters of Paul from revelation in the last book of the New Testament, the church henceforth had two Latin words for *apokalypsis: revelatio* and *apocalypsis*. The first was a classical word, going back as far as Ovid.[7] The second was taken over directly from Greek with the connotations that *apokalypsis* had acquired in the Jewish apocalypses and the Revelation/Apocalypse of John. The twofold history of revelation/apocalypse was established when Jerome (347–420) translated the New Testament into Latin. He used *apocalypsis* for translating the first verse of the book of Revelation/Apocalypse while he used (with one exception) *revelatio* for translating St. Paul.[8]

Apocalyptic Side

If we turn first to the apocalyptic side of the story in the first two centuries, we have mainly the Revelation/Apocalypse of John and a few other authors that we know directly or indirectly. One key author is Papias, but only a few fragments of his writings survive. We know from Irenaeus (and then from Eusebius and Jerome) that Papias claimed to be a "hearer of John," that is, to be directly in touch with the apostles.[9] And Irenaeus's own apocalypse, discussed below, may have been taken directly from Papias.

An important piece of writing in the early church was a book referred to by its author, the *Shepherd of Hermas* (c. 140). It was given a status almost equal to the scriptures because it was mistakenly thought to have been written by a Hermas referred to in Paul's letter to the Romans. The work is by no means a full-blown apocalypse. It is more taken up with moralizing commands. But its first part, called Visions, shows the influence of the book of Revelation/Apocalypse and other apocalyptic literature. The seer passes by a virgin bride who warns him that "you have escaped from your great tribulation on account of your faith, and because you did not doubt in the presence of such a beast." He is commanded to tell the elect of the Lord that this beast is a type of the great tribulation that is coming.[10] Although he is repeatedly told to "give heed to the judgment that is to come," he is not provided with any detail on the judgment itself and the state that follows judgment other than "your city is far away from this one."[11]

One of the first great thinkers in Latin Christianity is Tertullian of Carthage (c. 160–c. 225). In an early work, *On Spectacles,* he compared the vanity of the theater and athletics with the spectacle fast approaching when all will be consumed in one great flame. "What a spectacle is already at hand—the second coming of the Lord, now no object of doubt, now exalted, now triumphant."[12] In his work *Against Marcion*, he professed belief in a kingdom "before we come to heaven, and in a different polity—in fact after the resurrection for a thousand years, in that city of God's building, Jerusalem brought down from heaven, which the apostle declares is our mother on high."[13]

It seems safe to say that Christians in the first two centuries believed in the resurrection of the body, one of the elements in apocalyptic writing. Many heretical sects denied this doctrine and maintained that the spirit would be separated from the body and go directly to God. As the Synoptic Gospels and Paul's letters insisted, the resurrection of Jesus was the basis for the Christian's faith.

Belief in a messiah was a second element in apocalyptic writing that Christians held to. The appearance of God's anointed one was a sign of the endtime and the imminence of divine judgment. Writers such as Ignatius of Antioch, Polycarp of Smyrna, and the author of the *Epistle to Diognetus* surely held to these apocalyptic elements, but their views on a millennium can only be inferred. They seem to assume that the individual goes directly to God, although Polycarp explicitly refers to a bodily resurrection on the last day.[14]

In Justin Martyr (c. 160–230) we have a more thoroughly developed apocalyptic outlook, even if it is inconsistent throughout his writings.[15] In his two *Apologies* there is no mention of an earthly millennium. In the first *Apology,* he says we should not await an earthly kingdom. We should instead await resurrection, judgment, and an eternal kingdom.[16] Justin's *Dialogue with Trypho* contains many more apocalyptic elements, such as the second coming of the messiah in glory; the one that Daniel foresaw was "already at the door."[17]

Especially in chapters 80 and 81 of the *Dialogue*, Justin elaborates an "apocalypse." Although Justin allowed that there are "many who belong to the pure and pious faith and are true Christians" who disagree with him, he asserts that there will be a resurrection of the dead and a thousand years in Jerusalem. He interprets Old Testament texts, especially Isaiah, as "obscurely predicting a thousand years," and then he cites John, "one of the apostles of Christ, who prophesied by a revelation that was made to him, that those who believe in our Christ would dwell a thousand years in Jerusalem; and that thereafter the general, and, in short, the eternal resurrection and judgment of all men would likewise follow."[18]

Irenaeus of Lyons (c. 130–c. 200) was a bishop whose great concern was affirming the goodness of the body in opposition to gnostic views.[19] This insistence leads him into an elaborate apocalypse at the end of his major work, *Against the Heretics*. He writes that "the day of the Lord is as a thousand years; and in six days created things were completed; it is evident, therefore, that they will come to an end at the six thousandth year."[20] Irenaeus cites the Apocalypse of John, which foresaw the first "resurrection of the just" and the inheritance in the kingdom of the earth.[21] He insists the prophecies cannot be allegorized.[22] Irenaeus sees the resurrection of the just after the coming of the antichrist and the destruction of all nations under his rule. And "in the times of the kingdom, the earth has been called again by Christ, and Jerusalem rebuilt after the pattern of the Jerusalem above."[23]

The literal interpretation of the Apocalypse of John was soon to fall out of favor under the influence of Origen, Jerome, Tyconius, Eusebius, Augustine, and later church officials. After Irenaeus there were periodic outbreaks usually instigated by persecutions, such as in 249–251 or 303–311. The *Divine Institutes* of Lactantius (c. 240–c. 320) is the most prominent apocalyptic writing from this later period of persecution, describing the "extreme old age, as it were, of a tired and tottering world."[24] There will be a struggle between a great prophet and "another king will arise from Syria, born of the evil spirit. This antichrist will be overcome and the just will be rewarded."[25]

Irenaeus's work in particular was a source of some embarrassment to opponents of the literal reading of John's Apocalypse. Irenaeus was trusted and often cited as a staunch defender of orthodoxy. Thus the last eight chapters of his major work, *Against the Heretics*, was seen as an aberration and omitted from the Latin translation. That part of the work was suppressed until 1575, when it was recovered.[26]

Revelational Side

If we turn to the revelational side of revelation/apocalypse, there is no discussion of the concept of divine revelation before Justin and Irenaeus. Even then, the idea of revelation—the knowledge of God made known to the church—is more implied than discussed. Similar to the way that today's writers discuss "revelation" in the Old Testament, they find revelation in the early church fathers, even though the term is rarely used. For example, J. N. D. Kelly, in his standard *Early Christian Doctrines,* is sensitive to ambiguities in the early Christian use of "tradition," "prophecy," and "word of God." But Kelly seems not to notice any problem with "revelation." He frequently refers to what the fathers of the church say of revelation despite the fact that the term is seldom there. He even refers to their views of "Christian revelation" and "revealed religion," terms that are never used.[27]

One does find the verb "to reveal" used by church fathers to refer both to what humans do and what God does. Justin Martyr uses the term fairly frequently as a verb, a few times as a noun.[28] Clement of Alexandria (c. 150–c. 215) also uses it, though not with any of the technical sense it later has in the concept of "a divine revelation."[29]

What is sometimes cited as the first use of "revelation" that bears close resemblance to the later theological sense is found in Ignatius, bishop of Antioch (c. 35–c. 107). Ignatius does not use *apokalypto* or *apokalypsis;* he uses a related term in his *Letter to the Magnesians:* "There is one God, who has manifested himself (*phanerōsas heauton*) by Jesus Christ, his Son, who is his eternal Word."[30] Most often "reveal" is used as an ordinary term of description, similar to how we might use a word such as "discover" today. The verb "reveal" is used in the present tense as much as in the past; it is used in both the active and passive voices.

The idea of a divine revelation may seem to be implied in references to prophets and prophecies: what the prophet knows and speaks comes directly from God. Prophecy, in fact, is central to most of the writing of the first two centuries. Justin Martyr finishes his exhortation to the Greeks with the claim, "From every point of view it must be seen that no other way than only from the prophets who teach us by divine inspiration, is it at all possible to learn anything concerning God and true religion."[31]

Justin here uses "divine inspiration" rather than divine revelation. It was the usual way that the church fathers referred to the scriptures and the prophets; the Spirit of God inspires both of them. The church fathers also employ "word of God," a phrase taken from the Hebrew scriptures and applied to scripture and to the Christ. There is no extended attempt to defend a philosophical concept of inspiration, revelation, or word of God. Justin comes the closest in using *logos* to link the Greek term for reason with the Christ and the universal mission of the church. Other writers sidestep philosophical arguments in favor of directly pleading to people that they open their hearts to the church's message. Justin himself is more modest in his claims to knowledge than are his Platonist opponents; for Justin, we have only such knowledge of God that is necessary to obey and worship him.[32]

Besides scripture as the basis of doctrinal discussion, the term "tradition" took center stage as early as the second century. Similar to the use of "revelation," the verb form was used more frequently in the beginning. The image for tradition was of a "handing over," a "passing on" of the truth. As a distinct concept, tradition took a while to develop, but it eventually became a prominent part of Christian foundational language.

Although Justin uses "tradition" only twice, Irenaeus, who wrote shortly afterward, makes that term central.[33] Irenaeus was a bishop of the church, intent on the preservation of the tradition by means of the bishop's authority. In this context he refers to "the rule of faith" and the handing down of doctrine.[34] He seems to think that God is known or revealed both in the scripture and in the church's tradition. One of his images, destined to have a great influence, was a comparison of the apostles to rich men "depositing in a bank" all things pertaining to the truth.[35] Irenaeus, however, does *not* say that revelation is the deposit.

Irenaeus seldom uses the term revelation.[36] Where he does so, it is in arguing against his gnostic opponents' use of the word. Commenting on Matthew 11:25-27, Irenaeus argues that the "Father therefore has revealed Himself to all, by making his Word visible to all."[37] Although Irenaeus does not argue his case philosophically, he is not naive in the language and imagery he uses. He does not think that God "intrudes" in history to deliver revealed truths.[38] Neither Irenaeus nor any writer in the first two centuries uses "revelation" as a term that includes scripture and tradition. Nor does any writer refer to scripture alone or scripture plus tradition as the source(s) of revelation. It might be said of Irenaeus that he set the stage for revelation as knowledge passed down from the apostles.

Origen and Augustine

Origen (c. 185–254) represents a new stage on both sides of revelation's history . On the apocalyptic side, his allegorical method of reading scripture had the effect of defusing expectations of an imminent end to the world. Although Origen did not live long enough to write his commentary on the Revelation of John, he often cites the book and insists on a spiritual rather than a literal interpretation.[39] He considers a literalist interpretation "unworthy of the divine promises."[40] Revelation in Origen moves away from present and future expectation to a systematic knowledge handed down from the past. He still expects that "the end of the world and the consummation" will come, but it will be at that time when "every soul shall be visited with the penalties due for its sins." The time of the end is known to God alone.[41]

On the doctrinal side of revelation, Origen was a daring thinker who eventually was accused of heresy. Nevertheless, he professes belief that "the teachings of the church, handed down in unbroken succession from the apostles, are preserved and continue to exist in the churches up to the present day."[42] He goes on to distinguish between what he thinks are obvious facts that have to be accepted and secret truths that are hidden in scripture. He says that people who do not realize that there is a deeper sense to biblical prophecy are reading in a "judaistic" sense.[43]

Origen's metaphors are usually visual, drawing on the root meaning of "revelation" as an unveiling of secrets. In his commentaries on John's Gospel and on Matthew 11:27, he says that Christ reveals the Father whom he knows.[44] In Origen's grand philosophical vision, "the splendor of Christ's advent has, therefore, by illuminating the law of Moses with the brightness of truth, withdrawn the veil which had covered the letter of the law and disclosed for everyone who believes in him, all those 'good things' which lay concealed within."[45] Origen even accepts Philo's false etymology of "Israel" as meaning "he who sees God."[46]

Origen does not say that the scriptures are revelation or revealed by God. Rather, "the scriptures are divine, that is, are inspired by the Spirit of God."[47] The fact that the Bible is inspired does not relieve the reader of the effort to get at the deeper meaning. Origen distinguishes three levels of meaning: the bodily meaning, which refers to the historical; the psychic meaning, which carries moral weight; and the spiritual meaning, which might also be called mystical. Variations on these three levels of meaning run throughout the Middle Ages.[48]

The importance of the reader or listener provides an interesting twist on how Origen can refer to reveal/revelation. Although Origen is a key player in objectifying the idea of revelation—making it an object somewhere—his own use of reveal/revelation is often close to what I argue as the most appropriate meaning, namely, a present, personal relation between the divine and the human. Origen beseeches the Word "that he, pouring himself by his grace into our minds, may deign to enlighten what is dark, to open what is shut, to reveal what is secret."[49] Especially when referring to the Holy Spirit, Origen uses "reveal" in the present tense: "The Holy Spirit reveals spiritual knowledge"; "he opens and reveals a consciousness of spiritual knowledge."[50] Even for the wicked, Origen holds out hope that "it is better for them to be put off and abandoned for a time . . . then at last the word of God may be effectively revealed to them."[51]

This last quotation affirms the need for a moral openness so that the word can be effectively revealed. In many other places Origen suggests that intellectual preparation is needed. The theme of education is central to the writings of Clement, Origen, and their fourth-century successors. Christ is called "the teacher," the Christian is a "student," and Christianity is a knowledge (*gnosis*).[52]

At times their writing veers close to the heresy called Gnosticism, which made an escape from the evil of a material world dependent on possession of secret knowledge. C. Northrop Frye, in his study of biblical literature, comments that throughout Christian history both gnosticism and agnosticism have been unacceptable.[53] Christianity has always been engaged in finding a language that is between knowing and unknowing or is a paradoxical combination of knowing and unknowing.

When scripture is thought to have esoteric knowledge buried within its text, then the Bible passes from listener to reader, from reader to student, from student to specialized scholar. Origen in his sermons could speak to plain folks about enjoying the Bible with a humble heart.[54] However, the image of peeling back the literal meaning to get at levels underneath the surface could lead and did lead to a revelation understood as an object dug out by a clerical class and taught to "lay people."

A two-class system in the church arose in the second, third, and fourth centuries; it remains a serious problem for a church that started out by proclaiming equality before God. Origen should not be blamed for this development. I have noted that his use of revelation remained vital and relational. But his allegorical interpretation of scripture and his production of the first great systematizing of Christian doctrine had unfortunate results when people of lesser talents and narrower minds took over the tools that he had left.

One of the people who followed in Origen's wake and was his intellectual equal was Augustine, bishop of Hippo (354–430). While Alexandria continued to be the intellectual center of the East, Augustine was the giant through whom Western Christianity survived and eventually prospered. Some of Augustine's personal struggles became entwined with the theology of the Western church. His attitude to sin, which included quirky ideas on sex, draws criticism today.[55] He is the person chiefly responsible for formulating the doctrine of original sin, but he also had a significant part in most of the important doctrines of Christianity: Trinity, Incarnation, grace, sacraments, redemption.

The only element in Augustine's writing that I wish to comment on is his assumed or implied meaning of revelation (*revelatio*) and his interpretation of the book of Revelation (*apocalypsis*). His best-known work is the *Confessions,* which is only obliquely related to the topic at hand. The two works most directly relevant are *The City of God* and *De doctrina christiana* (which has several English titles, including a recent translation with the title *Teaching Christianity*).

Augustine's works, similar to Origen's, contributed to the twofold history of revelation: the apocalyptic history and the historical discussion of a knowledge of God that Christians claim. Augustine's success in reining in the millennialist impulse shifted church emphasis toward the elaboration and appreciation of Christian doctrine. In the first part of that project, controlling the millennialist tendency, Augustine continued the lead that Origen had provided in interpreting the book of Revelation. But for Augustine to follow Origen's allegorizing approach did not sit comfortably with his overall method of interpreting the scriptures. He viewed his own reading of the Bible as a middle way between literalism and allegory. And, in fact, Augustine's attempt to respect the literal meaning of the book of Revelation left open a sliver of light for later millennialist or millenarian assumptions.

In his approach to the book of Revelation, Augustine sided with the great biblical scholar Jerome. Concerning the belief that the saints would enjoy an earthly paradise, Jerome wrote: "The fable (*fabula*) of a thousand years must cease."[56] Commenting on the same material, Augustine remarks that some Christians "construe the passage with ridiculous fantasies."[57] Augustine candidly admits that "though this book is called the Apocalypse, there are in it many obscure passages to exercise the mind of the reader, and there are few passages so plain as to assist us in the interpretation of others."[58] The northern Africa of Augustine's time has been described as the "Bible belt of Christianity." A reading of the book of Revelation as prophesying a cataclysmic end is not so surprising at a time when the sack of Rome in 410 C.E. was imminent.

Augustine does not deny that the world will end; he assumes it will. But he interprets the thousand-year kingdom in the book of Revelation as the history of the church. He was unsure whether to take the number one thousand literally or figuratively. The more important point is that

Augustine brought this kingdom of saints within history as the story of the church. "The church even now is the kingdom of Christ, and the kingdom of heaven."[59] Here and in most writing until the twelfth century the church is not a human and reformable institution. It is the gathering of God's elect, which, temporarily but not eternally, is a mixture of saints and sinners.

Augustine has a doctrine of two resurrections: the first is spiritual, the second is bodily. The first applies only to the saints—a resurrection of mercy—while the second is for all—the resurrection of justice. Augustine allowed that this final judgment might be preceded by a period in which the antichrist would rage and by a short time between the antichrist's death and the final judgment.[60] Jerome had introduced the idea of a sabbath after the death of the antichrist. This idea sprang from his attempt to explain a discrepancy in Daniel between two ways of reckoning the time of the end. Jerome was also concerned with the text of Revelation 8:1: "When the lamb opened the seventh seal, there was silence in heaven for about half an hour."[61] Augustine and subsequent commentators, such as Venerable Bede, emphasized the shortness of this sabbath, but the idea nonetheless was formative of millenarian movements in the Middle Ages.

The entire plan of *The City of God* revolves around Augustine's belief that the city of man does not progress toward a paradisiac fulfillment. "Salvation history" for Augustine was an interior struggle. He compared the history of the human race to the development of the individual, but Augustine's "recapitulation" has a twist that distances it from modern theories of progress. The parallel between history and the individual is between "the experience of mankind in general, *as far as God's people* is concerned, and the individual man."[62] Thus, the idea of human history as continuous progress is excluded, but a progressive church history is not.

Does that mean there could be progress toward a more spiritual era for the church and the individual Christian? Augustine's main objection to the thousand-year sabbath in the future seemed to be because of the image of "carnal banquets." This millenarian opinion "would not be objectionable if it were believed that the joys of the saints in that Sabbath shall be spiritual."[63] Here the door was left open to groups proclaiming themselves as spiritual and thereby justified in trying to bring on the last days. Augustine did not go that route. For him, each soul struggles through spiritual crises and, as the *Confessions* suggests, the pattern of God's actions can be recognized only at the end.

Revelation (*revelatio*) is a term that seldom appears in Augustine's writing, but he does refer to the revelation (*apocalypsis*) of the last book of the New Testament. Since he interprets that book as a history of the church he could have spoken about revelation as present relation. Only occasionally does such language surface. Commenting on 1 John 2:18 ("Children it is the last hour"), he says, "So the very time in which the Gospel is being preached, up until the Lord is revealed, is the hour in which these things have to be observed, because the revelation of the Lord belongs itself to the same hour, which will come to its end on the day of judgment."[64] True to the language of John the Evangelist, Augustine here locates revelation in the present with a future orientation.

Augustine's influence on the apocalyptic side of revelation was mainly negative and suppressive. As part of a long line of interpreters from the third to the eleventh century, Augustine interpreted the Revelation of John so as to domesticate its explosive possibilities. We shall presently see that these efforts were only temporarily and partially successful. Augustine could not go all the way with Origen in simply allegorizing the text and denying a direct relevance to historical events.

On the other side of revelation's history, in which revelation is knowledge from the past, Augustine stands almost alone as the founder of the rules by which the Bible (and even much of secular literature) is interpreted. In the battle between the Humanists and Scholastics a thousand years after Augustine, both sides appealed to the same book, *De doctrina christiana*.[65] In that book Augustine drew on classical scholarship as far back as Aristotle and contributed his own mastery of the scriptures and church fathers.

As noted above, Augustine believed that his way of reading the scriptures was a middle way between Jewish legalism and Greek allegorism, or between attachment to the "letter" and association with a cosmic dualism of matter and spirit.[66] Augustine thought that Christians should read the scriptures for their spiritual meaning. What that phrase means was spelled out in fine detail and with numerous examples. But the complexity of his answer led to misunderstandings of his writings.

Augustine demanded much of the reader. He is perhaps the first thinker in history to place the reader at the center of the picture.[67] I noted of Clement, Origen, and other fathers of the church that they suggested revelation can occur only if there is a human recipient, that is, a listener or reader. Augustine goes beyond that in giving philosophical attention to the nature of reading itself. While the minimum knowledge which is necessary for salvation can be grasped by anyone (with the help of the Holy Spirit), much more is to be found in scripture. Those who approach the reading in a "light-minded" spirit will not only make mistakes, "they cannot guess at a wrong meaning."[68] God wanted "to save the intelligence from boredom." Thus, the truths have to be worked for, and "the more thoroughly indeed they seem to be wrapped up under metaphorical expressions, the sweeter they taste when they are finally unpacked."[69]

The main ambiguity in Augustine's method of interpretation resides in the term "literal." We obviously have some difficulty with this term today. There is frequent criticism, even ridicule, of people who take the Bible literally. But how else is one to read? Can one read any text if one does not attend to the words and the letters? Is not the basic principle of modern biblical study a return to what the words mean in their historical, social, and literary contexts?

Augustine lacked the resources of modern scholarship and, not surprisingly, he makes mistakes of detail in interpreting the Old Testament. But most of his principles are enlightened and have stood up well. He regularly asserts the need to try to find the author's intention. "Any who understand a passage in the scriptures to mean something which the author did not mean are mistaken though the scriptures are not deceiving them."[70] The complication here is that Augustine believes there is a divine authorship, too, so that the mind of the author includes mysteries beyond both (human) author and reader. That would allow the possibility of a meaning in the text not intended by the human author, but Augustine immediately adds that such an assumption would be a risky habit of interpretation.[71]

Augustine drew from two different traditions of interpretation: legal and literary. He may not have been fully conscious of how he was relating them. The two traditions overlap at points, but "literal" functions differently in each of them. The result is a confusion in Augustine's meaning of "literal." Or perhaps more fairly and accurately stated, the problem is that the English word "literal" translates two terms that Augustine usually distinguishes.[72] The "spiritual" reading of scripture that Augustine advocates has a different relation to these two meanings of "literal."

First, Augustine drew on a legal tradition of interpreting a text. This tradition of interpreting came down from Aristotle through Cicero and Quintilian. In the context of applying laws, a difference can arise between what the words seem to say (*scriptum*) and what the lawmaker may have intended (*voluntas*). The farther away one is from the time and conditions of the law's writing, the more likely there is to be a problem. For example, in discussions of constitutional law in the United States there is regular appeal to "original intent" or "the mind of the founders." Of itself, this appeal cannot resolve how the law should be interpreted.

Aristotle had introduced a principle that bridges original intent and present application. The principle of equity (*epiekeia*) meant that, having searched for the will of the lawmaker and having put the law into the context of all the laws, one should not apply the law in a way that leads to inequity. Augustine took over this contrast of *scriptum* and *voluntas*, combining it with St. Paul's contrast of letter and spirit. While one should not reject the letter (*littera*) of the law, one has to go more deeply to get at the will of the author—the spiritual meaning.

The ultimate author of the scriptural text is God, so Augustine changes Aristotle's principle of equity to love (*caritas*). One should not read scripture in such a way that its application would do violence to God's love and the love within the community. Thus, to remain with the literal meaning can be to misunderstand the text.

Second, Augustine also drew on a tradition of literary interpretation. Here, he contrasts literal (*propria*) and figurative (*figura*). The issue in this case is stylistic, but style implies substance. Here, too, one usually starts with a literal meaning to which can be *added* a figurative or metaphorical meaning.[73] But sometimes in a work of literature the metaphorical meaning is precisely what is intended. And then "when something that is said figuratively is taken as though it were meant in its proper literal sense (*propria),* we are being carnal in our way of thinking."[74] By using the word "carnal" in this context, Augustine crosses back to St. Paul's legal contrast of literal (or carnal) and spiritual. This conflating of legal and literary meanings of "literal" is the reason that the English word can be used to translate both *scriptum* and *propria*. It is also the reason for confusion about Augustine's insistence on a spiritual reading of scripture, which may or may not require going beyond the literal.

In summary, Augustine's spiritual meaning—as legally understood—goes beyond the literal. But, stylistically speaking, the spiritual meaning can be either literal or figurative. Stated differently, the spiritual can be the opposite of the literal (in his legal context), or it can be the same as the literal (in the literary context).

For Augustine, "practically all the doings of the Old Testament" have a proper literal meaning that must be attended to. But a Christian's spiritual reading of the Old Testament finds a figurative meaning as well. A neglect of the proper literal meaning leads to flights of allegory, as frequently happened in the monastic theology of the early Middle Ages.[75] Paul's spiritual reading of the Old Testament, however, leaves behind the letter of the law in order to find the will of the lawmaker.

Did Augustine really have to make the story so complicated? Possibly not, although the human attempt to communicate the most complex thoughts through written words is a complicated matter. Augustine's own contrasts are fairly clear. The main problem is subsequent imprecise language in talking about literal meaning and spiritual meaning. John Rist, in his biography of Augustine, notes that as a young man Augustine read Cicero, Virgil, Plotinus, Quintilian, Porphyry, and many others; but Augustine's successors read only him.[76]

Augustine does not use "revelation" as identical with the Bible. God speaks in the interior of the soul, although reading—silently and aloud—is part of the process.[77] He says that the Bible is inspired. Aware of mistakes in the Septuagint translation, he theorizes that the translators "were also directly inspired." They said things differently "to encourage the reader to concentrate on searching out the spiritual sense."[78] One commentator says that this shows that for Augustine revelation is pre-textual or post-textual.[79] But Augustine does not use "revelation" at all in this section. Perhaps it is implied that revelation is pre-textual, but for Augustine that does not diminish the significance of the text. He challenges the reader to put aside willful desires (*cupiditas*) so as to be open to the deeper meaning of life.[80]

Augustine pairs the terms reading (*lectio*) and meditation (*meditatio*), a combination that would continue throughout the Middle Ages. One cannot simply see the truth; here Augustine diverges from Plato. In the phrase later used by Isidore of Seville and John of Salisbury, one must listen to the "voice of the pages." Memory becomes the central power for grasping the truth. For Augustine and his successors, memory extends the present to include the past. Augustine is acutely aware of memory as the connection between the wisdom of the past and the community of today.

Most puzzling about Augustine's imagery is that he equates going in and going up. One finds God above by going into the interior of the soul.[81] The image of up/down, as I previously noted, runs deep in human history; it was especially strong in Augustine's day. Augustine's challenge to the reader, however, is with the language of inner and outer. To be "outside oneself" is to be unaware of God's presence. One must be quiet and meditate, recollect oneself, to find God at the center of the soul.[82] An emphasis on interiority has the danger of severing our connection to the political world, but in the *Confessions* Augustine is well aware of the political and social context of his life.

Augustine is not so aware of the dangers in the use of the metaphor of going up to God. The disparagement of the body and its pleasures is usually tied to the image of ascending above the earth to join the pure spirits. The equation of inner/outer and down/up is illogical, and it links the two dangers of the retreat from the political and the disparagement of the physical world. Augustine seems to have had a blind spot to this illogical equation of inner and higher. More remarkable is the fact that commentators today do not seem bothered by this problem.[83]

The story of revelation in Western Christianity was given a direction by Augustine that survived as the dominant strain for at least seven centuries and still has considerable influence today. The book of Revelation, interpreted as church history, was generally under the control of church officials and official interpretation. Revelation could increasingly be referred to as something not occurring in the present and the future but as something given once and for all time in the past.

Revelation, as apocalyptic future, declined in importance within Christian theology. Emphasis shifted to personal death and the sacraments. Frank Kermode captures this movement in saying "no longer imminent, the End is immanent."[84] Liturgical prayers, including the Eucharist and the creeds, kept some tension between past and future. Christians continued to pray for the "resurrection of the body" even when the immortality of the soul became the dominant belief. The sense of a final judgment was kept alive in medieval iconography. The gathering of the elect before the glorified Christ was prominent in churches and dominated the artwork in graveyards. Because of the visual meaning of revelation, art was a more effective means than writing for preserving this meaning of revelation. It is not clear, however, whether portrayals of a judgment were seen as evidence of a second coming at world's end or of the triumph of the church.[85]

The outstanding writers of the time did keep a tension between a possible end to their world and the need for vigorous activity to lay the foundations of a new world. Gregory the Great (540–604) is a striking example of this combination. During the time that he was pope (590–604), Gregory witnessed the collapse of governments in the West and the invasion of the Lombards in 593. He took a pessimistic view of history, which was the impetus for his sending missionaries to pagan lands. He wrote to Ethelbert, king of the Angles: "We also wish Your Majesty to know, as we have learned from the words of Almighty God in Holy Scripture, that the end of the present world is already near and that the unending kingdom of the saints is approaching." He goes on to list all the signs of impending doom.[86]

Ironically, Gregory's efforts as pope had enormous influence on future generations. His biographer, John the Deacon, wrote that "the more he noted the end of the world to press more closely, as its manifestations mounted, the more carefully he considered the affairs of all."[87] Something similar can be said of the monastic leaders of the time. The English monk Venerable Bede (c. 672–735) expressed a general pessimism about the times while nonetheless contributing to future history. The monasteries preserved ancient texts by the painstaking process of copying them by hand. The monks had removed themselves from "the world," but they still managed to be conduits of both literate knowledge and scientific techniques of agriculture.[88]

The Eastern church retained a more intellectual and mystical pattern to church life and the understanding of revelation.[89] Although Augustine in his early life had been influenced by Neoplatonic mysticism, he later turned away from any mystical reading of the scriptures and avoided the language of mystical union. Neoplatonism took a different route in the East, eventually providing, together with Aristotle's writings, the intellectual framework for medieval philosophy. The author now known as Pseudo-Dionysius, a Syrian monk of the fifth century, was mistakenly thought to be an associate of St. Paul. He thus had an authority far beyond what he would have had as a fifth-century monk. Without his authority, Neoplatonism might never have become the intellectual framework for much of Western philosophy. Medieval mysticism would surely have taken a different path.[90]

I have previously suggested that the split in the history of "revelation" comes closest to being healed by mystics who combine a reverence for the text from the past with an intense awareness of divine presence. In the West it was only after a ninth-century translation by John the Scot that Pseudo-Dionysius began to have an impact. And it was much later through Thomas Aquinas and fourteenth-century mystics such as Meister Eckhart that Neoplatonic mysticism flourished. The pattern of exit/return that Thomas Aquinas uses as the structure of his work had its source in the writings of Pseudo-Dionysius.

In the East, the images and language of Neoplatonic mysticism were more integral to the culture as early as the third-century fathers of the church. The Byzantine liturgy with its more than visual symbols was a crucial force in resisting a complete split in the meaning of revelation. So also was a mysticism that was firmly rooted in the sacramental principle of spiritual embodiment. Plotinus, the founder of Neoplatonism, went beyond Plato's visual metaphors for encountering the One who is "beyond being." The visual bias inherent in "revelation" is compensated for in Plotinus and Pseudo-Dionysius by metaphors of speech and touch that win out over vision.[91]

When Dionysius struggles with the metaphor of light, he is forced to use paradoxical language. "Darkness and light . . . it is none of these. So it is both darkness and light; it is a luminous darkness and a dark brilliance."[92] At the limits of speech, the mystic's only way to make positive statements is with double negatives. It is seldom noticed that revelation is itself a double negative: the negating of closure or the removing of what blocks the light. Mystics have sensed that revelation does not signify truths or clear doctrines; rather revelation provides a not-not-light or a not-not-openness.

This peculiar language, which can sound vacuous, is in need of tactile metaphors that keep the mystic rooted in body, earth, and community. That need was one of the main reasons for the central place of icons in the Eastern church. An icon is a physical representation that conveys a sense of divine presence.[93]

The more apocalyptic side of revelation did not disappear in the East. What has sometimes made it difficult to identify apocalyptic themes in Byzantine writing is that this literature was mostly in defense of the imperial office. In the midst of crisis, help could come only from the most powerful Christian leader, the *basileus* at Byzantium. The visions in Daniel 2 and 7, as well as Revelation 20, could be interpreted to glorify the emperor as the defense against the antichrist.[94]

The occasion for this new spurt of apocalyptic writing was the rise of the third of the Abrahamic traditions which uses the term revelation (*wahy*).[95] Muslims do not believe that their religion was founded in the seventh century C.E., but rather that the text of the Qur'an, which was dictated to Muhammed, is a recitation from an eternal book.[96] The metaphor of God speaking has a stronger role in Islam than it does in Christianity. Not "what we have seen" but "what we have heard, what we have recited" is the anchor of Islam.

Of the three traditions of Abraham, Islam is the most insistent in identifying scripture and revelation. To an outsider the result is likely to seem a legalistic and mechanical religion. The Qur'an, far more than the New Testament, is a series of practical commands that control behavior. Yet Islam is also the most insistent in identifying revelation with all of creation. The result is a strong mystical sense of God's presence everywhere. This paradoxical tension between literal and mystical, and between text and creation, is illuminated by a Sufi master: "No understanding of the Holy Book is possible until it is actually revealed to the believer just as it was revealed to the Prophet."[97] A reader or listener is needed to complete the act of revelation. The similarity to Origen or Augustine and many medieval mystics is striking.

As is true of Judaism or Christianity, Islam can end in a narrow fundamentalism. But when revelation is understood as the present relation of divine and human, Islam can be an ecumenical force for love and justice. A plurality of names veils the One who is far beyond us but at the same time is "closer than the vein in your neck."[98]

A direct Muslim influence on the Christian meaning of revelation is difficult to trace. For most of the Christian Middle Ages, Islam was the frightening shadow at the edge of Europe or the beast of the Apocalypse. Nonetheless, Islam made inestimable contributions to the intellectual life of the Christian Middle Ages. Most of what was known of Aristotle came from translations and interpretations of Arab Muslims. Much of the science, mathematics, and medicine was also a gift from Islam.

Unfortunately, no real religious dialogue occurred. Instead, as I noted above, a re-emergence of the apocalyptic was spurred by the threat of Islam. The most famous of these treatises is *The Revelations of Pseudo-Methodius*. Written about 660, it was attributed to Methodius of Patara, who lived in the fourth century. It rejected all collaboration with the Muslims. By interpreting Daniel's fourth kingdom as applying to Byzantium, it is the first source we have of the legend of the last world emperor, the one who would defeat the antichrist. Unlike earlier apocalyptic literature, Pseudo-Methodius encouraged active resistance, a theme that was to emerge in conflict with Muslims throughout the Middle Ages. Even in 1683, at the last siege of Vienna, excerpts from Pseudo-Methodius were used to encourage the Christian defenders.[99]

TWELFTH AND THIRTEENTH CENTURIES

The twelfth century is a turning point for the Christian Middle Ages. Among the changes at the beginning of that century was the introduction of translations from the Muslim world that brought in both Neoplatonic works and a flood of Aristotle's writings.[100] Modern science, especially anatomy and physiology, had its beginnings here. There was also the development of an ethic based on nature, both human nature and non-human nature. The theme of the human as microcosm of creation emerged along with an interest in the humans' artistic and technological reshaping of the world.[101]

The effect of this shift in outlook was an intensifying of both parts of "revelation" history. The split was now complete: *revelatio* above; *apocalypsis* below. On the upper path, a fully formed concept of revelation, as something to be investigated philosophically, occupied the great minds of the twelfth and thirteenth centuries: Anselm, Bonaventure, Albert, Aquinas. The lower journey was along a newly invigorated apocalyptic trail. The emergence or re-emergence of apocalypse was much to the chagrin of the professors in the newly founded universities and of the popes, who were trying to establish their own supremacy.[102]

Joachim of Fiore

One name towers above others for the inspiration of apocalyptic movements in the Middle Ages: Joachim of Fiore (1135–1202). As could be said of many great thinkers, Joachim would have been surprised, perhaps appalled, by movements that used his name and his writings for inspiration. He was a biblical scholar who introduced a complex and esoteric method of reading the scriptures. But reverberations from his writing ignited popular uprisings, most of them utopian and many of them violent. The crusades were not fought in Joachim's name, but his work was an ingredient in the ferment that included the crusades and other impatient thrusts to bring on the kingdom of God.[103]

Joachim took the book of Revelation not as a mere conclusion to the New Testament but as "the key of things past, the knowledge of things to come; the opening of what is sealed, the uncovering of what is hidden."[104] That is, *apocalypsis* is the key to *revelatio*. All of the revelation attainable by reading Old and New Testaments has to be seen through the book of Revelation/Apocalypse. In his commentary *Expositio in Apocalypsim*, Joachim elaborates a method called *concordia*, a highly symbolic correlation of Old and New Testaments. Neither the popes who eventually condemned him nor the new class of theologians who dismissed him could understand the nature of his appeal.[105] But what he offered to people was an answer to the complexity of history. A prophetic reading of the future was (and still is) highly attractive to many people.

The "irrational" attempt to see the future may seem to be a strange development in a century that was reining in the miraculous, perceiving an autonomy in nature, and establishing a rational system of theology. But it would not be difficult to draw parallels between the twelfth and twentieth centuries. When reason (*ratio*) becomes equated with a discursive form of speech that organizes the visible world as if that were the whole of reality, then part of human life and part of the human race is driven out of sight but not out of power. Unless *ratio* is accompanied by *narratio*, that is, another logic than the inductive/deductive method, then *irratio* is inevitable and crisis is imminent. "The Joachite 'transition,'" writes Frank Kermode, "is the historical ancestor of modern crisis . . . the age of perpetual transition in technological and artistic matters is understandably an age of perpetual crisis in models and politics."[106]

Joachim came to occupy this powerful position in the history of the West by interpreting the book of Revelation. His interpretation drew on a tradition of a thousand years of reading the text (although Augustine is the only writer that we are certain Joachim had read). Like much of the tradition, he contrasted a "carnal reading" (also called judaistic) with a "spiritual reading." But Joachim carried the contrast much further than Augustine had. Joachim's symbolic reading is a world apart from Augustine's attention to the literal meaning as the basis for both spiritual and figurative meanings.

Augustine, as we saw, took the book of Revelation as church history. The church was enjoying a thousand years (appoximately) of peace before the final judgment. There would be some kind of crisis near the end followed by a moment of sabbath rest. Joachim also took the book of Revelation as a story of the church but with one big difference: the thousand years of peace had not begun. By Joachim's reckoning, it was to occur in his lifetime, perhaps at the turn of the century (1200). This thousand-year reign of Christ would be introduced by a world-shaking struggle with, and eventual victory over, the beast/antichrist. Joachim, in contrast to Augustine, was an optimist. His is the first theory of progress, a notion that did not fully flourish until the eighteenth century but has been part of nearly all Western thought since the end of the twelfth century.[107]

Joachim has been regularly misunderstood both in the Middle Ages and in modern times. The basis of this misunderstanding can be pinpointed in a single word: *status* (state).[108] The standard way to summarize Joachim is to say that he is the initiator of the "third age," a belief that the age of the Father and the age of the Son would be followed by the age of the Spirit. In this third age, the Old and the New Testaments would be superseded. Institutions would disappear along with the authority of office. In this language of the third age, one can see the outline of Marxism as well as the "new age" spirituality that exploded into view in the late twentieth century.

The strange thing is that Joachim did not advocate a third age. In his complicated numerical system he had seven ages (*etates*), and the world is currently in the sixth age. Within this sixth age there will be a third state (*status*) in which the church will be reformed in the direction of a more spiritual or contemplative mode of life. Joachim described the rise of two new "orders" that would lead this reform. The foundings of the Franciscan and Dominican orders shortly afterward contributed much to Joachim's reputation as a prophet of the future.

To understand the place of the spiritual in Joachim's thinking, one must see it in its trinitarian setting. The Holy Spirit does not simply follow the Father and the Son; the Spirit is the bond of love between them. That may seem to be an esoteric distinction. It can be the difference, however, between dedication to reforming the church and the impulse to burn it down. A third age unrealistically expects to live with no authority and no institutions. Joachim's third state of the sixth age called for practical reforms to improve existing institutions, and he does not suggest that the Old and New Testaments should be transcended.

The contrast between these two mindsets was played out in the early history of the Franciscan order. The main part of the Franciscans looked to reform. Inspired by the gentle revolutionary from Assisi, the monks reestablished evangelical simplicity in a reformed church. The result was a new depth of spirituality based upon the life, suffering, and resurrection of Jesus. In contrast, the revolutionary group known as spiritual Franciscans demanded absolute perfection here and now. Such a demand could not be reconciled with an evolution of history and a reform of institutions. Conflict with the papacy in the thirteeth century was inevitable for these groups. Outbreaks of conflict with ecclesiastical and secular authorities continued for three centuries.

The year 1260, by one mode of calculation, was to signal the beginning of the third age. But except for uprisings by flagellants (those who practiced extreme forms of asceticism), the year passed quietly. As regularly happens when predictions about the end of the world prove inaccurate, some believers fell away, but others intensified their belief ("the end did not come because of our lack of faith and activity").[109] After 1260 the Apostolic Brethren emerged, led by Fra Dolcino, who indeed believed in a new age that would leave behind institutions. The church and its authority were repudiated as the *meretrix* (whore) of Babylon. Fra Dolcino expected the new age to come about with the extermination of the pope and the clergy in 1305. Instead, he himself came to a bad end after Pope Clement V preached a crusade against him; Dolcino and his followers were killed.[110]

One should note the prominence of women in the church heresies of the eleventh, twelfth, and thirteenth centuries. A group known as the Guglielmi (c. 1275) believed that in the new age spiritual roles would primarily be exercised by women. There was to be a new incarnation of Godhead in the opposite sex. Another movement indirectly related to

Joachim was led by Prous Boneta, who said in her confession of 1325 that she had been chosen to be the giver of the Holy Spirit to the world. The Christian church's failure to find outlets and serious roles for women resulted in talented women leading movements either of radical reform or radical opposition.[111]

Joachim of Fiore should not be blamed for all the irrational forces that he helped to unleash. In most ways he was a conservative exegete rather than the "great prophet," which was a title later bestowed on him.[112] Like numerous interpreters before him, Joachim sought the truth by reading an ancient book. His use of *revelatio* seems to bury knowledge of God deep in the text, recoverable only by scholarly analysis. According to Joachim, one of the three ways that God speaks in Scripture is *in revelatione imaginum*.[113] He gives as examples the wheel inside a wheel in Ezekiel 1:16 and the beast in Daniel 7:1-7. One might gather from that use of Joachim's phrase that revelation is the communication of supernatural knowledge fixed as an object for speculative inquiry.

Joachim, however, like mystics throughout the ages, had a sense of revelation as present, personal relation. Commenting on the appearance of the angel with an open book in the book of Revelation, Joachim writes: "That revelation was not made public at the time it was shown to John, nor even when it was begun in the Lord's resurrection, but rather in the church at the sixth age, whose beginnings we already grasp."[114]

In line with the main thesis of this book—revelation as a present relation—I find much to sympathize with in the above passage. Revelation is not an object located in the past; one must listen today for a divine word which is spoken now. At the same time, Joachim illustrates only too well the inherent problem with revelation as visual metaphor, as the unveiling of secrets. There was logic on Joachim's side in going through the book of Revelation to find the revelation in biblical images. But this procedure needed a base to stand on, including an appreciation of divine presence in the lives of ordinary Christians and in the broader tradition of Christianity. A trust in one's own visions leads inexorably to unforseen irrational effects. Until Christianity can heal some of its splits—rethinking its use of "revelation" in dialogue with its own past, with other religions, and with secular thought—the world is likely to experience continuing fascination with apocalyptic literature and frenzied movements to bring on the end of history.

Above this perpetual crisis on Christianity's lower path, the twelfth and thirteenth centuries represent a great moment of rationality. A somewhat peculiar alliance developed between the newly available works of Aristotle and an attention to the historical, literal meaning of the scriptures. The Christian idea of incarnation came to the fore, an idea that included respect for secondary causes. This appreciation of the natural world was reflected in a distinction between natural and supernatural. Far from disparaging the natural by placing something above it, this distinction was a recognition of the limits of the supernatural, especially the miraculous. In the twelfth and thirteenth centuries the world remained wholly supernatural, but the relative autonomy of the natural within that world gave birth to the beginnings of modern science and technology.[115] Here is where one finds treatises on revelation as a partner with reason.

Thomas Aquinas

The undisputed genius in the systematizing of the revealed (*revelata*) was Thomas Aquinas (1225–1274). Aquinas was sternly opposed to the millenarian movements that were swirling about Europe. He forbade his students to read Joachim, calling him "uninstructed" and condemning his concordance of Old and New Testaments.[116] Aquinas was opposed to searching for signs about the end of the world; he appealed to Augustine for the dismissing of apocalyptic literature. Aquinas would probably have shared the official view expressed by Pope Boniface VIII regarding the Joachites: "Why are these fools awaiting the end of the world?"[117]

The question seldom asked in Thomistic literature is how his anti-apocalyptic attitude may have influenced his assumptions about revelation and consequently his whole body of writing. A second coming of Christ is not denied, but neither does it play a prominent part in this writing. For Aquinas, revelation is centered on Christ, but his strong reaction against a future, apocalyptic Christ tends to locate revelation in the past. Fortunately, Aquinas's mystical link, to be explored below, does keep revelation in the present and saves his work from being a rationalistic system.

Thomas Aquinas's writing is the most brilliant attempt along the upper path of revelation to provide a Christian interpretation. Employing all the resources of Christian history, together with the available Greek philosophy, Aquinas created an original synthesis, which to this day remains a staggering accomplishment. He did not live long enough to complete his *Summa Theologiae*. He had an experience shortly before his death that made him consider everything he had written as "straw." Fortunately, those who survived him did not agree with his final assessment, and they preserved his work.

A common misunderstanding of Thomas Aquinas is that he juxtaposed Aristotelian philosophy and Christian revelation. Both elements in this pair are inaccurate. He was not simply an Aristotelian; he combined Aristotle with other philosophical traditions. And his writing does not deal with an object called Christian revelation, a term unknown to him. Thus, the idea of a pairing is itself misleading as in this summary by Ernest Becker: "In the hands of St. Thomas, philosophy, with 'deductive' logic as its instrument of precision, was a method of building a rational world, its aim being to reconcile experience with revealed truth."[118]

Aquinas drew upon the scriptures and the writings of the church fathers. He also drew heavily on Neoplatonic tradition, as mediated by Pseudo-Dionysius, whom he cites 1,700 times. Harder to trace but profoundly influential were the Muslim writers Avicenna and Averroes. The great Jewish scholar Maimonides is also cited with respect by Aquinas. Out of this extraordinary collection of sources, Thomas Aquinas wove a grand synthesis. In the foreword to his monumental project, the *Summa Theologiae*, Aquinas says, apparently without irony, that it is "for the training of beginners."

Any attempt to summarize this complex work is beyond my scope. My interest here is how Aquinas speaks of revelation in the *Summa Theologiae* and other works. In contrast to the preceding writers in this chapter, one does not have to search far for the use of "revelation." In the first question of the first article in the *Summa,* Aquinas uses the word seven times. At first glance Aquinas seems to have a naive attitude in his assumption that there is an "objective" world. But what obstructs our understanding of his writings is the tendency to read into them formulas that came much later. Writers casually refer to Thomas Aquinas's view of "revealed theology," "revealed religion," and "the Christian revelation," even though he does not use these terms.[119]

Even such a careful student of Thomas Aquinas as the great twentieth-century commentator Etienne Gilson sets up contrasts with the term revelation that are not in Aquinas's writings. Gilson, in his widely read *Reason and Revelation in the Middle Ages*, neatly arranges the book's three chapters according to those who exaggerated reason, those who exaggerated revelation, and finally Thomas Aquinas, who harmonized reason and "Christian revelation." The neat symmetry offers a solution to the problem but only for those people who accept that the problem is the harmony of two things called reason and Christian revelation. Gilson assumes on every page that there is such a thing as Christian revelation. He says of a "Thomist family" that "all its members will grant that there is a true revelation: the Christian revelation."[120] Concerning Archbishop Etienne Tempier's condemnation of Aquinas in 1277, Gilson says that proposition 175 reads: "Christian revelation is an obstacle to learning."

Archbishop Tempier, however, does not refer to "Christian revelation" in this proposition (he refers to *lex Christiana*). Nor does the archbishop refer to "Christian revelation" in any of the 219 propositions.[121]

An obstacle to understanding Thomas Aquinas's meaning of revelation is the assumption that he is writing theology. Despite the title, *Summa Theologiae*, Aquinas describes the work as an exploring of sacred doctrine. The usual translation of *sacra doctrina* as "theology" obscures the active and relational meaning of Aquinas's understanding of revelation. *Doctrina* for Aquinas means teaching; sacred doctrine is what God engages in with humans. The reception of that teaching is *disciplina*, the learning of doctrine. Aquinas occasionally interchanges doctrine for discipline, something that was done in translations of Aristotle. For both Aquinas and Aristotle, teaching–learning is a single process seen from opposite ends.[122] This principle, which runs counter to most twentieth-century writing on teaching and learning, will be explored in the last chapter of this book.

Revelation, for Aquinas, is a case of God teaching and humans learning. Thus, he usually refers to divine revelation (not Christian revelation) as an action on God's part, one that exists only if there is a reception or learning on the human side. But just as the word "doctrine" migrated from action to content, so "revelation" also came to refer to a what, the object grasped in the human reception. The element within the revelational process that *represents* the presence of the divine to the human is called the *revelata*, what has been revealed. Although Aquinas can speak of "revealed truths," there is not an identity between these truths and whatever can be stated in human language.

For this reason, Aquinas says that sacred doctrine is based on articles of faith (*articula fidei*)—not articles of revelation. Articles of faith involve articulation by the church of its understanding of revelation that has been received by believers.[123] The premises of sacred doctrine are held *ex revelatione*, that is, the articles of faith come to exist by the action of God's revealing and the action of the human reception in faith. The usual way for Aquinas to use "revelation" is with a preposition: *by, through, from, according to.* This construction is similar to the way St. Paul often uses the term in the New Testament. "Revelation" in later history becomes identified with statements of doctrine. But Aquinas had a much more sophisticated understanding of language than to think that statements were revealed by God.[124]

Thomas Aquinas, like Augustine, insisted that sacred doctrine must rest on the literal meaning of the scriptures. He allows for a diversity within the literal meaning. Since God is the ultimate author of scripture, the literal can include more than the human author intended. Aquinas also has a complex spiritual meaning based on the interrelation of the Old Testament, New Testament, and the "glory to come."[125] Any knowledge we have of divine things is by intention, not comprehension: "Things of faith are not proposed in themselves but by certain words or likenesses which fall short of expressing or representing them; consequently they are said to be known as through a mirror in a dark manner . . . they are not unknown."[126] The last phrase, "they are not unknown," is an accurate indicator of the modest claim that is at the heart of Aquinas's work and a link to the language of double negatives in the mystical tradition.

Aquinas was profoundly influenced by the mystical tradition, which came to him by way of Plotinus and Pseudo-Dionysius (and to a lesser extent, Avicenna). This central fact was neglected by centuries of commentators up through the beginning of the Thomistic revival in the 1890s. It was possible to read Aquinas simply as an Aristotelian because material from Aristotle is the obvious content within the Neoplatonic framework. But that was like seeing a jumbo jet as a room where people sit reading newspapers, without noticing that the plane is forty-thousand feet above the earth.

I will not try to trace all of the reverberations that the Neoplatonic framework has in Aquinas's writings. But by raising every question to the level of "being" (*esse*)—something not found in Aristotle—Aquinas provides a new approach to God, knowledge, goodness, nature, truth, and teaching, all of which affect his meaning of revelation. Consider these three points:

1. The plan of the *Summa Theologiae* is exit/return (*exitus/reditus*). The movement in the universe that Aquinas traces is not up/down, although that aspect is included. The overall journey of creation is out from the creator, around, and back to the creator (*circulatio*).[127]

2. Aquinas is the first philosopher to treat knowledge not physically but metaphysically. Knowing is simply a form of "to be." In creatures, knowing is indicative of a deficiency, and thus knowledge functions as a "remedy for loneliness." In God, however, to be and to know are identical.[128] Simplicity in God means that God's presence is his revealing. As every creature is capable of revealing God, God is implicitly known in every act of human knowing. God's truth is everywhere but humans have the weakest intellects in the universe and a confused love life.[129]

3. All things in the universe are interconnected because each participates in "to be." They are related through "sympathy" and by the overflowing of "to be." The refrain that runs throughout Aquinas's moral

thinking is that "the good is diffusive of itself." That principle means that to be a good person is not to obey rules (although good persons usually do) but to share one's life with others.[130]

The influence of Greek philosophy in Aquinas's writing gave a pre-eminence to visual metaphors. Heaven is described as a "beatific vision." But Aquinas, like numerous Christian writers stretching back to St. Paul, had a countercurrent in the form of faith as hearing. "Faith has a knowledge that is more like hearing than vision."[131] The centrality of word of God, which Christianity learned from the Hebrew scriptures and applied to Christ, meant that Aquinas often contrasts hearing God and human seeing. "Anyone is far surer of what he hears from the infallible God than of what he sees with his own fallible reason."[132]

Lest it seem naive that God is known in every act of knowing and that the word of God is spoken through every creature, one should keep in mind Aquinas's principle that we simply cannot grasp what God is. "Revelation does not tell us what God is and thus joins us to him as an unknown."[133] This human predicament is signaled by the use of a peculiar language of negatives. The commonly used phrase "negative way" is misleading because this path is actually one of double negatives. We know God by denying to the divine what limits or negates us. For example, Aquinas agrees with Maimonides that to say God is alive means that he is not dead.[134] A journey down that mystical road can end in terrifying darkness. If light/darkness is the mystic's only metaphor, then the mystic is lost. But if the mystic is rooted in a community with its aural, oral, tactile, and tasting metaphors, then the soul's dark night is also one of joy.

No sentence in the *Summa* is more important than the one in the preface to the third question of the first article: "Now we cannot know what God is, but only what God is not; therefore, let us consider the ways in which God does not exist."[135] Anyone who takes Aquinas at his word here cannot read the *Summa* as a grand rational system that explains God and the universe. Everything said about God, including his simplicity, is a double negation.

While Aquinas does not negate reason, he places it in a literally unimaginable universe where all the senses must be alive to the truth, goodness, and beauty of every creature. Humility ("of the earth") is called for when the humblest of creatures may speak the greatest truth. Responding to an objection that scripture should not portray God through creatures of the "baser" sort, Aquinas writes: "Understatement is more to the point with our present knowledge of God. For in this life what he is not is clearer to us than what he is; and therefore from the things farthest removed from him we can more fairly estimate how far above our speech and thought he is."[136]

I mentioned above metaphors of eating or taste as one of the bonds that keep our endarkened knowing continuous with ordinary daily life. Throughout the Middle Ages, metaphors of digestive activity were central to knowledge. Meditation on what has been read is called *ruminatio*, a chewing over what the mind has ingested. Reading at meals has always been standard practice in the monastery. The metaphor is especially prominent in medieval mysticism, both Jewish and Christian. "It is this tasting and seeing, however spiritualized it may become, that the genuine mystic desires."[137]

The image of revelation as food is related to the prophet being given a book to eat (Ezek. 3:13; Rev. 10:9-11). But the image also draws on our most elemental relation to vegetables and to other animals. Eating food is a symbol of the human desire for union with oneself and others. Knowledge partially satisfies the desire. Wisdom is knowledge at its best, a knowledge that brings savor. "Taste and see that the Lord is sweet."

The mystical possibilities of Aquinas's writings were developed by Meister Eckhart (1260–1327), a Dominican preacher of the next generation. Eckhart rattled church officials by carrying the dazzling obscurity of Aquinas to extremes.[138] He was condemned in 1327 for a series of propositions; "a great man pulled down by a lot of little men," in the words of Thomas Merton.[139] Aquinas was also placed under a shadow of heresy shortly after his death. But while Aquinas was quickly restored to the mainstream, safely confined as an expositor of Aristotle, Eckhart had to wait until the twentieth century to get some restitution. Neglected by theology along the upper path, Eckhart, along with Joachim of Fiore, influenced the lower path of Christianity, as well as modern thinkers from Hegel to Heidegger.[140]

Aquinas's mystical bent allows one to understand his meaning of revelation as a twofold speaking: God speaks through the preacher and also speaks an interior word by the inspiration of the Holy Spirit.[141] The words do not act as signals to inform us but as invitations to himself.[142]

Aquinas distinguished between common and private revelation. Any individual claim to know God must be tested against the whole tradition. He also distinguished between natural and supernatural revelation. He failed to grapple very well with the question of the salvation of the non-Christian, but he does not speak of revelation as if it were a possession of the church. His distinctions are not separations; they are within the one divine revelation, an activity which is ever present and calls for a daily response.

4

Revealed Religion

THIS CHAPTER EXPLORES the revolutionary change in the understanding of religion from the Reformation's beginnings until the end of the eighteenth century. In this period, the use of "revelation" also underwent a revolution, especially linked to changes in the new mathematical sciences. In one part of the story, revelation becomes a system of ideas or statements. In the other part of the story, revelation becomes a more intense demand for utopia, for the realizing of paradise on earth.

Throughout the sixteenth and seventeenth centuries, Christianity could not think out its position vis-à-vis the rapidly rising sciences because it had its own internal conflict. Protestant and Catholic churches mounted separate defenses; Protestants eventually attached the term revelation to the text of the Bible; Catholics associated the term with defined doctrines. To the skeptical scientist, these Catholic and Protestant beliefs seemed very little different. Jews increasingly used "revelation" in this period, but there was no significant conversation between Christians and Jews about its meaning.

The latter part of the Middle Ages was typified by a growing use of human reason for solving small problems but a parallel sense of reason's limits in solving the big problems of life. A radical split developed between scholastic logic in systems of philosophical theology and various nonrational movements that sought salvation in mysticism, fideism, humanism, and millenarian uprisings.[1]

As reason reached its perceived limits, mysticism had the greatest flowering it has had in all of Christian history. Especially in the Rhineland and in England, the fourteenth and fifteenth centuries were a mystical garden. When Pseudo-Dionysius's *Mystical Theology* was translated into English, "it ran across England like a deer."[2] The anonymous author of *The Cloud of Unknowing* provided a practical, experimental handbook for all Christians to find a knowing that is an unknowing.[3] The mystic, as I noted earlier, strains at the idea of revelation because it provides only the choice of light or darkness. Unless language is well used

75

and a community's meaningful rituals support the mystic, mysticism can end in barrenness or violence. Johan Huizinga, in his famous *Waning of the Middle Ages,* says that the great mystics "never lost their way back to the Church awaiting them with its wise and economic system of mysteries fixed in the liturgy."[4] That seems to me much more accurate than the same author's statement that "mystics, it has been said, have neither birthdays nor native land."[5]

I referred in the previous chapter to Meister Eckhart, the greatest of the fourteenth-century mystics. In the liturgy, and specifically in preaching, Eckhart's mysticism is to be found. Not in his Latin treatises on theology but in his German sermons preached to ordinary people, Eckhart pushed beyond scholastic logic to new notions of intellect, knowledge, and language. Eckhart challenged the visual as the dominant metaphor for knowing. His sermons are studded with metaphors of pregnancy, overflowing rivers, sparks of fire, music. All of these have their visual aspect but their appeal is to all the senses.

Visions are generally distrusted by the mystic not because they are based on the senses but because they are not sensual enough. According to Eckhart, even Christ, the image of the Father, had to leave so that the Holy Spirit could inspire the apostles and future generations.[6] The Spirit has to free the mind from its usual way of seeing so that the soul can taste the wisdom of the Lord. For Eckhart, intellect is not so much a matter of seeing but of letting be. God's presence is an absence, a divine abyss.[7]

Eckhart was acutely aware that God cannot be captured within any human language. He did not disparage doctrine, but he maintained that any doctrine contains less truth than it omits. Statements about God, even if valid, may be no more true than their opposites.[8]

While mysticism pushed at the limits of scholastic reason, humanism pulled in the opposite direction: namely, to the classical and mostly forgotten roots of medieval thought.[9] In its early phase, humanism tended to be anti-theological but not anti-Christian. The recovery of ancient sources included a return to the scriptures and to the fathers of the church.

Where humanism and mysticism differed was in their conceptions of the human individual. Mysticism exalted the human by a paradoxical relinquishing of all that human individuals hold dear. Even the "self" must go, in order to be "oned" with God. Humanism, in contrast, stoked the sense of selfhood and consciousness. The beginning of humanism has sometimes been dated to a precise moment in April, 1336.[10] The great scholar Petrarch described his feelings of that day as he ascended Mt. Ventoux in the Alps. Petrarch's feelings are not about the grandeur of nature but about the self-conscious reflection of the individual. Nature is but the backdrop to consciousness, soul, and will. Petrarch turned to Augustine's *Confessions* for interpreting his experience, although Petrarch's connection to Descartes' *Meditations* and Rousseau's *Confessions* is easier to trace than is his Augustinian ancestry.

The Renaissance humanist theme is embodied in a phrase that survives to this day, "the dignity of man." Pico della Mirandola (1463–1494) in his remarkable *Oration on the Dignity of Man* probably thought that he was stating Christian belief in saying of the individual, "it is given to him to have that which he chooses and to be that which he wills."[11] Pico puts these words into God's instructions to Adam, but the sentiment was novel in the fifteenth century. Its breathtaking claim is that a human being is whatever he chooses to be.[12]

SIXTEENTH-CENTURY REFORM

One of the greatest attempts at a humanistic theology was the work of Desiderius Erasmus (1469–1536).[13] Although he became Luther's enemy, Erasmus shared many qualities with Luther at the start. Both men had no tolerance for scholastic theology, and they led the return to sources, retranslating the Bible from its original languages. Both men saw Christ as the regulative principle of biblical interpretation. For Erasmus as much as Luther, the phrase "word of God" applied to both the scriptures and to Christ.

Erasmus thought that images of Christ can be an obstacle to Christian thinking, but not so the scriptures: "These writings bring you the living image of his holy mind and the speaking, dying, rising Christ himself."[14] Luther excoriated Erasmus for writing a "diatribe," a word that then meant conversation.[15] For Erasmus, conversation was the way to truth and God. In his translation of *logos* in the opening sentence of the fourth Gospel, Erasmus used *sermo* (a flow of speech) instead of the Vulgate's more static *verbum* (word). He said that his first choice would have been *oratio* except that it was a feminine noun.[16] *Oratio* is the word Erasmus wished to apply to Christ—"the eloquent persuasion of God."

Erasmus was accused both by Luther and Catholic officials, and by commentators ever since, of being indecisive, weak, and lacking in conviction. But perhaps he was only being consistent with his humanist love of rhetoric and conversation. He sought a middle ground at a time when no compromise was possible.[17]

Martin Luther

Most of the different currents of the late Middle Ages run through one person, Martin Luther (1483–1546). Luther shared Erasmus's disdain for scholastic theology and Aristotelian philosophy, preferring the new and simpler piety. Luther was profoundly influenced by mysticism even though he renounced the mystic's presumptuous search for divine union. Luther accused Erasmus of being corrupted by humanism, and yet Luther cites classical authors as frequently as does Erasmus. And although Luther was appalled by the eruptions of millenarian movements within the Reformation, an apocalyptic theme runs throughout his own work. In short, Martin Luther was a complex person whose inner struggles were a microcosm of the Christian church's struggle.[18] His greatest personal strength and his great contribution to the church was a recovery of Christian sources. Luther translated the Bible into German and passionately preached a return to the pristine "word of God."

The Reformation, it is often said, began in 1466 with the printing of the Bible. Church tradition had already been affected by the printing press before Luther came on the scene.[19] For Luther, the spread of books that was made possible by printing was God's "highest act of grace." The word of God could no longer be kept under wraps by church officials. What Luther could not foresee was the long-range effect as "the word" was endlessly reproduced on the printed page. A century after Luther the focus had shifted from the preaching of Christ crucified to the infallible text of God's words.[20]

Luther did not put much stock in "revelation," but his writings are pivotal in the transition to modern theology and its accompanying secular philosophy. Compared to his use of "word of God" and "faith," the term revelation is but an occasional visitor to Luther's writings. He uses the term most often in his commentaries on the Bible, especially Genesis, Psalms, John's Gospel, Romans, Galatians, and the book of Revelation. In his New Testament commentaries he usually uses "revelation" only because St. Paul or St. John bring up the word. Nonetheless, his somewhat casual use of "revelation" is instructive when placed in relation to his governing metaphor of "word of God."

The phrase "word of God" had been used since the beginning of Christianity. As noted in chapter 2, it is central to the Old Testament/Tanakh for describing the relation of divine and human. The church fathers used "word of God" to refer to the Bible and to Christ, or, as in Luther, to the Bible read through the interpretive prism of Christ.

As I have noted previously, "word of God" and "revelation" did not start out as equivalent in meaning. The first is an oral metaphor (God says), the second is visual (God shows). Perhaps more important, "word of God" is obviously a metaphor. Some people may have thought that God actually spoke Hebrew words, but it is unlikely that many people did so. In Christianity, as the Bible was translated into several languages, it became nearly impossible to take "word of God" in a literalistic way. The term revelation, in contrast, could be taken quite literally as the making known of a secret. The contrast of light and dark, known and unknown, could be taken as a simple matter of fact.

Luther was acutely aware of the "word of God" as an oral metaphor. Preaching plays a central role, above all other rituals in importance.[21] The word was to be spoken in the assembly; faith comes by hearing. Luther does not generally speak of reason as negative, despite a few famous phrases denouncing Aristotle and the work of reason. Reason is blind, however, when it comes to spiritual things.[22] For salvation one must have faith in the word of God rather than in any works of men.

Luther's use of revelation is closer to its medieval usage than it is to its modern usage. Much of what was said earlier about Thomas Aquinas could be repeated for Luther. Only very occasionally does he use a phrase that suggests the beginning of the modern use of the term. I will summarize his main uses of revelation and then give a few examples of the inkling of change.

1. Luther uses the verb "reveal" more often than the noun "revelation." This contrast is most obvious in his commentaries on John's Gospel, Galatians, and Romans, but it is true throughout his writings. Furthermore, when he does use the noun, in nearly every case there is either no adjective modifying it or if there is one it is the adjective "divine." One should note the crucial significance of this fact: the noun qualified only by "divine" retains a meaning of action. Revelation is what God does, not the name of an object that is under human control.

2. Although Luther never reflects at length on the meaning of revelation, he keeps close to the New Testament meaning where the etymological root is evident, that is, the uncovering of a secret. One of the few places where Luther comes close to defining revelation is in his Commentary on the Psalms. Criticizing the allegorical method of Origen and Jerome, Luther writes: "Revelation is, of course, something more than allegory, namely, the capacity to hit upon something in Scripture that not everyone discovers."[23] Like many exegetes before him, Luther was caught between affirming the simple, direct meaning of the "word of God" and

at the same time admitting that a deeper meaning is hidden in the text.[24] Particularly in regard to the Revelation of John, Luther has to admit that it contains words and allegories that are not easily understood.[25]

3. Luther always distinguishes between word of God and revelation. When the two terms come together, revelation is identified with the Holy Spirit's work in the interior of the believer. "The Gospel is a divine Word that came down from heaven and is revealed by the Holy Spirit."[26] The contrast here is not so much between the visual and the oral, but rather between internal and external. Luther did not seem to sense the danger- ous possibility that this use of language opened. He assumed that the preached word of God has a preeminent position. At the same time, Luther was responsible for a new attention to interiority, to belief as an act of the individual: "Each man must do his own believing." If revela- tion is the present act of the Holy Spirit in the heart of the believer, it was not a big step for many people to follow their hearts wherever they led.

4. Compounding this danger of equating revelation with an interior movement, Luther often uses "revelation" with a future orientation. Here he is usually following St. Paul. But the effect—not in Luther but in those who followed—could be to undermine the authority of the words spoken and written in the past. What takes over is the movement of the heart directed to secrets to be revealed in the future. Luther is faithful to the New Testament contrast between hearing now, seeing later. The Greek apotheosis of vision—the truth is what you *see*—survives in Luther despite his predilection for "word of God" and his infrequent use of "rev- elation." At the end of everything there is revelation: "The kingdom of grace is and remains a secret kingdom concealed from this world, main- tained in word and faith until the time of its revelation."[27] The word of God, for all its importance is still a stepping stone to the revelation. "We began by faith, we persevere by hope, and we shall have everything by that revelation."[28]

5. Luther is opposed to any special revelation. "Now that the Apostles have preached the Word and have given their writings, and nothing more than what they have written remains to be revealed, no new or special revelation or miracle is necessary."[29] This reference to spe- cial revelation is not the language of general and special revelations that later took hold in Protestant circles. In this later usage of general and spe- cial, special becomes equated with biblical or Christian. That is the oppo- site of what Luther means by special revelation.

While discrediting any special revelation, Luther nonetheless uses "revelation" to refer to his own mission of reforming the church. He cas- tigates the "unlearned" for seizing on obscure books, including the Revelation of John, to claim new revelation.[30] But in the same volume he writes: "Formerly—before God revealed the light of the Gospel—much was said and written about the contemplative and active life."[31] The time indicated here is clearly the sixteenth century and not the first. Similarly, in the Commentary on Galatians, he writes: "[Sorcery] was a common sin in our time before the Revelation of the Gospel."[32] The distinction that for Luther justifies this presumptuous use of revelation for his own time is indicated in his Commentary on John's Gospel. While saying that "no further words of revelation are to be expected," he can also say that the doctrine of the apostles "was not restored without the Holy Spirit's revelation; for our predecessors also had the same Scripture, Baptism and everything. Yet it was so soiled with mud."[33]

In summary, Luther nearly always uses "revelation" to refer to a divine activity, common in biblical times but also found in the Holy Spirit's action in the heart of the believer. He presumes that this inner activity, whose effect is to uncover what has been hidden (for example, human sinfulness), is within a context of the preached word of God. With a mystical element still present, Luther plays with the opposition of light/dark, hidden/revealed. God hides himself, his secrets are unknown to us. God is absent to our sight, but as in Eckhart and other mystics, God is present by word, taste, and touch.[34]

In a handful of cases Luther uses a formula that goes counter to his usual meaning, opening the way to modern developments. For example, in *Bondage of the Will,* he writes, "We should be content with the words of God and simply believe what they say, for the works of God are utterly indescribable."[35] The plural "words" is probably just a stylistic pairing with "works," but it foreshadows a shift from the metaphor "word of God" to a belief in the Bible as the infallible words of God. Similarly, he uses the plural "revelations" in several places, although the context seems to dictate that use.[36]

More startling is the one place where the word "Christian" appears as a qualifier of "revelation." In referring to "Christian revelation and preaching," he seems to have misplaced the adjective.[37] The existence of Christian preaching is doubted by no one, Christian or non-Christian. But the existence of a Christian revelation is not asserted by Luther, Aquinas, Augustine, or any church father. There are admittedly occasions in Luther, as in Aquinas, where the referent for revelation seems to be a human possession rather than a divine activity. In Luther's referring to "revelation of the Son of God or the knowledge of Jesus Christ,"[38] the parallel of revelation and knowledge is not much at variance with his usual way of describing the work of the Holy Spirit. Since "revelation" is a noun, however, a slight shift of emphasis can suggest a thing from the past rather than present activity.

That is the reason I said above that the printing press was initially Luther's great asset, but in the contrast of visual and oral metaphors the printed page became a double-dealing friend. The word of God could now be seen by everyone. It was an object in a book (*the* book was now *one* book in a multitude). Books can be put on the shelf or in a motel room desk drawer. The knowledge can be stored away for the individual who some day may "take a look." As "word of God" came to mean a visual object and "revelation" moved toward becoming a knowledge that Christians possess, the two metaphors tended to merge into one literal claim: God told us his secrets.

Luther's cry of *sola scriptura* left the Bible in the vulnerable position of being identified with words of God and revelation. Luther did not, in fact, reject tradition, even though for centuries the difference between Protestants and Catholics was stated in the formula of scripture alone versus scripture and tradition. Jaroslav Pelikan applies to Luther the principle "Tradition is the living faith of the dead, traditionalism is the dead faith of the living."[39] When arguing with his Catholic opponents and playing down the value of ritual, Luther could seem to be opposed to tradition.[40] But in arguing with Zwingli over infant baptism, Luther appealed to tradition.[41]

Finally, as I have suggested earlier, Luther's identifying of revelation with the inner working of the Holy Spirit has links to both mystical and millenarian traditions. The mystical implications were consciously suppressed by Luther after his early writing. The millenarian tendencies were also opposed by Luther in his condemning of the Anabaptists and the Peasants Revolt.[42] Thomas Muntzer's millenarian uprising that began in 1520 with his interpretation of the Revelation of John was opposed by Luther even to the extent that Muntzer identified Luther as the beast of the Apocalypse.[43]

Nonetheless, Luther became increasingly concerned with the apocalyptic element as can be seen by comparing his two prefaces to the book of Revelation. While in 1522 he all but dismisses the significance of the book, in 1545 he goes through a detailed application of the book to the church's history. The thousand years has already occurred and we are now in the last days. The evils of the papal regime are part of the church's suffering.[44] The pope might be the antichrist, "for all his nature, works and doings are against Christ for the destruction of Christ's nature and work."[45]

As in other apocalyptic interpretations, a frightening aspect of this view is his attitude toward Judaism and Islam. Luther called the Turks "the devils' helpmates" and saw the advance of Islam as a sign of the end-time. Even when the siege of Vienna was lifted in 1529, Luther saw this event not as a disproof of his beliefs but as a period of grace.[46] Luther's disgraceful comments about the Jews are better known, but they are not usually placed in an apocalyptic context. While advocating "sharp mercy" and Christian love toward the Jews, Luther was unyielding in his attack (even up to three days before his death). The Jews were a "compass" for determining the devil's penetration into the contemporary church.[47] How much Luther contributed to modern anti-Semitism is debatable. But what is clear is that the split in the meaning of revelation was not healed by Luther. As the church encountered the challenge of a new world, it not only lacked a united front with Judaism and Islam but even lacked a unified Christianity.

One other sign that Luther interpreted as signifying the end of the world was the discovery of America. A German map maker in 1507 had invented "America" as part of a mythical interpretation of the journeys of Columbus, Vespucci, and their successors. Columbus himself thought that he had discovered the entrance to paradise. To this day "America" retains an apocalyptic meaning. Of course, the land mass to Europe's west had been met by explorers before Columbus. But "America" was invented or discovered in the late fifteenth and early sixteenth centuries. The occasion could just as well have been named the "revelation of America."[48]

"America" was central to the transformation of time and place. Henceforth, there was no longer the "island earth" surrounded by water; now there were to be continents separated by oceans. And now the future came to exist with the openness of human possibilities. In secular thinking, "America" became a name for the future and for progress. In religious terms, "America" became the place where God's kingdom was beginning to be revealed. We shall see in chapter 5 that the nation that calls its citizens "Americans" has been and continues to be a hotbed of apocalyptic activity.

RELIGION AND RELIGIONS

The emergence of the modern concept of religion both followed upon the Protestant Reformation and was in reaction to the uncertainty unleashed by the loss of church authority in the early sixteenth century. The beginnings of change are foreshadowed in the fifteenth-century writers Nicholas Cusanus (1401–1464) and Marsilio Ficino (1433–1499).

Both men make a connection between Christian religion and a wider humanity, using "religion" here much as Augustine or Aquinas had used the term.[49] But instead of condemning paganism, Cusanus and Ficino recognized that the doctrine of Christ could embrace all peoples. In *De Christiana Religione*, Ficino writes, "Every religion has something good in it; as long as it is directed toward God the creator of all things, it is a true Christian religion."[50] There is no wavering here from the orthodox belief that true religion is Christian religion, but a plural use of "religions" is on the horizon. Ernest Cassirer sees the preparation for a dialectical reversal within Ficino's concept of revelation: "If *all* spiritual values embraced by the history of humanity can be reduced to and based upon a single revelation, it would also seem to imply conversely that this desired unity of revelation is to be sought in the *whole* of history and in the totality of its forms."[51]

John Calvin

John Calvin (1509–1564) provides a main link in the evolution of "religion." His main work is entitled *Institutes of the Christian Religion*. Like Ficino's "Christian religion" the term reflects a medieval meaning while foreshadowing the "religion" and "religions" that began to appear at the end of the sixteenth century. One could as easily translate Calvin's title as *Instructions in Christian Practice* or *A Guide to Christian Living*. That is, Christian religion was not yet one of the world's religions but instead the personal practices of reading scripture, praying, and practicing virtue.[52] And yet Calvin's work, following upon Luther and systematizing the gains of the Reformation, was a step toward "the Christian religion" as one institution among many. In Karl Barth's view, Calvin was a tragic figure because he was the most mature, most successful of the Reformers, so that by 1555 the Reformation had ended by taking on historical form.[53]

Calvin opens the *Institutes* with the statement that "true and substantial wisdom (*doctrina*) principally consists of two parts, the knowledge of God and the knowledge of ourselves."[54] That statement and his subsequent contention that the two knowledges are inseparable, form the framework for the entire work. There are not two knowledges of God. No abyss separates knowledge of the Creator and knowledge of the Redeemer.[55] On this point, Calvin is closer to the thirteenth century than to the seventeenth century.

Calvin has a structure for this knowledge that parallels Luther's use of word of God and inner revelation. Through the Scriptures the knowledge of God is made known to the believer. Scripture testifies that the whole creation speaks of God. Commenting on Romans 1:22, Calvin proposes that revelation is offered to all people but is not accepted by most of them. Human misperception, which is traceable to sin, is the cause of ignorance. In his *Commentary on Romans,* Calvin says that humans are blind but they are not so blind as to be faultless.[56] In the *Institutes,* he changes the metaphor of persons being blind to "persons who are old or whose eyes are by any means become dim." If someone is blind, failure to see is a physical not a moral failure, but the person whose eyes are dim needs "the assistance of spectacles," the scripture that "dispels the darkness and gives us a clear view of the true God."[57]

The scriptures can only succeed as spectacles when the Holy Spirit speaks within the believer. "For as God alone is a sufficient witness of himself in his own word, so also the word will never gain credit in the hearts of man, till it be confirmed by the internal testimony of the spirit."[58] Like Luther, Calvin tends to reserve "revelation" for the interior movement. "The Office of the Spirit . . . is not to feign new and unheard of revelation . . . but to seal in our minds the same doctrine which the Gospel delivers."[59] "Belief requires such a sentiment as cannot be produced but by a revelation from heaven."[60] Karl Barth explains that because for Calvin there was a conversation of the Spirit with itself—the Spirit in the inspired word and the Spirit dwelling within the believer—there was not a twofold truth but a single point above the antithesis of subject and object, inner and outer."[61]

Calvin undoubtedly saw it that way and thought that the connection of outer word and inner testimony was obvious. "I speak of nothing but what every believer experiences in his heart."[62] To succeeding generations it was not so clear. One part of the seventeenth century latched on to the inner voice of God as the basis for either natural religion or a religion of the Spirit. Another stream of thought found God in a book, either the Bible or the book of Nature. For many Christians, revelation became another name for the Bible. For other people, Christian and non-Christian, the knowledge of God was sought in the book of Nature (a metaphor in use since the twelfth century but one with a new meaning in the seventeenth century).

SEVENTEENTH-CENTURY RELIGION

The plural "religions" was initially used for the many Christian denominations that had sprung up in the sixteenth century. It was first used in German in 1563 and in English in 1593.[63] This way of speaking about

Christian sects or denominations ceased in the seventeenth century but the use of "religions" in the plural had come to stay.[64] The successor to an intramural Christian use was "natural religion" and "revealed religion." The debates in the second half of the seventeenth century centered on whether natural religion prepares and leads into revealed religion or whether they are separate bodies of truth. More important than how the two are related was the assumption that these two things exist. The language of natural and revealed religion remains to this day.

So successful was this seventeenth-century invention that this distinction is thought to be obvious and traditional. W. Cantwell Smith, countering this view, writes: "The concept of revelation had been standard in Christian thinking from New Testament times. Yet no one before the eighteenth century had ever supposed that what was revealed was a religion."[65] Smith is inaccurate in ascribing this change to the eighteenth century. More than a dozen books published between 1670 and 1700 have the term "revealed religion" in the title.[66] But his main point remains, namely, that the introduction of "revealed religion" was a revolution from which we have never recovered. The term "revealed religion" made little sense in the seventeenth century and makes even less sense today. Yet it continues to float through discussions of religion and revelation as a common currency. Its effect is to obstruct thinking about reason, revelation, and religion.[67]

An even stranger term, and just as common, is "revealed theology." Peter Byrne begins his book on natural religion by attributing to Thomas Aquinas the view that "natural theology contains a body of truths about God and his relationship to the world discoverable by the use of unaided human reason and is contrasted with a body of truths—revealed theology—discoverable only by reflection on God's special revelation in history." On the following page, Byrne allows that "the substance, if not the terminology, of the distinction between natural and revealed theology is certainly to be found in Aquinas."[68] But the terminology is decisive here if one wishes to understand Aquinas, as well as the novelty of natural and revealed religion. Byrne cites the one place in Aquinas's writings that he uses "natural theology," but it has nothing to do with the distinction at issue; it is used in contrast to the mythical and civic theology of the Greeks.[69] And the phrase "revealed theology"—theology as what God has revealed—would have struck Aquinas as absurd.

"Natural religion" could be a meaningful term, depending on what it is contrasted to. At its origin, the clearest opposite to natural religion was conventional religion. This contrast is first developed in the writings of

Lord Edward Herbert of Cherbury (1583–1648), early in the seventeenth century. For Herbert, natural religion is what is stamped on every soul at birth. The term natural here is not the opposite of supernatural; in fact, the origin of this natural religion is similar to the origin of what the Middle Ages called supernatural, that is, it is directly from divine infusion. Natural religion for Herbert was not the opposite of revealed religion, a term that did not yet exist.

By emphasizing what is given to (human) nature, Herbert makes the externals of religion not only secondary but mostly a cause of religious decline. Herbert attributed corruption to ceremony and priesthood, thereby echoing Reformation themes. But the "word of God" now gets included in what is to be judged. Mankind has the liberty of passing judgment on "what in Sacred Scriptures may be called the pure and undisputed word of God."[70] "Disputed doctrine can be tested adequately by no evidence save that of revelation made directly to ourselves."[71] While the "historically revealed" is allowed to exist, it does not fare well in this framework.

Writing at the same time as Descartes, Herbert takes an epistemological approach to religion, searching for certainty amid "diverse and sundry religions." He assumes that human beings are "the same or very little differing in all ages and countries."[72] This human nature is good, the doctrine of human depravity is a fiction. And since God is good, then the means of salvation must be available to everyone in all ages. The "only Catholic and uniform church" is the means of salvation but this church is a set of ideas, not an institution.

Herbert believed that there are five "catholic articles or common notions" that "by no means depend on some faith or tradition but have been engraved on the human mind by God . . . acknowledged as true throughout the world by every age." His five articles are: (1) that there is some supreme divinity (*numen*); (2) that this divinity ought to be worshiped; (3) that virtue joined with piety is the best method of divine worship; (4) that we should return to our right selves from sin; and (5) that reward or punishment is bestowed after this life is finished.[73]

Although critics were quick to point out that actual history did not confirm these notions as universal, Herbert's five articles continued to have some currency for two centuries. He built in the provision that these ideas are often obscured in actual history, which meant that contrary historical evidence did not disconfirm his theory. For example, he maintained that "almost all ancient religion is symbolic" so that what seems to be a pantheon of gods is not really idolatry. Wise men knew that God could not be discovered in one thing.[74] Priesthood has corrupted the practice of religion, but behind these corruptions the five articles survived everywhere. His claim was not directly refutable with any evidence.

For Herbert, reason was an instrument for inference. This movement of the mind to infer conclusions was called "discourse." Reason was thus very limited in power; it was not a competitor with revelation. The choice is between revelation/religion on one side and the corruptions of society and conventional religion on the other side.

A different direction for the meaning of natural religion was taken by a group of thinkers known as the Cambridge Platonists. There were echoes of both Neoplatonism and Stoicism in their views of nature and reason. In contrast to Herbert's reason as mere instrument, the Cambridge group took reason to be the voice of God. In Neoplatonic thought, human reason is a participant in divine reason.

Benjamin Whichcote (1609–1683) was the leader of this group. In his writings, revealed truth is superimposed on natural truth, and what we have is "more of the same thing." The only difference between natural and revealed was "in way of descent to us."[75] He employs the Neoplatonic term "emanation" in distinguishing these two kinds of descent. Thus, a natural religion and a revealed religion work seamlessly together. He introduces the interesting term "after-revelation" for what scripture brings to reason. "God has set up Two Lights: to enlighten us in our Way; the light of reason which is the light of creation; and the Light of Scripture, which is After-Revelation from him."[76]

The great emphasis on reason and knowledge may seem to be a kind of gnosticism, in which intellect is all that is needed for salvation. But the knowledge that Whichcote describes presupposes a "concomitant affection" for God. Knowledge and love must come together. He also places Christ at the center of a mediational process concerned with redemption. Christ is not merely a model for humans or a teacher of truths, but he is also the focus of moral transformation.[77]

With his emphasis on reason, Whichcote is able to take a surprisingly modern attitude toward the interpretation of scripture. Like Origen, Augustine, Luther, and Calvin before him, Whichcote insists that "Scripture is clear, full in all matters of life" while at the same time acknowledging that God is hidden and the work of the Holy Spirit is necessary to reveal the deeper meaning of scripture. He thinks that it is not enough to cite texts of the Bible: "Scripture as a rule of faith is not one Scripture but all." One must "see what is said" but not think it is enough that it is "barely related in that book."[78] He would no doubt have appreciated the work of modern scholarship that came two centuries later.

Ralph Cudworth (1617–1688), one of Whichcote's disciples, tried to show that even the complex doctrines of revealed religion can be known by reason. Thus, the Christian doctrines of Trinity and Incarnation were able to be discovered by the light of reason. *The True Intellectual System of the Universe* in 1678 is one of the first places where "revealed religion" is used. In that work, Cudworth scoured ancient sources of Greece, Rome, Egypt, and Persia to show that dogmas, which were being attacked as irrational, had in fact been held throughout history on rational grounds.[79] Ironically, while he was trying to close the split between reason and revelation, his introduction of "natural and revealed religion" created an unbridgeable gap.

Four years later a work by John Dryden (1631–1700) also opposed Herbert's split between a natural religion and historical Christianity. Dryden criticizes what had come to be called "deism." In a work whose title (*Religio Laici*) was nearly the same as Herbert's, Dryden takes aim at the belief that humans discover the truth of religion from within their own minds:

> These truths are not the product of thy Mind,
> But dropt from Heaven, and of a Nobler Kind.
> Reveal'd religion first inform'd thy Sight
> And Reason saw not till Faith sprung the Light.[80]

Here the concept of revealed religion has congealed into something "dropt from heaven." Herbert's ideas of a natural religion infused at birth were vulnerable to criticism, but Dryden's assumption of the term "revealed religion" boxed him into an opposite corner. Revelation is now an external object. Another line in Dryden's poem, "Tis Revelation what thou think'st discourse," is intended to affirm that knowledge is a gift ("dropt from heaven") rather than a human achievement ("the product of thy mind"). What disappears in this contrast of natural and revealed religions is the spoken word, language as public utterance. The result was that discussion of revelation, discovery, and enlightenment passed from religious thinkers to mathematical scientists.

Scientific Takeover

The previous section on the Cambridge Platonists dealt with one strand of seventeenth-century thought that struggled with religious formulas. The names of Herbert, Whichcote, and Cudworth are not well known, even though they shaped the religious language still in use today. The section to which I turn now includes the names of Copernicus, Kepler,

Bacon, Galileo, and Newton, names that are among the most famous in history. These men also contributed to today's religious language, each of them maintaining that their scientific study gave support to a divine maker and a virtuous human race. Johannes Kepler called the scientist the "priest of God"; Robert Boyle saw his scientific vocation to be a "priest of nature."[81] There is no reason to doubt the sincerity of their religious devotion. But there is good reason to think that the church and its theologians sided too completely with the mathematical scientist.

The main conflict of the seventeenth century pitted Platonist against Platonist. The group known to history as the Cambridge Platonists would be better called Neoplatonists. Their opponents were Platonists of the Pythagorean kind, that is, believers that the universe is explainable in mathematical terms. The opposite of both kinds of Platonists were the Aristotelians, many of whom were not true to the spirit of Aristotle, a biologist and physicist. Aristotle described the world we sense. The new scientist distrusted the world of the senses in favor of what lies behind and above. The world was now to be understood with the mathematics of Plato, Pythagoras, Descartes, Leibniz, Newton. The metaphors for knowledge and truth were visual; eyesight did not provide the truth, but sunlight and sight were the stepping off points for mathematical insight.

The Neoplatonic stream of thought, which had a continuous tradition since the third century, offered the only sustained alternative to the mathematician. In the early Middle Ages, Neoplatonic thought received a boost from the writings of Pseudo-Dionysius. The late Middle Ages was enlivened by the publication of the *Corpus Hermeticum,* which purported to be an ancient Egyptian book of wisdom.[82] Although the work was later shown to be a product of the Roman Empire, the "hermetic tradition" was an important impulse for an organic philosophy in which God is the soul of the universe and the human being encounters the divine directly in sensual and rational experience.

This mystical way of thinking about the universe is prone to irrationalism. It was lumped together with magic and condemned by both scientist and theologian. Obviously, this philosophy did conflict at points with Christian orthodoxy. It set an impossible task in trying to fit itself within revealed religion. The result was often irrational. But a revelation in the form of ancient wisdom known through secret oracles was attractive to part of the human race and a part of the mathematical scientist.

People are surprised when they find out that Isaac Newton spent more time on alchemy and the study of biblical prophecy than he did on his mathematical science. Newton even cites the *Corpus Hermeticum,* which had been discredited almost a century earlier. In the most rational of centuries in which the secrets of the book of Nature were revealed to be mathematical, the search along the lower path did not cease, the search for an emotionally engaging contact with the source of all meaning.

The choice that confronted the seventeenth century was whether God is in or out, whether God is the inner force of the created universe or an outside maker and governor. The great astronomer Johannes Kepler (1571–1630) was a convert in 1605 from the former to the latter: "My aim is to show that the machine of the universe is not similar to a divine animated being, but similar to a clock."[83] For two centuries the image of God as clock maker (or clock winder) dominated Christian apologetics. The image was terribly reductive but one that was consonant with the seventeenth-century approach to science and religion.[84] For Kepler, God was still to be found in the world's design, in the way that the clock is made. A generation later with Galileo, God was consigned solely to the role of efficient cause. God starts the world, but we cannot infer anything of the nature of God from the created product.

The men of powerful influence in the seventeenth century all spoke with reverence of revelation. Descartes, Bacon, Boyle, Newton, and Locke paid their respects to the scriptures as the source of revealed truths. With greater enthusiasm they also believed that God was revealed in the discovery of the laws of nature. Whereas the book of scripture is often ambiguous, mathematical science offered the absolute certainty to which the century aspired.[85]

Such was the mind-set of Galileo (1564–1642) in his famous conflict with the church. The church had not condemned Copernicus in the previous century for saying that the earth goes around the sun (while many astronomers did condemn Copernicus's view). Church officials were anxious to work out a compromise with Galileo, who had many friends and supporters among the clergy. Galileo suggested that the text of the Bible in which Joshua stops the sun should be interpreted metaphorically. Galileo had a good point. But the cardinals who insisted that Galileo's theory was a mathematical but not a factual explanation were not entirely off the mark.[86]

The celebrated myth of Galileo has the courageous individual who is dealing in fact up against the oppressive institution that is concerned not with truth but only with its own power. The actual story is one of stubbornness on both sides. Galileo, as much as the church officials, could not admit the limitations of his point of view.[87] Lewis Mumford accuses Galileo of a crime much greater than what he was accused of by the church. Galileo, according to Mumford, divided the world into subjective and objective, "dismissing as unsubstantial and unreal the cultural

accretions of meaning that had made mathematics—itself a purely subjective distillation—possible."[88]

Mumford may be unfair in loading the whole problem on Galileo's
shoulders. Galileo was but one of a cast of many, stretching from Kepler
at the beginning of the century to Newton at the end. But the project was
as Mumford describes it, namely, a split of the world into objective and
subjective spheres, followed by the application of mathematics to discover
the laws of the objective world. The slate of past history had to be wiped
clean so that a perfectly logical system could be built, a system that could
be described in a single, unambiguous language. There were several
attempts in the century, most notably by Johann Comenius and by Gottfried Leibniz, to invent a universal language. "There will be universal
peace over the whole world," wrote Comenius in his *Via Lucis;* "there will
be no ground for dissenting when all men have the same truth presented
to their eyes."[89]

Marin Mersenne, a Catholic priest, was a champion of Galileo and a
friend of Descartes. Mersenne believed that the establishing of a natural
order was a precondition for certifying miracles. Without laws of nature
how can we be sure that God intervenes miraculously by breaking the
law?[90] Descartes himself needed a kind of miraculous intervention to
establish a connection between the inner and the outer.

Francis Bacon (1561–1626) was not one of the scientific leaders of
the seventeenth century, but there is probably no one in the century who
did as much to shape the political, practical, and religious implications of
the new science. In the *Advancement of Learning* Bacon warns against
"confounding the two different streams of philosophy and revelation
together." Revelation and sense differ in matter and manner, yet the spirit
of man and its cells are the same; we receive them as "different liquors
through different conduits."[91]

Bacon believed that it was a religious duty to use natural philosophy
to restore man's control over nature. Although Bacon is the first writer
clearly to pit "man against nature," he professes that this power is to be
used with humility. Natural philosophy "is rightly given to religion as her
most fruitful handmaid since the one displays the will of God, the other
his power."[92] In the Garden of Eden, "uncorrupted natural knowledge"
was not the occasion of Adam's fall (the desire for moral knowledge was).
Bacon's millenarian hope was for the restoration of this pure state before
the fall.[93]

Was this humility genuine or was Bacon simply hiding his true
motives behind religion? No one can say with certainty, but one should

not be overly harsh in judging him in the light of much later developments. He was perhaps naive in not recognizing an inevitable violence in the use of power to "conquer nature" and to extend the "human empire." Unlike most philosophers who only speculate about power, Bacon was chancellor of England and court counselor to Elizabeth I and James I. His extension of the "human empire" was not clearly distinct from the policies of the British Empire.

Given the historical setting of Bacon's writing, the "man" who is conqueror included only a small slice of upper-class European males. That makes Bacon a special point of attack for modern feminism. In his division of man and nature, women came in on the side of nature, part of the realm to be conquered by man. One does not have to engage in big jumps of inference for this conclusion. Bacon used overtly sexual language in describing man's relation to nature. Far from being arrogant, however, the good scientist is a gallant suitor who has to establish a chaste and lawful marriage between mind and nature. Science provides a nuptial couch for the mind and the universe. The profession of humility here is not convincing to his many feminist critics today. Bacon's most ominous comparison was to the investigation of witches. "If the inquisition of truth is his object, neither ought a man to make scruple of entering and penetrating into these holes and corners."[94]

Bacon lived at a time when the myth of a social contract began to be elaborated by Hobbes, Locke, Rousseau, and others. The salvation in the future will be a return to a previous "state of nature." A secularizing of the Christian doctrine of original sin turns historical man into an exile from the state of nature. The (present) society is a necessary evil, but now a future could be imagined where man would not be alienated from himself. For Bacon, the millennial expectations depended upon science and its power to create new mechanical arts (technology). While the Christian revelation now functioned as an object of faith, the real revelation of truth was the scientific project of inventing or restoring paradise.

Isaac Newton (1642–1727), a more complex character than Bacon, is probably the most famous mathematical scientist in all of history, but a man obsessed with religious themes in his private life. Although he was as insistent as Descartes and Bacon in keeping science and religion separate, his greatest hope was to give support to "the belief of a Deity." In his mechanistic picture of the world he left open a place for "the very first cause, which certainly is not mechanical."[95] Even the limitations of his system were seen to be additional proof of God. "Some considerable irregularities . . . will be apt to increase, till this Systeme wants a Reformation."[96]

It is perhaps unfortunate that Newton succeeded so well. "Nature and Nature's laws were hid in night: God said, Let Newton be! And all was light."[97] His laws of gravity were an inestimable contribution to science. But he also convinced his contemporaries and many theologians of the next generations that his mathematical system was the appropriate way to support religion. David Hartley wrote in the preface to the second edition of Newton's *Principia Mathematica*: "Newton's distinguished word will be the safest protection against the attacks of atheists."[98] That may have been true, given the choice at the time between theism and atheism. To the question of a great being outside the universe, the atheist's answer was no; the theist said yes. But neither answer had much to do with a living religious tradition.

If the world consists of passive bits of matter, then a great outside force must be the first mover. Newton's proof of God's existence bears some superficial resemblance to Thomas Aquinas's "first way," but without any of the rich historical context that Aquinas presupposed. In addition to the empirical proof of a first mover, Newton also believed in a revelation, consisting of truths that were given to Noah. This revelation had been preserved unchanged in the New Testament and in other esoteric sources.[99] Newton did not have an apocalyptic expectation, but he did have an irrational context for his mathematical beliefs.

John Locke (1632–1704) forms an appropriate cap to the seventeenth-century development of revealed religion. While he seems to want a balance of faith and reason, his meaning of "revelation" tips the balance toward reason, which is "our last judge and guide in everything."[100] Faith is assent to a proposition. This assent is based on "the credit of the proposer, as coming from God in some extraordinary way of communication. This way of discovering truths to men we call revelation."[101]

Locke's reference to "the way of discovering" is reminiscent of a use of revelation during the Middle Ages. But it is *propositions* that crowd out any alternative meaning for revelation. Locke is skeptical of any internal, private movement of the Spirit. He thus distances himself from Herbert's common notions of religion, as well as the way Luther and Calvin used revelation. Outward signs (especially miracles) have to accompany propositions that can be above reason but not against reason. Revelation is "natural reason enlarged."[102]

Just as for Newton, Locke needed a deity for both epistemological and political reasons. The universe is a tidy place under the control of this deity. Similar to his contemporary Gottfried Leibniz and to Alexander Pope, who was to follow, Locke's God was in his heaven, and all was right with the world. The role of Christ was no longer as redeemer; he came to clarify matters already knowable by reason.

Like many others who struggled with the problem, Locke seems to be inconsistent in his view of the Bible. He contrasts the clarity of natural religion ("plain and very intelligible to all mankind") to the "revealed truths which are conveyed to us by books and language . . . liable to the common and natural obscurities and difficulties incident to words."[103] On the other hand, Locke believed that for people who cannot find the truth by the use of reason "there needs no more but to read the inspired books to be instructed; all the duties of morality lie there clear and plain, and easy to understand."[104] The key word is "morality"; the Bible has clear precepts of morality for the simple folk.

Locke posits a state of nature in his political theorizing. ("In the beginning all the world was America").[105] Unlike Hobbes or Bacon he does not seem to have any millennial urge, no dark underside to which the book of Revelation might appeal. He was nearly a pure rationalist. On one point, however, Locke opened the door to a major shift in the conflict of theism and atheism. He speculated that although matter itself cannot give rise to thought, God could superadd thinking to matter.[106] That started some people wondering whether matter has to be imagined as being passive and whether a great first mover is necessary. The change from British theism of the late seventeenth century to the French atheism of the eighteenth century required just a minor shift in the relation of atoms and motion.

EIGHTEENTH-CENTURY ENLIGHTENMENT

The eighteenth century is known as the age of enlightenment. In the most famous essay on that topic, Immanuel Kant defined enlightenment as daring to be wise, "the escape of men from their self-incurred tutelage."[107] Kant said that he placed the main point of enlightenment in matters of religion. He cautioned that the century was not an enlightened age but an age that was becoming enlightened. The leaders of the French Revolution took inspiration from Kant's call in their rebellion against revealed religion.

After Newton and Locke, lesser minds took up the task of articulating the relation between natural and revealed religion. Samuel Clarke, John Toland, and Matthew Tindal were among the most prominent writers who tried to balance the natural and the revealed. Nothing they did could prevent a slow erosion of credibility for the category of revealed religion. In his study of nature in the eighteenth century, Basil Willey concludes that "nature was to furnish the principal evidence of religion, while a somewhat embarrassing Revelation must be harmonised with it as best might be."[108]

Samuel Clarke (1675–1729) stayed close to Newton's mechanics and to the great mover behind the universe. Few people would have read Newton or followed his reasoning from the mathematics of his astronomical calculations to a deity. Clarke spread the gospel of theism as a simple, clear, and certain system of religion. He devised a series of twelve categories to describe the divine being: eternal, immutable, self-existent, and so forth. Clarke was still being cited by Rousseau a century and a half later, but his arguments and his reputation largely faded from the history books.[109]

John Toland (1670–1722) was intent on taking any mystery out of Christianity. Everything is reduced to clear definitions. He was especially interested in reducing the distance between natural and revealed religion. His main work is a rather uninspiring exposition of a rational religion. In one of his letters, however, he suggests that motion is essential to matter, a point on which the eighteenth century turned.[110]

Matthew Tindal (1655–1733) argued that natural religion "differs not from the Reveal'd but in the manner of its being communicated." Tindal and those who followed this line of thinking had a way of addressing the problem of universality. Christianity—in its essence—was thought to have always existed. "True Christianity" is identical with human reason. Theism is an acceptably rational religion, while doctrines as accretions over time are unnecessary and divisive. Herbert's "common notions" survived here, freed from the divine stamp on the soul that Herbert had assumed. Human reason establishes the necessary doctrines of religion.[111]

The most systematic exposition of natural and revealed religion belonged to Bishop Joseph Butler (1692–1752) in his *Analogy of Religion*. Butler tries mightily to give a boost to revealed religion. He accuses Tindal of rejecting revelation, an accusation that is not entirely fair. Both men have a natural religion, and for Tindal, revelation is a repetition of the same material. For Butler, "though natural religion is the foundation and principal part of Christianity, it is not in any sense the whole of it." Furthermore, Butler argues that revelation is "an authoritative publication of natural religion and so affords the evidence of testimony for the truth of it."[112]

Butler acknowledges that "neither the Jewish nor Christian revelations have been universal" so that "both revelations have had different degrees of evidence."[113] This admission is a key issue in a century when equality and humanity became rallying cries. Once the category "Christian revelation" is accepted, Christians are caught in a dilemma: either admit that these truths apply to only one group of people in only one slice of history, or else, arrogantly claim that Christianity already has the universal truths that everyone else is searching for.

Neither Augustine, Aquinas, Luther, nor Calvin had this problem. For any Christian writer before the seventeenth century there could not be two revelations. There was divine revelation, which, of course, is universal. Not all Christian writers grasped that the Christian interpretation of that revelation had limits and biases. But a divine revelation implies the possibility of Christian–Jewish–Muslim dialogue on the meaning of revelation. No such dialogue is possible from within a Christian revelation or a Jewish revelation (Muslims were seldom mentioned by Christians as legitimate players in this religious search, and Muslims did not accept the phrase "Muslim revelation").

Butler's attempt to defend revealed religion or Christian revelation led him to claim that "the natural and revealed dispensation of things" are equally obscure. The general drift of the eighteenth century was toward simple truths and what the Puritans in North America called "the art of plain speaking." Jonathan Swift ridiculed the idea that "unless a proposition can be presently comprehended by the weakest noddle, it is no part of religion."[114]

Butler, too, was counterattacking this demand for simplicity. While other Christian apologists had argued that the Bible was as clear as the book of Nature, Butler went in the opposite direction. Both sources are unclear, and "we are incompetent judges of both nature and religion."[115] In a longer view of history, Butler had a good point. The eighteenth century's obsession with simple, clear, certain ideas proved to be temporary and illusory. But arguing for mystery in religion because there is also mystery in nature was not convincing to people who were certain that all the obscurities of nature would soon be eliminated. Butler's defense of revealed religion or Christian revelation did not stop the tide of British philosophy, which tended to view propositions "dropt from heaven" as useful fiction for the masses but not a serious philosophical question.[116]

In France, a more direct attack on Christianity was made in the name of nature. The century can be seen in miniature as played out in the experience of Denis Diderot (1713–1784). Starting out as a Catholic boy who considered holy orders, Diderot passed to deism, then to skepticism, finally to atheism. Early in his life, Diderot still looked to Newton as a necessary defense against atheism. "Only the deist can oppose the atheist. The superstitious man is not so strong an opponent."[117] But eventu-

ally by combining Newton and Descartes, Diderot concluded that he had
no need of God, that the very question was irrelevant.[118] If matter is
active—something that Newton denied and Descartes affirmed—then
there is no need for a first mover. And if matter is all there is in our experience—something that Newton affirms and Descartes denies—matter or
nature is the name for all that is. The two greatest thinkers of the seventeenth century became mutually corrective.[119]

Diderot was a dramatist and the editor of the first *Encyclopedia*. In
both roles his work was far reaching, and it helped to undermine traditional forms of authority. What remained to be done was for a great sys-
tematizer to lay out the case for eighteenth-century atheism. The person
who did that was Baron Paul d'Holbach (1723–1789) in his three volume *The System of Nature or Laws of the Moral and Physical World*. Holbach simply ascribes to nature the qualities that Samuel Clarke had
attributed to God. That is, nature is eternal, immutable, self-existent, or
necessary. There is no need for a mover outside of nature. "Motion is a
manner [of being] which matter derives from its own existence."[120] Holbach rejects any special revelation as self-contradictory: why would a God
of universal love be revealed to only one small group?[121]

In 1770 the Assembly destroyed Holbach's books and called upon
Abbé Nicolas-Sylvain Bergier to respond to the rising tide of atheism.
Bergier's argument relies on the premise that "movement is not essential
to matter" and "we are forced to believe that there is in the universe a substance of a different nature . . . a motor that is not itself matter."[122] Here
was the best defense Christianity seemed able to offer, one formulated
entirely in terms of matter and motion.

Holbach's apotheosis of nature has an echo in both first-century
Stoicism and twentieth-century ecology. He begins his *System* by saying,
"Man is the work of Nature: he exists in nature; he is submitted to her
laws: he cannot deliver himself from them even in thought."[123] Stoicism
was consistent in drawing the moral that we must yield to nature
"whether it asks for our children, our country, our body or anything
whatever."[124] One of the Stoics' founders compared man to a dog tied to
a cart; the dog's choice is to run freely along with the cart or else be
dragged along by the cart. The eighteenth century, for all its talk of reverence for nature, did not have the same humility as the Stoics. The
premise now was that the dog had grown up, and it would decide where
the cart went. "Man" was now in charge.

Holbach, similar to many writers today, did not see the severe problem caused by asserting that man is part of nature.[125] Unless one con-
ceives of freedom as submission to the inevitable, the question of the

relation of nature and freedom remains. Although the human being cannot step outside of natural processes (for example, the food chain), human life is not simply determined by natural laws. The human being has the ability to say yes or no to what nature offers, thus altering many natural processes.

Jean-Jacques Rousseau (1712–1778) avoided a simplistic reducing of everything to nature but at the cost of having a complex and confusing meaning of nature. Rousseau started out as a friend of Diderot and the other *philosophes,* but he became their enemy. The break was precipitated by Voltaire's mockery of the Christian's faith in providence after the Lisbon earthquake of 1755. Rousseau's *Letter on Providence* was one of the inspirations for Voltaire's *Candide.*[126]

Rousseau's views on revelation and religion are best captured in a long sermon in *Emile* and in the final section of the *Social Contract.* These two pieces of writing are as good as any sources for understanding today's discussion of religion. Karl Barth began his tracing of modern Protestant theology with Rousseau: "It is from Rousseau onwards and originating from Rousseau that the thing called theological rationalism, in the full sense of the term, exists."[127] Many people have called Rousseau the first modern man. All the conflicts of modernity are evident in his self-conscious, candid, and boastful *Confessions.* Hannah Arendt's comment put it succinctly: Jean-Jacques was at war with Rousseau.[128]

Book 4 of *Emile* outlines the boy's introduction to religion (from which he has been shielded until the age of fifteen). Rousseau, through the mouthpiece of a renegade priest, presents natural religion, which, he explains, is another name for theism or true Christianity. Whereas Diderot used Descartes and Newton against each other, Rousseau has traces of both of them to support his position. The universe shows an intelligible design, the work of a providential deity who created man free and innocent of evil. All of Rousseau's doctrines of natural religion are argued from what he takes to be the obvious facts of experience.

In his *Confessions,* Rousseau says that the attack of the encyclopedists had strengthened his faith. "The study of man and the universe had everywhere shown me the final causes and the intelligence which directed them." He goes on to say that he had devoted himself for several years to reading the Bible, especially the Gospels.[129] In *Emile,* Rousseau stitches together a sentimental attachment to Jesus and a description of natural religion.[130]

Following this description of natural religion in *Emile,* Rousseau makes a sustained attack on revealed religion. "We have three principal religions in Europe. One accepts a single revelation, the second accepts two, the third accepts three."[131] His statement is not true since each of the religions accepted only one revelation. Rousseau, however, might have argued that Christian revelation claims to supersede Jewish revelation and Islam claims to transcend both. Rousseau rightly judges that such religious claims lead to wars fought in the name of God.

Rousseau's main adversary was the Catholic church and all its eighteenth-century apparatus. In the *Social Contract*, Rousseau names three kinds of religion but immediately dismisses the religion of priesthood as so bad that it is not worth discussing. The "religion of man" (equivalent to the true Christianity that Jesus taught) is a beautiful but impractical ideal because a true Christian is unconcerned with this world. Practicality requires a "civil religion" with state-imposed rituals and the one virtue of tolerance.[132]

Reason and emotion play important roles in Rousseau's religion (and ethics) but revelation is illogical and expendable. In a letter to the archbishop of Paris, Rousseau asked, "Is it simple, is it natural that God should go in search of Moses to speak to Jean-Jacques Rousseau?"[133] Although Rousseau's question is typically self-centered, it is a legitimate question. The church, instead of working on that question, simply condemned Rousseau and his view of revelation in *Emile*. The Assembly declared the book "subversive of religion, morals and decency, seditious, impious and sacrilegious, besides much else."[134] The church agreed with this political judgment, and Rousseau spent the years after 1762 in flight and exile.

Central to Rousseau's idea of a social contract was a state of nature (which he admitted may have never existed but was needed as a regulative ideal).[135] In *Emile*, more so than in the *Social Contract*, society is presented as something negative, the source of all evil. The boy Emile is prepared by his tutor to live in a world beyond society—beyond *this* society—where the general will of the people will be reunited with nature. Rousseau has a prescient comment in 1762 on the coming of revolution and the end of European monarchies.[136] As early as 1791, there were books that credited or blamed Rousseau as the author of the French Revolution. Edmund Burke called him "the insane Socrates."[137] In 1794, Rousseau's remains were disinterred from the Isle of Poplars and brought to the Paris pantheon, there to be buried opposite Voltaire.

Its partisans saw the French Revolution as a moral and spiritual crusade. "Everything has changed in the physical order; everything must change in the moral and political order."[138] The hope that the slate could be wiped clean and that the world calendar could be set at zero has been a recurring hope in the West as far back as Plato. As we have seen, the book of Revelation became the handbook for total transformation. And Joachim of Fiore in the twelfth century gave rise to millenarian movements throughout the Middle Ages, with new energy being generated in the sixteenth-century Reformation. By Rousseau's time the search for the end of *this* time was being transformed into a theory of historical progress. The leaders of the French Revolution would hardly have cited the Christian church's millenarian movements as their predecessors. Nevertheless, the impulse toward a "third age," toward a radical reconstruction of society was in continuity with the lower path of revelation's history. Karl Marx and other exponents of revolution would recognize the continuity.

The logic may be paradoxical but not entirely surprising. Revelation along the upper path became almost completely rationalized: it was a series of propositions that any reasonable man could figure out for himself. The alliance of science and religion was victorious in its battle against superstition and magic. At least on the surface, science and rational religion appeared to be the victor. But as Alfred North Whitehead remarked of the eighteenth century, "if man cannot live on bread alone, neither can he live on disinfectants."[139] A revelation promises vision. If all there is to see is propositions, then the vision of a future world will be fueled by other emotions and energies. In the eighteenth century, the possibilities of the future were opened by science, technology, explorations, and discoveries. Those who were not part of the scientific thrust toward the future looked to religious visions for the end of suffering and entrance into paradise.

The United States of America emerged in the late eighteenth century as an uneasy alliance of rationalists and evangelicals, deists and apocalypticists. Henry May, in *Enlightenment in America,* contends that the United States Constitution could not have been written a few years later; it would have been overwhelmed by a more revolutionary force of enlightenment.[140] The secular framework of the Constitution has for the most part restrained and channeled the religious energies of the United States. The traditions of the church and the synagogue have also managed to keep rooted in history the religious drive that is implied in the apocalyptic term "America." In the following chapter, the United States plays a central role in the apocalyptic side of revelation.

5

Liberal and Conservative Religion

T HIS PRESENT CHAPTER brings the story of revelation up through the twentieth century by discussing some representative individuals and movements of the past two centuries. The previous chapter led up to a discussion of England and France during the seventeenth and eighteenth centuries. The main thread of the story shifts now to Germany and its impressive array of philosophers in the nineteenth and twentieth centuries. During this same period, the apocalyptic side of the story emerges most dramatically in the United States of America.

At the beginning of the nineteenth century, the philosophers and theologians of Germany dismissed Judaism as a dead religion of the past.[1] In the twentieth century, however, Jewish writing on revelation documents the vitality of Judaism and offers a new challenge for Christian writers. This chapter culminates in a discussion of Martin Buber and Franz Rosenzweig, two brilliant Jewish writers in the first half of the twentieth century. In this post-Holocaust era, a serious conversation between Christians and Jews is needed, and it is more likely to occur in the United States than in Germany.

The beginning of the modern world, on the political side, was heralded by the American and French revolutions. This double transformation completed the move to modernity that had begun in the literary and fine arts and moved through economics, empirical science, and the "mechanical arts" (technology). In every sphere of human activity it was now assumed that we in the present know better than our distant ancestors.[2]

Until the eighteenth century "tradition" was usually a very positive term, as was a related term, prejudice. To live according to tradition is to be prejudiced, that is, some things have been prejudged before we were born. Hans-Georg Gadamer, in trying to recover the value of tradition, writes that "the prejudice of the eighteenth century was the prejudice against prejudice."[3] Henceforth in the modern world, calling someone prejudiced would be one of the worst accusations possible. But without a form of prejudice, Christian, Jewish, and Muslim traditions become subsumed under modern concepts of reason and enlightenment.

IMMANUEL KANT AND FRIEDRICH SCHLEIERMACHER

The philosopher most responsible for the meaning of reason and enlightenment in modern philosophy and theology is Immanuel Kant (1724–1804). Kant was a rather timid fellow who was reared in a pietistic family in Konigsberg, Germany. He lived a sheltered, academic life but his philosophy had a wide-ranging effect. His major work, *The Critique of Pure Reason*, was published in 1781, but it was not until the end of the decade that it reverberated throughout Europe. Heinrich Heine, looking back from the mid-nineteenth century, drew a parallel between Kant's philosophy and the French revolution: "On both sides of the Rhine we see the same break with the past. All respect is denied to tradition; in France every right, in Germany every thought must justify itself. And as the monarchy fell here (France), so there fell deism, the keystone of the spiritual regime."[4]

Kant has often been compared to Luther, and on the question of revelation they do show some similarity. Neither of them put much stock in the concept of revelation, but their remarks on the subject placed a stamp on the decades and centuries that followed. But while Luther could unleash a new vitality in the Christian church, Kant could only, in the words of Karl Barth, offer terms of peace to the Christian church.[5] Or as Nietzsche would say, Kant was the "great delayer," still propping up his own form of deism.[6]

Kant was enmeshed in a dichotomy that Luther did not have to contend with: revealed religion and natural religion. While Kant is careful not to attack revealed religion, it is superfluous in his system, except as a teaching tool for the nonphilosophical folk of his own day and for the human race of a less-enlightened age. Kant uses natural and revealed as the way of classifying religions according to origin. He tries to clarify "revealed religion" by adding the phrase "or the one standing in need of a revelation."[7] This acknowledgment of the term's inadequacy does not lead Kant to a reassessment of the distinction itself. Only in a couple of places, which I will examine later, does he suggest a meaning of revelation that is more comprehensive and vital than what revealed religion conveys.

The eighteenth century of Kant's Germany was split between a pious, devotional kind of religion and a highly speculative system of doctrinal beliefs. The former was one strand of the eighteenth-century pietistic movements that had spread across many European countries in both Jewish and Christian religions. In Germany, the movement was very strong, with its roots in the 1675 work *Pia Desideria*, by Jacob Spener. The pietists emphasized the Bible and devotion; religion was to be experiential and practical. On the positive side of its simplicity, pietism encouraged kindliness toward other denominations and help for the needy and poor. On a less positive note, it furthered individualism in religion and saw little need for an intellectual exploration of the history and doctrines of Christianity.

The intellectual defense of Christianity was taken up by Christian Wolff (1679–1754). Wolff's deism has similarities with John Locke's, but whereas Locke claimed to be an empiricist, Wolff was purely speculative. He allowed for the possibility of revelation but set many conditions for it. (He wanted God to speak in clear language and in proper syntax). The result was an undermining of any *external* revelation. Wolff invited Christians to rest their case on a foundation of speculative reason.[8]

Immanuel Kant, like most great and influential thinkers, brought together the opposing currents of his time. His aim, he said, was to establish a rational basis for the pious beliefs of his ancestors.[9] As often happens, however, the great synthesizer undermines both elements of the synthesis. For Kant the *speculative* reason of Wolff was not defensible as the basis of Christianity. What he calls *practical reason* is needed to support that piety. "I must therefore abolish knowledge to make room for faith."[10] But now Luther's call that "each man must do his own believing" was to be done without help from tradition or speculative philosophy.

The requirements of Kant's practical reason turn out to echo Edward Herbert's common notions of religion. Instead of Herbert's five articles, Kant has three "universal, true religious beliefs." God is understood according to the threefold parts of any government: (1) creator or holy legislator; (2) preserver of the human race or benevolent ruler; and (3) administrator of the laws or righteous judge.[11] Thus, there can be only one true religion, which is "hidden within and has to do with moral dispositions." Kant allows that there can be several kinds of faith, what he calls "ecclesiastical faiths" that appeal to the senses.[12] With this language Kant completes a rather remarkable reversal. Whereas for the Bible and the Qur'an "faith" means deep interiority and trust in God, Kant's "ecclesiastical faith" is all externals. And whereas "religion" began as ritual and practice, Kant's is "hidden within."

Kant is careful never to reject the *possibility* of revelation, which he usually associates with the Christian scriptures. Unlike Luther, he avoids using the term revelation for inner stirrings of the heart. He says that the wish to observe heavenly influences in ourselves—supposed inner revelations—is a kind of madness.[13] But no one can deny the possibility that scripture "may (with respect to what is historical in it) be regarded as a genuinely divine revelation."[14] That seems to grant an impressive role to scripture, except that "to discover in Scripture that sense which harmonizes with the *most holy* teachings of reason is not only allowable but must be deemed a duty."[15] Notice that now it is the teachings of reason that are deemed most holy.

The *practical* reason that is at issue in revelation supplies the basis for approaching scripture: "The highest principle of all Scriptural exegesis is the moral improvement of men."[16] Even politico-civil law, when not immoral, takes precedence over what is held to be divine statutory law.[17]

Despite Kant's protest that no one can reject the possibility of revelation, his combination of natural religion and practical pietism left no place for revelation, except among historians. Revelation is superfluous for morality. Since the moral law must be obeyed by everyone, it must be simple enough to be grasped by "the commonest unpracticed understanding."[18] Kant does praise the Christian scripture for enriching philosophy in the past. But the religion that once was revealed is now natural.

With the collapse of revealed religion into the standards of reasonableness, Kant has no place for the apocalyptic side of revelation. He was aware that the pietistic movements were prone to having messianic leaders and visions of another world. He was also aware that the New Testament, which he acknowledged might be a divine revelation, ended with the Apocalypse. Similar to exegetes since Origen, Kant interpreted the Revelation of John as "a symbolic representation intended merely to enliven hope and courage and to increase our endeavors to that end." To the apocalyptic visions of John, Kant opposed the teachings of Jesus, which "revealed to his disciples the kingdom of God on earth only in its glorious, soul-elevating moral aspect."[19] In support of this interpretation, Kant cites the scriptural text most favored by nineteenth-century liberal theologians: "The kingdom of God is within you" (Luke 17:21).[20]

In a few places, Kant allows a wider meaning for revelation, a meaning which if pursued might lead to a language different from the deadly pair of natural and revealed religion. In *Religion within the Limits of Reason Alone*, Kant says "all that we need concerning the objective rule of our behavior is adequately revealed to us (through reason and Scripture), and this revelation is at the same time comprehensible to every man."[21] In this passage, Kant subsumes reason under revelation; thus, scripture and reason can appear side by side as expressions of revelation.

There is another passage more remarkable for both its content and placing. It is in the preface to the second edition of *Religion within the Limits of Reason Alone*: "Since, after all, revelation can certainly embrace the pure religion of reason, while the second cannot include what is historical in the first, I shall be able to regard the first as the wider sphere of faith, which includes within itself the second as the *narrower one.*"[22] Here revelation and reason are imagined to be concentric circles, and revelation is the wider circle. This statement would seem to indicate a reversal of the judge and the judged. Is it possible that some power beyond reason is the basis of religion? Kant did not go down that path, but the door was open for those in the nineteenth century who might try such a reversal.

Friedrich Schleiermacher (1786–1834) did not exactly reverse Kant's use of "revelation," but he did succeed in bringing piety to the foreground in a way that Kant had not. If Kant's aim was to support the pious beliefs of his ancestors, Schleiermacher provided support for the piety, if not for all the beliefs. Schleiermacher is one of the first writers to address directly the meaning of revelation. He is aware that the contrast of natural and revealed religions is very problematic.

The discussion of religion and revelation in the seventeenth and eighteenth centuries was largely controlled by scientists and philosophers. With Schleiermacher, the question is put back into the domain of theology. In his early work, *On Religion*, Schleiermacher refers to "theology" only a few times and usually disparagingly. In his mature work, *Christian Faith*, he is intent on defending theology and even has a large part in "professionalizing" theology.[23] He tried to situate his Christian faith historically and geographically. He came to his task well versed in the Enlightenment's newly developing sciences and the study of history.

Unlike many of his idealist colleagues, Schleiermacher saw the human self not as an incarnation of reason but as a member of a historically differentiated community.[24] Thus, Schleiermacher was a forerunner of the scientific study of religion which emerged toward the end of the nineteenth century. He had an appreciation of both the historical and psychological aspects of religion as a human institution. His stance also provided a basis for an ecumenical conversation, although, like so many of his Christian colleagues at that time, Schleiermacher viewed Judaism as a moribund religion.[25]

It is difficult today to approach Schleiermacher neutrally. In the early part of the twentieth century he became the whipping boy for those who were opposed to the Protestant liberal theology of the nineteenth century. Schleiermacher no doubt was the inspiration for much of that theology, but it is not so clear that he meant to say what his successors found him to say. The concepts and distinctions that he used were difficult to grasp and his writing style did not help. He is most famous for basing religion on feeling and for establishing knowledge of God on the feeling of absolute dependence. I will discuss these ideas to the extent that they relate to his meaning of revelation.

Schleiermacher defined his words carefully. When writers do that, they often assume that readers will accept the definitions and proceed from there. But the meanings of words spread out beyond the control of anyone's definitions. The history of a term and its current usage in ordinary language overcome any stipulated definitions. In this instance, such key words as feeling, dependence, and self-consciousness could not be kept within the boundaries of the definitions that Schleiermacher had assigned to them.

In arguing that religion is based on feeling, Schleiermacher says that he cannot accept that divine revelation "operates upon man as a cognitive being. For that would make the revelation to be originally and essentially doctrine."[26] In trying to give revelation a richer meaning than doctrine, he moves away from "man as a cognitive being." His alternative is that "God works upon us directly as a distinctive existence by means of his total impression on us; and this working is always a working upon the self-consciousness." He concludes, "That this does not exclude doctrine but implies it is obvious."[27] Unfortunately, the connection was not obvious to many people who saw here a reduction of religion to feeling and self-consciousness, along with the disparaging of scripture and doctrine.

Schleiermacher wanted to call attention to one kind of feeling and one kind of dependence. He describes several forms that dependence takes, such as that of child to parent and citizen to fatherland. Then he introduces the term "absolute dependence" to convey the human relation to God.[28] This absolute dependence "is always a working upon the self-consciousness." This self-consciousness is something deeper and simpler than self-absorbed reflection. "What is implied in this self-consciousness is to be designated by the word 'God,' and that this is for us the really original signification of the word."[29]

Many Christian critics took from this description not "man's absolute dependence" on God but God's dependence on man's self-consciousness. I think that the two volumes of *Christian Faith* show that this accusation is unfair, but his early attempt at a psychology of religion was easily misinterpreted as conveying that God is a feeling of dependence that man has on the way to his becoming conscious of himself.

Schleiermacher's use of "revelation" has some similar problems. His most precise description of the term is, "we might say that the idea of revelation signifies the *originality* of the fact which lies at the foundation of a religious communion."[30] While he accepts the validity of a distinction between natural and positive religion, he denies that "positive" and "revealed" are synonymous.[31] Revelation has to do with an originating event, not the beliefs of Christianity or other religions. Schleiermacher thus frees the term revelation from where it was stuck for two centuries, cut off from what is "natural" in religion.

Schleiermacher, however, did not free the term revelation from confinement to the past. It would seem that he has a context to describe revelation as present, experiential, and relational, but he does not do that with any consistency. Early in *Christian Faith* he writes that "if we speak of an original revelation of God to man or in man, the meaning will always be just this, that along with the absolute dependence which characterizes not only man but all temporal existence, there is given to man also the immediate self-consciousness of it, which becomes a consciousness of God."[32] That description of revelation would seem to fit the present as well as the past but he refers only to the past when he gives his precise definition of revelation as the originating event of a religious communion.

There is a missing link here between the religious communion and the human individual. I suspect that Schleiermacher assumes that there is an inherent relation between person and community which links past and present. Much of his language, however—world, social, feeling, dependence, self-consciousness—is not up to the task.[33] A philosophy more focused on person in community is necessary to place revelation in the relation of each person to God, but without negating either the past or the communal and institutional structures of the present.

UNITED STATES RELIGION

The nineteenth-century story of "revelation" in the United States parallels seventeenth-century alliances and conflicts in England. Church writers in both centuries, contrary to what is widely assumed, were great supporters of science. The conflict that emerged in the United States toward the end of the nineteenth century pitted a theology based on one kind of science against a theology that claimed support from a different kind of science. Darwin became the point of division, but the demonizing of Darwin and Darwinism is more a phenomenon of the twentieth than the nineteenth century. When Christian writers rejected Darwin in the nineteenth century, they did so by claiming that he was insufficiently scientific. In contrast, they usually invoked "Lord Bacon," the seventeenth-century theorist of inductive method and scientific clarity.

The language that emerged in the nineteenth century for describing political and religious differences was liberal/conservative. The contrast was European in origin, especially derived from the French experience. In politics, liberal meant affirming freedom and rights for the individual; conservative meant the protection of class and privilege. In religion, the liberal was open to the future and new ideas; the conservative was intent on the preservation of traditional ideas and practices. By the mid-twentieth century, these two terms had lost their original clarity; what is called conservative today would often fit the profile of nineteenth-century liberalism.

In the nineteenth century, practically everyone in the United States was a political liberal, that is, open to the future, against class privilege, and concerned for individual liberty. Religiously, the situation was more complicated. Almost everyone was apocalyptic, although that stance had both liberal and conservative versions. As I noted earlier, "America" was from its birth in 1507 an apocalyptic term, the name of the promised land, the place for the appearance of the kingdom of God. When the United States was founded in the 1780s, it deliberately identified itself with the dream of America, calling its citizens "the Americans."

From the sixteenth century onward, "America" had a secular as well as a religious version. People came in search of paradisiac wealth, which could be material or spiritual. The fishermen in seventeenth-century Marblehead informed their colleagues in Boston that "your fathers may have come here for religious freedom, ours came here to fish."[34] Apocalyptic connotations of the term America could be and were transmuted into belief in an abundant material future. The nineteenth-century belief in progress blended religious and secular versions of America.

Liberal theology thus found a home in United States Protestantism. It flourished before the Civil War and re-emerged with new vigor after the crisis of the war.[35] In France and Germany, liberal theology took a strong inward route, dependent on romantic philosophy. The theology also became dangerously entwined with nationalism. "Instead of communicating with all creatures, as his namesake did, by means of Revelation, God no longer spoke *to* man in a universal tongue; He now spoke from *within* him, in the language of his nation."[36] In the United States,

God spoke the language of "America," which is not the name of the nation but a religious idea about the nation.

The United States talked about the separation of church and state. But the political policies of the United States were often conflated with the religion named America. Even when the United States was a small player on the world stage, it saw itself as leading the world into the future. No matter how difficult life was for immigrants in the United States, America meant that life would be better for their children and better still for their children's children.

The idea of religious progress, or at least progress in religious under-standing, was in the air before Darwin. "What preceding age can com-pare with ours, in general knowledge and the rights of man?" asked the *Presbyterian Quarterly* in 1853.[37] There were few takers ready to name a preceding age. What Darwin did was to place the human in the center of the great cosmic map and describe the mechanism of organic change. Darwin himself resisted the idea of progress—even the term evolution—but theories of moral and religious progress routinely invoked Darwinian support.[38]

I have said that nearly all the theology of the United States, under the aegis of America, was apocalyptic.[39] Even those writers who accepted the premises of the new science and the wonders of technological progress believed in an end to the world and Christ's judgment. But these pro-gressives also expected a thousand years of earthly paradise before the final appearance of Christ. Thus, they were known as "postmillennial-ists," believers in progress until the end of the millennium, when the final crisis would occur. Their opponents were known as "premillennialists," meaning that Christ would intervene in a sinful and declining world before the millennium. Only after that great crisis would the thousand years of earthly paradise begin.[40]

The great divide between pre- and postmillennialism became clear in the 1870s. By that time Christianity was being pressed on two fronts. The Darwinian revolution was in full swing, with moral and religious infer-ences being drawn from the biological theory.[41] In addition, the higher criticism of the Bible was threatening the foundations of Christian belief. The Civil War acted as a catalyst to force a choice: either place the "Chris-tian revelation" into a radically transformed and enlarged worldview or else mount an unyielding defense of the Bible's truths as superior to the mere theories and hypotheses of the new sciences.

Liberal theology chose to adapt Christian revelation to an evolution-ary world picture. The ambiguous phrase "historical revelation" now became commonly invoked. It could mean that revelation was located in the past when the Bible was written. But historical could also refer to the postbiblical era and to the evolution of Christian belief. Revelation, like other historical phenomena, was now believed to be progressing, "a continuous river of light and life, flowing through the ages with a constantly increasing fullness of development."[42]

The two metaphors of enlightenment and revelation were easily fused, but while "the continuous river of light" preserved the root meaning of revelation, the place of the Bible and Christian origins became clouded. William Newton Clarke wrote that "revelation is not a lightning flash: it is rather like the dawn, brightening into the full day." That image reduced the biblical era to a primitive beginning that had now been superseded.[43]

The marriage of Darwinism and liberal theology became evident at the meeting of the *Evangelical Alliance* in 1873. James McCosh, the president of Princeton University, spoke of science and scripture as parallel revelations that are mutually confirmatory. "Both reveal order in the world, the one appointed by God, the other discovered by man."[44] This theme of two revelations was carried out at book length by Henry Ward Beecher (1813–1887) in his *Evolution and Religion*. The seventeenth-century division of man and nature was still operative, but what Beecher placed next to nature was "a record of the unfolding of man."[45] The evolutionary pattern of history revealed the nature of man and the pattern of progress. Scripture became subordinate to that historical progress: "The oaks of civilization have evolved since biblical times. Should we then go back and talk about acorns?"[46]

Henry Ward Beecher was the most popular preacher of a somewhat complacent Christianity. He could write that "the general truth will stand that no man in this land suffers from poverty unless it be more than his fault—unless it be his sin."[47] Conversely, the accumulation of wealth was now interpreted as a sign of virtue, success in this life being a forerunner of the establishment of the kingdom of God: "Material prosperity is helping to make the national character sweeter, more joyous, more unselfish, more Christlike."[48]

Unlike European writers who imagined the kingdom to be internalized, United States writers saw the kingdom of God in the accumulating wealth of "Christian America." The kingdom of God is "not a kingdom lying in another world beyond the skies but established here and now."[49] But just as a spiritualized kingdom runs counter to the political connotations of the term kingdom, so also "kingdom" as meaning worldly success sits uneasily with Jesus' words "my kingdom is not of this world." H. Richard Niebuhr described this progressive theology as "a God without wrath brought man without sin into a kingdom without judgment through the ministrations of a Christ without a cross."[50]

Arrayed against the postmillennialist liberals were the premillennialist defenders of the Bible. And what the last book of the Bible revealed was not progress but a coming end to the illusion of progress and an end of human history. The United States from its beginning had been a hotbed of apocalyptic expectation. The Shakers, the Millerites, the Mormons, the Jehovah's Witnesses, and numerous other groups had in common the expectation of an imminent end. Sometimes the prediction was as precise as naming the day. October 22, 1844 is a day made famous by the Millerite prediction of the end. Similarly, Charles Russell, founder of the Jehovah's Witnesses, set October 1, 1914. In such cases, when the end does not come, part of the faithful drift away. The remaining believers resolve to work harder and believe more strongly in order to bring on the end.[51]

The main development of premillennialism in the nineteenth century was called dispensationalism. The idea of stages of history, which is found in Augustine, Joachim, and many modern theories, was recast as a series of "dispensations" by John Nelson Darby (1800–1882) and his popularizer, C. H. Mackintosh. A dispensation was defined as "a period of time during which man is tested in respect of obedience to some specific revelation of the will of God."[52] Each dispensation ends in crisis and a testing of faith. So it happened with Noah at the time of the flood, and likewise the captivity in Egypt. Today we are in the "great parenthesis" awaiting the final crisis, the great tribulation. God has two peoples: an earthly Israel and the heavenly church.

Dispensationalists believe that the events of the Apocalypse are to happen soon. Armed with this knowledge, they believe that there is an unholy conspiracy of an apostate church and the antichrist; that the Jews face terrible persecution before their redemption; that the church's main mission is to rescue souls from the wrath to come; and that God will take up the true believers—in what is called the rapture—before the final conflict. The most worrisome aspect of belief in a great tribulation is that the Jews have a special role to play. As in the millenarian movements of the Middle Ages, the Jews are likely to suffer when apocalyptic-minded Christians try to bring on the end of history.[53]

Since the seventeenth century much of Protestant Christianity has closely identified revelation with the words of the Bible. As nineteenth-century criticism of the Bible moved into high gear, a defense of revelation was mounted, word by word, sentence by sentence. In the 1880s the term "inerrant" came into prominent use to characterize the Bible. The term parallels the First Vatican Council's use of "infallible" for official pronouncements by the pope. The papal claim was startlingly large, but it is rarely invoked. The claim that the Bible is inerrant had to cover thousands of statements written millennia ago and subject to copying, editing, interpolating, and translating. Revelation had to be imagined as dictation from God, despite a mass of evidence that the text we have did not originate that way. William Hoyt, at a Bible conference on the "Inspired Word," said he did not accept a dictation theory, but he nevertheless spoke of biblical prophecy as a "photographically exact forecasting of the future."[54]

The premillennialists in the late nineteenth century did not view themselves as opposed to science. On the contrary, they believed they were applying science to the Bible. Reuben Torrey in *What the Bible Teaches* (1898) described his work as "simply an attempt at a careful, unbiased, systematic, thorough-going, inductive study of Bible truth."[55]

It is at this time that the language of "propositions" came into widespread use. It was often assumed in twentieth-century disputes that "propositional revelation" is the traditional view rather than what it is: a nineteenth-century novelty. It was also assumed that those who oppose "propositional revelation" are dismissive of the Bible. But approaching the Bible as a series of propositions, each proposition true on its own standing, is to be oblivious to the nature of the Bible as a collection of writings across a wide spectrum of literary genres.

Reuben Torrey offered as a principle for his five-hundred pages of biblical propositions: "Beauty and impressiveness must always yield to precision and clearness."[56] It apparently did not occur to Torrey that the impressive beauty of the Bible, its integrity as a literary composition, might be necessary to get at its precision and clarity. Dismembering the story of Exodus, the poetry of the Psalms, or the portrait of Christmas into propositions does violence to the Bible.[57]

The premillennialists continued a tradition that went back to the Puritans' art of plain speaking in the seventeenth century. The United States has always prided itself on talking candidly and simply.[58] The only European philosophy that flourished here was Common Sense Realism. Its name said almost all: the world is as it appears, and words mean just what they seem to mean. The clear distinctions and factual language of seventeenth-century Puritanism provided the basis for nineteenth-century premillennialism. William Ames had written in 1623, "There is only one meaning for every place in Scripture. Otherwise, the meaning of Scripture would not only be unclear and uncertain, but there would be no meaning at all—for anything which does not mean one thing surely means nothing."[59]

The greatest preacher in the closing decades of the nineteenth century was Dwight Moody (1837–1899). Moody kept his distance from the elaborate theories of the dispensationalists, but he was intent on preaching the imminent return of the Lord: "The word of God nowhere tells me to watch and wait for the coming of the millennium, but for the coming of the Lord. . . . I find that the earth is to grow worse and worse, and that at length there is going to be a separation. . . . I look on the world as a wrecked vessel. God has given me a life boat, and said to me, 'Moody, save all you can.'"[60] For Moody, the truth was simple and plain; all that was required was a decision to accept that truth. "It is 'I will' or 'I won't' for every man in the house tonight. . . . The battle is in the will and only there."[61] The premillennialists had little outreach or social involvement that would try to deal with harsh economic conditions. The millennium would come with the conversion of one soul at a time.

The premillennialists achieved their greatest success with the publication of the Scofield Reference Bible in 1909. Dispensationalist theory was incorporated as commentary into this edition of the Bible, which sold twelve million copies. Between 1910 and 1915 a series of twelve paperbacks called *The Fundamentals* were published. They summarized the simple, clear truths that had been preached in the previous three decades.[62]

In 1920 the term "fundamentalism" was coined to describe this movement, which showed surprising strength between 1920 and 1925. The patriotic fervor of the fundamentalists placed them in a strong position to fight German ideas and the atheism of the intellectual class. A counteroffensive was launched in a series of books defending liberalism; the case was summed up in a famous sermon by Harry Emerson Fosdick in 1922, entitled "Shall the Fundamentalists Win?"[63] European liberalism had been hard hit especially by the horrors of the World War. The United States's problem was an internal class struggle and the fight to preserve the deep religiosity of the country against the perceived encroachment of science.

What crystallized the conflict was the educational reform efforts in the 1920s. Waves of teachers who had been trained in "progressive education" came forth from the University of Chicago and from Teachers College in New York. They set out to enlighten the immigrants in the North and the rural population in the South. The fundamentalists were confident enough to take on the progressives. In 1925 they staked all on the Scopes trial in Dayton, Tennessee. A biology teacher named John Scopes stood accused of teaching evolution, something forbidden by Tennessee law.[64]

William Jennings Bryan led the fight against the forces of evolution. "Our purpose and our only purpose," Bryan said, "is to vindicate the rights of parents to guard the religion of their children." Clarence Darrow, on the other side, stated the issue as "every child ought to be more intelligent than his parents."[65] The trial issued in a conviction for Scopes, one that was later overturned. But the real significance of the trial was the ridicule it brought upon Bryan and the whole fundamentalist movement. The trial was seen by the country through the savaging reports of H. L. Mencken and later through the movie version of the play *Inherit the Wind*. Fundamentalists (or "evangelical Christians") were driven from the public square for fifty years until they re-emerged on the national stage in the mid-1970s.[66]

MARTIN HEIDEGGER AND HIS SUCCESSORS

In European circles of philosophy and theology the apocalyptic drive took a different route. After liberalism had disintegrated in the trenches of the World War, many Christian thinkers came to view the New Testament not as a series of reasonable sermons but as a stark call for repentance by a strange figure who thought he was living at the end of time. Does Jesus' preaching of an "eschatological ethic" make him irrelevant to the contemporary world or is that just what is needed in response to modernity's crisis? Toward the end of the twentieth century the term "postmodern" came into vogue, but for many thinkers the whole century was a challenge to the idea of the modern. The term postmodern added little but confusion; it did not suggest either the nature of the questioning or an alternative path. Modernity and enlightenment had been practically synonymous. Is enlightenment the wrong metaphor, and, if so, are we to believe in endarkenment?

Doubt about enlightenment is not necessarily good news for Christianity. Revelation in the form of "the Christian revelation" was a subordinate partner of secular enlightenment. A reaction against modern rationalism can lead to irrationalism and violence, something that is not merely a hypothetical danger in the past century. Amid the diverse, often chaotic, streams of twentieth-century philosophies, two themes stand out: (1) the attempt to get beyond the dichotomy of subject and object; and (2) a conscious reflection on the complexity and mystery of language. The two themes are connected in that the attempt to overcome the split of subject and object inevitably involves trying to find language that will accomplish that task. Both concerns go to the heart of the revelation question as it has evolved over the centuries.

Martin Heidegger (1889–1976), a dominating figure of the twenti-eth century, grappled with both issues. The early Heidegger began with the split of subject and object, while the later Heidegger was especially concerned with language. René Descartes is usually cited as the father of modern philosophy, with his sharp opposition between the thinking sub-ject and the external world. Numerous thinkers after Descartes were con-fronted with trying to prove that our knowledge matches the external world or even to prove that an external world exists. Heidegger, instead of giving one more answer to this question, rejected the validity of the question. Disagreeing with Kant's claim that it is a scandal of philosophy that there is no cogent proof for the existence of things outside us, Hei-degger writes that "the scandal of philosophy does not consist in the fact that this proof is still lacking up to now, but the fact that such proofs are expected and attempted again and again."[67]

The split of subject and object may be a philosophical problem, but it is also the basis of modern science. In its classic form, scientific method supposes a rational mind studying data and drawing inferences with mathematical precision. In the popular imagination, the empirical sci-ences proved their validity by their technological fruits. But in the second half of the twentieth century many people began to have doubts about some of the wonders of technology. Heidegger was one of the early doubters. "Calculative reason" brings forth only superficial truths, and modern technology is mostly dehumanizing.

Whether Heidegger offered a positive alternative remains debatable. Some people consider his work to be high-class obscurantism. In addi-tion, his personal reputation suffered since his death as one biography after another has documented his more than passing involvement with Nazism.[68] At the beginning of Heidegger's career there was great hope and excitement. Hannah Arendt, one of his students, said that "his name traveled all over Germany like the rumor of the hidden king. . . . Think-ing has come to life again."[69] Today, many people hold his philosophical accomplishments in the highest regard while acknowledging his moral obtuseness. The case is summed up by Hans-Georg Gadamer, one of his best-known students and successors: "Martin was the greatest of thinkers and the most petty of men."[70]

Whatever final judgments are rendered on the man, his philosophy undeniably had a wide and deep influence. His ambitious intention was to overcome philosophy's misdirection, which he traced not to the seven-teenth century but to the time of Plato. He wanted to recover the ques-tion of "being," which he claimed had been replaced by the search for certainty. His plan was to move from the human experience of finitude (or time) to the act of being that transcends individual existents. Then he would cover the same ground in reverse, starting with being. Only the first part of that plan proved feasible in *Being and Time*. In the half century that followed, the second part was accomplished only in fragments.

The beginning section of *Being and Time* describes in striking and penetrating detail the human experience of the world. Instead of beginning with consciousness or sense data, Heidegger begins with moods (for example, fear).[71] And before one gets to knowledge, one must move through understanding and interpretation. That is, interpretation focuses on an item (for example, a hammer) but interpreting that one item presupposes a prior understanding of tools or equipment. We understand and interpret our temporal world as we try to impose order on it. We know things because we have acted and been acted upon. Thus, Heidegger tried to get behind the dualism of consciousness and objects by starting with human beings dwelling in, acting in, and suffering in a surrounding world or environment.[72]

Actually, Heidegger usually refers not to the human being but to *Dasein*, which literally means "there among beings," the place where being (*Sein*) shows itself.[73] By identifying the human with *Dasein*, Heidegger combines a call for humility and an exaltation of the human. The human being is so far above other finite beings that an "abyss" separates him from other animals. And yet "man is not the lord of beings. Man is the shepherd of Being . . . with the essential poverty of the shepherd."[74]

Our lowly limits come home to us in the fact of our mortality; the human is a being-toward-death.[75] While the dark and fatalistic side of mortality is usually emphasized, Heidegger says that we should also rejoice in our finitude, appreciating that pain and death and love belong together.[76] As mystics know, there is a calm joy in giving oneself over to a power beyond human willing. In Heidegger's "letting be of being," there are echoes of St. Paul, Augustine, Eckhart, or Luther but without any faith in the One whom Jesus called father.

In trying to retrieve a more primordial experience of being, Heidegger returned not to Amos or Isaiah but to Heraclitus and other Presocratic philosophers. In Heraclitus, *logos* refers to a gathering of fragments; being and *logos* were interchangeable before *logos* came to mean "word" and then "idea."[77] Although Heidegger was critical of visual metaphors ("the mathematical"), he remained within the Greek part of Western tradition and was highly critical of the Hebrew prophets.

The later Heidegger concentrated on language, "the call of being." He criticized two common ways of understanding language: as the external expression of inner thoughts and as the representation of reality. For

Heidegger, language is not a tool that humans use; it is almost the reverse. "Language speaks, not man. Man only speaks when he fatefully answers to language."[78] Heidegger was fond of a line in Hölderlin's poetry, "We are the conversation," but it is not clear who are the conversationalists. The "we" does not seem to refer to two human beings.

Heidegger's later philosophy was attractive to some Christian theologians. Hans Jonas cautioned them that "being reveals itself" is not the same as "the world is God's handiwork."[79] Heidegger seemed caught between the metaphors of (visual) revelation and speaking. The old gods do not show themselves; what we await is a word of salvation. Refusing to accept the prophetic word of biblical tradition, Heidegger is left with a bleak present.

In his "Conversation on a Country Path" in 1944, he used the line "we can do nothing but wait." He came back to that line in his final interview in *Der Spiegel* in 1976.[80] We await a word that will compel our wholehearted assent to its gentle direction. He seems to end with a mystical stance which lacks the political and liturgical environment that every mystic needs. Although he can say that "insofar as we are dialogue, human being implies co-being," any signs of friendship or community seem aborted in the direction that his philosophy took.[81]

The themes that Heidegger introduced did open new discussions of revelation, the limitations of the metaphor and what might be necessary to rethink it. For Christians who are content with Christian revelation, located in a written text from the past, the overcoming of a dichotomy of subject and object is not good news. The theism founded in the seventeenth century was quite compatible with classical science's world of objects. It was not comfortable with Darwin's return to a world of organic relations and to the humans' place among the other animals.

Nietzsche, Heidegger, Freud, Wittgenstein, and most currents of twentieth-century thought have undermined seventeenth-century theism. Not that the result is atheism. As Heidegger and Nietzsche insist, atheism and theism are bound together. Heidegger refused the word atheist; Nietzsche did not call himself an atheist but the antichrist. What Heidegger, Wittgenstein, and their successors have opened up is a new appreciation of the humans as "hearers of the word." Speech is not reduced to factual reporting and rational calculation. Religious ways of speaking may again find a place.

Two Christian writers who were directly influenced by Heidegger for their ideas of revelation were Rudolf Bultmann (1884–1976) and Karl Rahner (1904–1988). They share little else in common because they moved in nearly opposite directions in rethinking revelation. Bultmann, working from the New Testament and preaching, took hold of the existential side of Heidegger, that is, the individual's decision to live an authentic life. Rahner, reworking the metaphysical tradition of Roman Catholicism, found support in Heidegger for the recovery of a deeper meaning of revelation within Christian tradition.

Rudolf Bultmann

Bultmann, like Jean-Paul Sartre, was inspired by Heidegger's description of the human predicament. What meaning can the individual find in a life that is limited by death? One answer is that humans have to invent the meaning of their lives. A second answer is to look for a challenge that comes from beyond the human. These two answers are sometimes linked together by the peculiar term "transcendent." Religious writing in recent decades has adopted "the transcendent" as a way to refer to God. But the word started out as an adjective to describe human experience. The human being is one that transcends or is always going beyond itself.[82]

In his essay "The Concept of Revelation in the New Testament," Bultmann approaches the text to find an answer to the predicament that Heidegger had described. Bultmann acknowledges that he brings to the New Testament a "preunderstanding" of revelation. He does not apologize for a bias; instead, he claims that such preunderstanding is a necessity.[83] I grant that "understanding" here has to be grasped in a Heideggerian meaning, that is, something that precedes knowledge. And it is true that one cannot go in search of a "concept" unless one already has a sense of what one is looking for. Bultmann, however, presupposes a quite specific meaning of revelation: "Revelation is the communication of knowledge by the word" or "revelation is an occurrence that puts me in a new situation as a self."[84] He claims that all religions choose between these two meanings.

I do not think it is obvious from history that revelation has these two meanings or that every religion chooses between them. Bultmann's preunderstanding of revelation leads him to treat the New Testament in cavalier fashion. He has more than a hundred citations to St. Paul and St. John, but he never examines the actual word revelation, its history and connotations.

Bultmann contends that the New Testament is entirely on the side of the second meaning of revelation; it is a personal address, not a set of doctrines. Throughout the essay, he repeatedly denies that there is any communication of knowledge. But at the end of the essay he allows that "there is indeed a knowledge that is also given in revelation. . . . I am given a knowledge, namely, of myself, of my immediate now, in which and for which the word of proclamation is spoken to me."[85] Bultmann can also say that "the revelation consists in nothing other than the fact of Jesus Christ." Calling Jesus Christ a "fact" (or an "event") is apparently clear to some Christian theologians, but it would be a puzzling use of language to most outsiders.[86]

Bultmann calls the occurrence of revelation an "eschatological fact," which means "the kind of fact in which the world comes to an end." One might surmise that he is here taking up the futurist or apocalyptic side of revelation. One expects a description of the last book of the New Testament, but nowhere in the essay does he refer to the Revelation of John. In other writing, he disparages the last book of the New Testament where "the peculiar between-ness of Christian existence has not been grasped." His summary judgment on the book is that "the Christianity of Revelation has to be termed a weakly Christianized Judaism."[87]

For Bultmann, "revelation is understood in its true nature only when it is understood as something that takes place in the present, in my particular present."[88] He immediately follows that statement with the claim that "the way in which it is made present, however, is through preaching," and "the preaching is itself revelation."[89] Since he has removed revelation from cosmic history, the end of the world seems to arrive in a sermon.

What is most attractive in Bultmann's concept of revelation is its present tense. God acts now; the human must respond in the present. "The kindness of God is new every morning; yes, provided I perceive it anew every morning."[90] I have repeatedly affirmed the principle that revelation has to be understood as a present reality. But two cautions must be attached to that principle: (1) the present must include the reality of the past and the possibilities of the future; and (2) my present has to be situated in the presence of a community.

Bultmann's premises seem lacking on both points. He constantly refers to the moment, the now, the event, the occurrence. This language tends to exclude the past from being found in the depths of the present. It also neglects a future that arises from the interaction of human decision and what the past presents.

On the second point, Bultmann's language is individualistic, cut off from both the human community and the nonhuman, natural world. The quest is for self-understanding, and the revelation is "the existential relation between God and man." Even if one takes "man" as generic rather than individual, no community or group of people responds with concerted action. Preaching is the central liturgical act in which the word of God challenges the listener's self-understanding. By taking the life, death, and resurrection of Jesus out of ordinary history, the explosive political meaning of the gospel may be lost. Revelation is not organically related to a people struggling for a better future and a just world.[91]

Karl Rahner

An alternative path from the influence of Heidegger was taken by Roman Catholic theologian Karl Rahner. He tapped into what Heidegger calls the ontological question: to be or not to be. The Roman Catholic Church at the First Vatican Council (1869–70) had tried to stem the tide of modernism by affirming revealed truths (*revelata*). A century later the church was confronted by the same problem; only now it was worse. The initial draft of a pronouncement on revelation would have simply dug the church deeper into a reactionary position. A small band of bishops, theologians, and exegetes were responsible for rejecting the initial document on revelation and thereby turning the church in a new direction. The preeminent theologian was Karl Rahner, whose work on revelation in the twenty-five years before the Second Vatican Council provided much of the groundwork for the council's conclusions.

It would be misleading to call Rahner a Heideggerian. He was closer to being a reincarnation of Thomas Aquinas in the sweep of his work. He rethought Catholic tradition through the lens of Kant, Hegel, Heidegger, and the Tübingen school of theology, which had brought to the fore the living and evolving tradition of the church.[92] On some particular points, Heidegger's influence on Rahner is evident. For example, Rahner's *Theology of Death* is a brilliant reflection on the doctrine of redemption by Christ's death in relation to the experience of each person as a "being-toward-death."[93]

On the question of revelation, Rahner interpreted Aquinas's philosophy within its Neoplatonic context. Each being is a participation in "to be." All questions, whether of knowledge, causality, or teaching, were raised to the level of being. The creature exists because of its act of being. While God is "subsistent to be," the creature is a composite of essence and existence (*esse*). Rahner viewed the question of revelation as the supreme example of the creator/creature relation and the question of causality. God is not a "second cause" or a being apart from other beings. God is loved not apart from but through and in creatures.[94]

Like Aquinas, Rahner was more mystic than rationalist. He described Christianity as "a religion which sets man face to face with the Incomprehensible which pervades and encompasses his existence and makes it impossible for him to construct an ideology . . . a calculable root formula of existence."[95]

While avoiding an extrinsic God who intervenes in history, Rahner also had to avoid a progressivism that identified revelation with the unfolding of history. He always kept together two aspects of revelation: "the transcendental experience of the absolute and merciful closeness of God" and, at the same time, the concrete, historical reality, what he calls "predicamental" revelation. While he can say that revelation is coextensive with the spiritual history of humankind, he always insists on Jewish and Christian histories as intrinsic elements of revelation. As a Christian, Rahner keeps "the experience accomplished in Jesus Christ" at the center.[96]

Rahner is well known for the phrase "anonymous Christian." He is often criticized, sometimes ridiculed, for describing the salvation of the non-Christian in this way.[97] Yet I know of no better phrase that anyone has proposed—from within the language of Christian theology. Perhaps "anonymous follower of the Christ way" might have been clearer, if less catchy. A Christian theologian simply cannot abandon Christ-language. Furthermore, what is usually neglected is Rahner's argument for the positive and salvific role of non-Christian religions.[98] The phrase "anonymous Christian" was intended as intramural language for Christian theology; its purpose was to bring about humility on the part of the Christian. Rahner could also speak of the non-Christian in other terms: "Anyone who courageously accepts life—even a shortsighted, primitive positivist who bears patiently with the poverty of the superficial—has already accepted God."[99]

Despite his soaring into the rarified air of metaphysics, Rahner never lost touch with simple Christian piety and the biblical "word of God." The language of listening—the humans as hearers of the word—guided his philosophy.[100] There is no Rahnerian system of abstract ideas. His typical essay is a digging down into the history of theology to rediscover the meaning of grace, concupiscence, *ex opere operato,* or revelation. What looked like barren, overworked soil produced startling new life. But the novelty was always modestly situated within a context set by the Bible, the church fathers, and the great theologians of the past.

Rahner's notion of revelation is a relational one. It is God's act but not without a human response. "There is no proclaimed revelation except in the form of a believed revelation. A believed revelation, that is, heard revelation, always includes . . . a synthesis of the Word of God and the word of a particular man."[101] The relating of externally spoken word and interior movement of the Holy Spirit links Rahner with Aquinas, Luther, and Calvin. While Luther and Calvin tend to restrict the word revelation to the interior pole of the relation, however, Rahner's language is closer to Aquinas's in that revelation is the relation. "God is not merely an object and efficient cause of a created utterance concerning him. By his self-communication as the grace of faith, he is the interior principle within man both of the occurrence and the hearing of that occurrence."[102]

Rahner wrote many essays on resurrection and the last things. He certainly believed in a present and future Christ whose " second coming takes place at the moment of the perfecting of the world into the reality which he already possesses now, in such a way that he, the Godman, will be revealed to all reality and within it, to every one of its parts in its own way, as the innermost secret and center of all the world and of all history."[103] Still, I do not think his usual meaning of revelation has an inherent relation to the endtime. He does not incorporate the book of Revelation into his reflection on the nature of revelation. Like theologians from Origen onward, Rahner took the last book of the New Testament as allegory. This stance keeps Christianity from a futurist obsession that could undermine care for the creature and struggles for justice.

The disadvantage is that "Christ" becomes located in the past. If revelation is to be present and at the same time centered on Christ, then "Christ" has to refer to what happens now as a realizing of what will be completed at the end of history. This use of "Christ" takes nothing away from Jesus of Nazareth, whose life, death, and resurrection orient the life of the Christian toward the fullness of Christ. Although Rahner's theology tends in this direction, he did not succeed in reversing the language of Christian theology that is weighted in another direction. I suspect that Christian theology cannot and will not change until it has a more serious dialogue with Judaism.

MARTIN BUBER AND FRANZ ROSENZWEIG

In this last section I turn to two outstanding Jewish thinkers of the twentieth century: Martin Buber (1878–1965) and Franz Rosenzweig (1886–1929). Buber is the better known of the two, but for my purposes Rosenzweig is the more important figure. They shared many ideas, including that of revelation, but Rosenzweig created the more consistent and complete theology. Neither writer has the trust of the whole Jewish community. Buber was embraced by secular and Christian thinkers, but his attitude to Jewish law was suspect. Rosenzweig nearly became a Christian, and he retained a positive attitude to Christianity. Dialogue between Christianity and Judaism requires participation by people deeply immersed in their respective traditions. Dialogue can also use a few individuals exploring the margins, people whose loyalty is bound to be questioned.

One could make a case that the twentieth century is divided between Heidegger and Buber. They are joined in their opposition to the dichotomy of consciousness and world. They are also joined in the conviction that the key to overcoming this opposition is in language, or more precisely, the spoken word. But whereas Heidegger goes back to the Presocratic Greeks to recover "being," Buber grounds his work in the Hebrew prophets. Buber starts from a word that has been spoken and a word that is spoken to humans today. Heidegger, while commenting on the poetry of Hölderlin, could only wait in silence. Buber's philosophy is first and last dialogical, not the dialectical interplay of concepts but the unpredictable exchange between beings who speak and respond.[104]

Buber starts by dividing the world into two primary words: I-Thou and I-It. Two problems immediately present themselves. The first is the danger of trivialization. The title of Buber's book, *I and Thou*, can convey to people a romantic picture of two lovers resisting the depersonalized world of "it." Buber suffered the fate of many other philosophers who have had a central insight turned into a cliché.[105]

The second danger is a problem inherent to his division. Any philosophy that begins by dividing the world into A and B creates a dualism that is difficult to overcome. Depending on the principle of division, the width of the split between A and B varies. Buber's A and B are intriguingly simple and yet complex: two dialogical words. The title *I and Thou* is misleading in the inclusion of "and." The first word is I-Thou; similarly, the second word is I-It. Both words are "attitudes," a term that suggests movement between the two. But I-Thou, as an attitude within the speaker, seems incapable of overcoming the subject-object dichotomy of modern philosophy.

Before demanding too much of Buber's philosophy, however, one should acknowledge his brilliant poetic insight that brought the dialogical and interpersonal to center stage. Perhaps, as Rosenzweig argued, we need a "We-It" and a "He-It" relation to do the whole job of philosophy. But as Rosenzweig would have agreed, one can see the need for further relations only because Buber has pointed the way with dramatic simplicity.

Much of twentieth-century thinking has followed or accompanied Heidegger down the road of the lonely individual who is inevitably absorbed into the great All. From astrophysics to evolutionary biology, the human organism is portrayed as an accidental and insignificant speck. The best that one can hope for is to invent some meaning for oneself. Buber contends that meaning can only be discovered (revealed) not invented.[106] He starts with the personal as central reality; everything else is of lesser significance.

This picture of the world is not a simple anthropocentrism. At the center is not the human individual but speaking and listening. (Here there is a parallel to Heidegger placing *Dasein* at the center.) The human speaker is confronted by others who address him or her. For Buber this call can come from a tree, an animal, or someone greater than the human.[107] If the voice of God is to be heard, it can only be from the center and not from above. The sensual world is "the outermost and thickest shell of God."[108] And the community of speakers and listeners can exist only because each member stands in a living, reciprocal relationship with the center.[109]

One can also say that at the center is presence or the present. "Only as the thou becomes present does presence come into being."[110] Here is where Buber locates the term revelation: "Meaning is found through the engagement of one's own person; it only reveals itself as one takes part in its revelation."[111] Thus, the encounter, the present relation, is revelation. "He who takes what is given him, and does not experience it as a gift, is not really receiving; and so the gift turns into a theft. But when we do experience the giving, we find that revelation exists."[112]

Buber's emphasis on the present makes him vulnerable to criticism. If the present is opposed to the past, then to locate revelation in the present is to disparage the past. Buber does not intend to do that. His present is not a point that excludes the past as a series of preceding points. Instead, the present is a relation that is intended to include the past. But for many people, the I-Thou relation does not seem able to encompass the past. And Buber seems not inclined to identify revelation with the I-It relation.

The criticism is often formulated around the question of content. In trying to avoid making revelation into an object, Buber seems to deny that revelation has any content. Critics take that to mean a dismissal of Bible and tradition. But the question of content is itself not clear. The person who demands to know the content is most likely looking for information, data, statements of truth, doctrines, beliefs, and so forth. For Buber, these are abstractions from a living relation. Separated from a living relation, no object can be identified as revelation. The relation itself is the content.

Consider the nature of a living, personal relation. A man who is on intimate terms with a woman is unlikely to have a catalogue of information about her. If asked about her height, the color of her eyes, her shoe size, he might know a precise answer or he might have to guess. If he is asked whether she is trustworthy, he would say yes. If asked to prove that claim he would have to marshall pieces of evidence that would not necessarily be conclusive to the interrogator. The person within the relation has a different perception from the outsider. The outsider in asking questions about content may be oblivious to the reality of the relation itself.

Consider a parallel case in Christian history. For centuries, Protestants and Catholics were supposedly split over the question of whether revelation is contained in scripture alone or is contained in scripture and tradition. From the middle of the twentieth century onward, it became increasingly acknowledged that Protestantism needs tradition in the interpreting of scripture. Likewise, Catholic scholars admitted that the basis of all doctrine lies in scripture. Catholic and Protestant differences did not disappear with these admissions but better conversation became possible. The answer to the question of where revelation is *contained* is: nowhere. Revelation is not a content that can be contained anywhere. It is a present and living relation between the divine and the human.[113]

One way that Buber tried to counter the criticism regarding the content of revelation was to link the term revelation with creation and redemption. He gives credit to Rosenzweig for this fruitful insight. Creation, revelation, and redemption point to three aspects of time. Creation, imagined as past, is origin; redemption, as hoped for future, is the goal. Revelation is the present relation that links creation and redemption. "Revelation is not a fixed, dated point poised between the two. The revelation at Sinai is not this midpoint itself, but the perceiving of it, and such perception is possible at any time."[114] Later in the same essay, Buber says that creation, revelation, and redemption "actually coincide, that God every day renews the work of the beginning but also every day anticipates the work of the end."[115]

This acknowledgment by Buber of overlapping processes would seem to soften the harsh criticism that he often makes of Christianity. He argues that Christianity has "fused the essentials" of revelation and redemption in Christ. Christian followers have therefore been guilty of "pressing the end," claiming that redemption has already occurred and that only the final judgment remains.[116]

While the previous pages have offered many examples of Christians trying to hasten the endtime, there has always been a restraining tradition to warn that the fullness of redemption is yet to come. Christians, like

Jews, are enjoined to work for justice in the present. The Jew looks forward to the coming of the Messiah; the Christian looks forward to the coming of the (fullness of) Christ. The two traditions will always differ in their emphases, but the difference is not a simple, factual question of whether redemption has or has not happened.

For both traditions, revelation can be understood as the present, living relation on the way to a transformed world-to-come. Buber writes beautifully of the experience of redemption in the present, that is, revelation as promissory of future redemption.[117] Christians can concur even though their preeminent interpretation of the experience is through the life, death, and resurrection of Jesus.

Franz Rosenzweig was a colleague of Buber; he was eight years younger than Buber, but Buber outlived him by thirty-six years. They translated the Bible together; and while Rosenzweig was indebted to Buber for some of his foundational ideas, he was not averse to offering pointed criticism. Rosenzweig had a brief and brilliant career from 1913, when he decided against conversion to Christianity, until his death in 1929, after seven years of terrible illness. His greatest work was *The Star of Redemption,* which, like many works of twentieth-century theology, emerged from the experience of World War I. But while most of the Christian theology from the war reflected bitter disillusion with nineteenth-century theories of progress, *The Star of Redemption* is a positive and hopeful reaffirmation of traditional Judaism.

Rosenzweig often commented on the medieval poet and philosopher Judah ha-Levi, who found a positive place for Christianity in the Jewish scheme of things.[118] The Christian nations "are the readying and preparation of the Messiah for whom we wait."[119] Rosenzweig described Christianity as a tree that grew from the seed of Judaism and has cast its shadow across the whole world. But while Rosenzweig viewed Christianity positively, he conceived of Islam as the "other." He was incapable of seeing Islam as anything but a reactionary force over against Jewish and Christian traditions.[120]

From his first published writing in 1914, Rosenzweig was concerned with saving or restoring the idea of revelation.[121] He had been challenged by his Christian friend Eugen Rosenstock-Huessy to decide whether he had a religion based on reason or revelation. His remaining a Jew was thus tied to his finding revelation a meaningful term. For Rosenzweig, revelation is simply the love of God made present, that is, God's love in the historical present directed toward a specific "I" and the human response of obedience to his commands.

Rosenzweig expressed two points of disagreement with Buber: the nature of the present and the place of the law that has been given in the past.[122] Buber, as noted above, did try to incorporate the past within the present, but it is doubtful that his I-Thou relation can bear the weight. Rosenzweig insisted that even to talk about I-Thou requires a third person perspective, a language that is not simply I-It. And for the past to be available for the "I," there has to be a "We-It," that is, a community that keeps alive the past in its rituals and moral practices. "For Judaism, the Torah is not a book, it is a living, growing oral law."[123]

The Star of Redemption is structured around three irreducible realities: God, man, world. The relations among these three bring forth creation, revelation, redemption. Like Heidegger, Rosenzweig begins with the threat of death, the ever-present awareness of one's own mortality. From this present experience, Rosenzweig moves to the gift of creation and the hope for redemption. At the center of the picture is revelation: "Revelation is of the present, indeed it is being present itself. . . . The past creation is demonstrated out of the living, present revelation."[124] As in Rahner's Neo-thomism, Rosenzweig's creation is not an event in the past but a living relation most fully expressed in the present revelation.

Some of Rosenzweig's formulations left him vulnerable to the same criticism directed at Buber, namely, a slighting of "content" in favor of the present encounter. But Rosenzweig showed an increasing concern with Jewish law, as shown by his letter to Buber in 1923.[125] He continued to say, "I do not believe that revelation is ever a formulation of law." But his objection is to a conception of law as objects ("content") cut off from the present community. The law is a command that requires response.[126]

Redemption is a present experience insofar as it is implied by revelation. The "continuing availability of revelation" becomes actual in decision, commitment, daring—what Rosenzweig calls a messianic theory of truth.[127] He avoids the two traps of modern theories of revelation: either an external truth confronting every individual in a timeless moment or else a truth unfolding as historical progress. Instead, God speaks today to the singularly specific situation of the person who must act in response so as to understand revelation. "Not that doing necessarily results in hearing and understanding. But one hears differently when one hears in the doing."[128]

Rosenzweig uses an interesting term for what he calls the "Archimedean point" of his thinking: "Revelation is orientation (*Orientierung*)." That was the answer his friend Rosenstock-Huessy gave Rosenzweig in response to the question of how he understood revelation.[129] Orientation suggests a direction for acting in the present. No concrete knowledge of future events is contained in the orienting of one's life, but neither is one left stranded in a present of timeless ideas. The person is aware of having something and also waiting. "He has a feeling that both the waiting and the having are most intimately connected with each other. And this is just that feeling of the 'remnant' which has revelation and awaits salvation."[130]

Rosenzweig's use of "orientation" can be compared to a word that has been prominent in recent Christian theology, namely, promise.[131] In trying to incorporate the other side of revelation, the apocalyptic element in Christianity, many theologians have emphasized the future. Christian faith is said to be faith in the promise of redemption. The change of emphasis can be fruitful. There is a danger, however, of simply jumping from the past to the future, which is Christianity's oldest problem. Where and how is the promise located? A promise can be one more thing located in the text of the past. The fact that the promise is about the future does not of itself connect the present and the future. And the denial that the future is found in the "potentialities of the present" severs the future from the present.

Instead of saying that "revelation is promise," one might say "revelation is promising." The quickening possibilities of the present, funded by the community's past, have a promising aspect. The future *is* in the potentiality of the present, although humans are not capable of understanding the full depths of the present. And the future does not mechanically unfold from the present. The future depends on God's promising revelation and also on the decision, commitment, and daring of the human response.

Just as Rosenzweig can do a better job with the past than can Buber, so Rosenzweig's orientation better links present and future. Redemption is not an event at the end of days but a process that goes on daily. It remains a reality that is mostly hoped for, but the hope is an aspect of present experience.[132]

There are rich possibilities here for a Christian–Jewish conversation about concrete acts in the present oriented toward future redemption. Rosenzweig refers to the irreconcilable hopes of Jews and Christians.[133] That is probably true, but the differences need not be as sharp-edged as Rosenzweig leaves them. Despite his positive attitude to Christianity he nonetheless can say, "At the bottom of his heart any Jew will consider the Christian's relation to God and hence his religion a meager and round-about affair. . . . Why should a third person have to be between me and my father in heaven?"[134]

If Christianity is so misunderstood by such a sympathetic observer, then Christianity has not done a very good job of educating its own members or conveying an intelligible picture to outsiders. For Christians, Jesus is the embodiment of the divine–human relation, the activity of God and the response of the human. Jesus is the firstborn of his brethren, the downpayment of the future redemption of the world. But unless Christians can give an intelligible answer to Rosenzweig's question, no Christian–Jewish dialogue can get beyond mere tolerance. A joint effort to explore the meaning of revelation remains a hope for the future.

I have to admit the paradox of ending this historical survey with two Jewish writers since in the preceding material I have focused on Christian writers. I have not presumed to tell the Jewish story of revelation. But I end with Jewish writers in the twentieth century to indicate that the future belongs to an ecumenical discussion that would certainly strengthen Christianity and most likely help Judaism as well.

I could end this fifth chapter with authors I referred to in chapter 1. Later writing in the twentieth century by Barr and Barth, Pannenberg and Bultmann, Schillebeeckx and Latourelle, Dulles and Van Beeck, as well as biblical, patristic, and medieval scholars on apocalypticism, could end this chapter. I think, however, that some of the changes in Christian discourse that are necessary for fruitful conversation with Judaism are still to be accomplished. The Holocaust remains today an enormous rift in the possibility of such conversation and much of the twentieth-century discussion of revelation is based on modern German scholarship. No individual Christian writer of the last half century could accomplish the needed changes, however good his or her intention. I prefer, therefore, to leave a space between the end of the historical survey and the present situation.

I turn instead to reflections of another kind, drawn from philosophy, ethics, and education. In the analysis that follows, I will refer at times to Judaism and Islam. Since I am not working in the second part with Christian texts but reflecting on logical and practical issues of today, I think it is appropriate to make some references to Jewish and Muslim traditions as sources for theoretical and practical considerations.

PART TWO

6

Responsibility and Revelation

A MAIN THEME in modern philosophy during the last two centuries is that we know only as we do.[1] Instead of our getting a clear view of the world and then moving to act, we wake up in the middle of activity and try to make sense of what we are already involved in. This modern notion that practical action encompasses theoretical knowledge is compatible with Christian, and even more, Jewish religions. Both Christianity and Judaism are sets of practices, within which knowledge serves as a guide to a proper way of life.[2]

If revelation is assumed to be theoretical knowledge, that is, the unveiling of an object which is gazed upon, then the practice of a religious way of life begins with a separation between beliefs and practices. In contrast, if revelation is itself practical, emerging only as one practices the religion, then the moral life, intellectual understanding, and education in religion take on a different shape.

In this chapter, I am interested in the aspect of the practical that is called ethical or moral. Neither of these terms is entirely satisfactory. The ethical in modern speech is most often restricted to academic discussions. The moral tends to be restricted to a behavioral meaning. Cicero invented moral to translate the Greek ethical. Since then, the two words have had varying connotations according to time and place. Early Christianity absorbed large chunks of Greek ethics, especially Stoicism. Medieval Christianity added schemes of Aristotelian virtue. Despite the Reformers' attempt to erase much of this Greek material, the moral codes of churches still reflect this influence. Jewish religion absorbed less of Greek and Latin morality; however, modern ethics made considerable inroads to liberal forms of Judaism.

If revelation/word of God had been thought through with all of its implications, some of this moral/ethical material would be either different or unnecessary. That may be asking too much. Christianity, Judaism, and other religions are subject to the influence of surrounding moral practices that do not flow from the core ideas and practices of the religion. In this chapter, I do not attempt to strip away false practices but simply suggest how the meaning of revelation that has been proposed might simplify and clarify the demands of a Christian or Jewish moral code.

I have put forward the thesis that revelation should be understood as a present relation. The present understood as a relation, not a disappearing point, can include the past; it can also include the possibilities of the future. The present relation is a relation of presences: the activity of the revealer and the response of the one to whom there is revelation. This idea of revelation, especially when clarified with "word of God," has considerable, if not universal, support from writers examined in the first part of this book. From Origen and Augustine to Rahner and Rosenzweig, the human being is portrayed as dialogical partner. There is not first an object called revelation, followed by acceptance of the object of belief. The reader or listener must be present for revelation to occur. The present tense of the relation is not consistently emphasized in the historical record, although many writers have searched for a way to say just that while remaining orthodox.

Since acting as a recipient is truly acting, and not simply being acted upon, the humans are actively engaged in revelation. It is real dialogue even if a peculiar sort of dialogue in which the recipient first has to be given the power to say yes or no. The attempt to separate God's part and the human part into discrete portions is bound to fail, although the question constantly recurs.[3] Doctrine and law are integral to divine revelation, flowing from the life of the relation, but when isolated as objects of belief or codes of conduct they are not revelation. The closest we can get to the divine voice and divine will is to examine the moral/ethical life as a response within the deepest and broadest set of relations that are humanly imaginable.

RESPONSIBILITY

The moral/ethical idea that most clearly meshes with this idea of revelation is "responsibility." This term is especially prominent today. If one is looking for Christian and Jewish relevance to today's discussions, the omnipresence of the term responsibility is both an advantage and a disadvantage. The term responsibility is constantly used as if everyone knows what is being talked about and that the only problem is that we do not have enough of it. I think that one has to dig down into the historical and philosophical roots of responsibility before deciding how helpful the term can be.

The term responsible originated from a mixture of Jewish, Christian, and Roman elements about two thousand years ago. The word has a Latin origin and did not have an exact equivalent in Greek. Like "revelation" being attributed to Old Testament literature, "responsibility" gets attributed to Aristotle. Aristotle's visual imagery, however, clashes with responsibility as an oral/aural metaphor.[4] The Greeks also lacked the idea of psychological freedom or a freedom of the will which is closely related to responsibility.

Responsibility originated in connection with the emergence of the individual—the child of a heavenly father—in pharisaic Judaism. The other necessary element for the origin of the term was the sense of judgment; that is, the belief that the individual must answer for his or her life's actions. Apocalyptic thinking, Jewish and Christian, was the seedbed of the idea of responsibility. The legal thinking that blossomed in both Latin Christianity and rabbinic Judaism joined with the Hebrew Bible's central theme of "word of God" to produce a description of the human being as responsible. Thus, revelation/apocalypse and responsibility have been closely related from the beginning.[5]

As was the case with "revelation," it is important to bring into the discussion every voice that can contribute to exploring the meaning of responsibility. I am not looking at the term from within moral theology or Christian ethics. Those studies usually assume a body of Christian revelation that limits the possible range of exploration. I do not presume that responsibility is exclusively the concern of ethicists or people who are said to be ethical. Much of contemporary discussion assumes that some people are responsible and other people are not. I do not wish to exclude people who for whatever reason have already been classified as not responsible.

Being responsible is widely praised, especially by rich, powerful, successful, and upright people who confidently assume that they have "taken responsibility for their lives." Sometimes responsibility is simply a synonym for human autonomy; that meaning would make responsibility a competitor with Jewish and Christian religions. The distinctions in this chapter are needed to show that responsibility can be the ethical/moral translation of revelation instead of a secular substitute for revelation.

I would first argue that responsibility is a characteristic of all human beings and at least some nonhuman beings. The root meaning of responsible is "able to answer a word that has been spoken." This spoken word can be human speech or a metaphorical extension of it. And the answering can be performed by every human being, including very young infants, people who are called mentally retarded, hardened criminals, people dying of old age. The answer might take a form other than the words of human language. Some physical or mental act could be the acknowledgment of the word that has been spoken and heard.

Some nonhuman animals clearly fall within this meaning of responsible. Anyone who spends time with a dog, a cat, a horse, a dolphin, a chimp knows that at least some animals are able to respond to a word that has been spoken. One of Descartes' strange doctrines was that (nonhuman) animals are mechanisms.[6] From Descartes' era until Darwin's revolution, the "beast" did not fare well; it was an object for disposal by rational man. Darwin's work began a restoration of continuity between human and nonhuman animals.

The record on the medieval treatment of animals is by no means faultless, but medieval philosophy did presume that animals have souls and that humans could learn lessons from their next of kin. On some occasions in the Middle Ages, animals, such as dogs, were put on trial.[7] It was assumed that the animal is a responsible being. That belief may strike us as bizarre but we still make demands on some animals (racehorses, police dogs, parrots) and expect them to respond. A horse or a dog can be disciplined (taught) by a trainer to respond in some ways and not in other ways.[8] Sometimes we even hold something close to a criminal trial. If a pit bull attacks a child, it is likely to be restrained or killed. Words such as vicious, savage, or criminal are used to describe the animal. We stop short of imputing guilt to the dog, but we do hold it responsible for bad behavior.

Is an elephant responding to another elephant an instance of responsible activity? The choice is ours as to how far we extend the metaphor of answering a word that has been spoken. I see no problem in extending "responsible" to the entire living world so long as human responsibility is not deemphasized. The inclusion of nonhuman animals can in fact throw light on key distinctions within human responsibility.[9] But the use of "responsible" as a synonym for an impersonal cause can obscure the distinctive character that the term responsible had at its origin and still most often has.

Responsibility has always been more important than simply one of the virtues. William Bennett, in his popular *Book of Virtues*, includes responsibility as one of the traditional virtues that needs to be reaffirmed.[10] But there are no classical accounts of a virtue of responsibility and no medieval treatises on the subject. The word itself lay mostly hidden until the eighteenth century, but it underlies the Jewish and Christian sense of what a human being is: the being who listens and responds to the one who is creator of the universe and its ultimate judge.

Responsibility plays a central role in the twentieth-century writers discussed in chapter 5, especially Buber and Rosenzweig. Heidegger uses some of the same words as they do, although his rejection of Jewish and Christian traditions leaves him with a truncated description of responsibility. For Heidegger, language seems to take over the position of that ultimacy to which humans are responsible. "Language speaks, not man. Man only speaks when he fatefully answers to language."[11] Heidegger's formula that *Sprache spricht* (language speaks) leaves some people wondering if Heidegger short-circuits personal responsibility. Was the infamous inaugural address of 1933 with its praise of the Nazis *Sprache* speaking or Martin Heidegger speaking?

This example of Heidegger's speech crosses the line into "moral responsibility." In discussions of responsibility nearly all the attention is directed to moral responsibility. This emphasis is understandable, but the nonmoral part of responsibility in human life should not be eliminated from consideration. The line between moral and nonmoral is very often unclear, and the line can move during the course of one's life. The context for understanding morality is lost if responsibility is equated to moral responsibility. It is important to recognize that we often do not know if a person is morally responsible for a bad action (deserving of blame), even when we judge that the behavior is unacceptable. Courts have to judge whether a defendant is legally responsible, that is, guilty or innocent before the law. Fortunately for all of us, the judgment of moral guilt is reserved for God.

The history of "revelation" and the history of "responsibility" have similarities and differences. Each is a foundational term that more often than not has been implied rather than explicitly stated. While revelation is a visual metaphor and responsibility is oral/aural, a cooperation between the two can be mediated by the biblical word of God. The recognizing of responsibility as central to moral/ethical life helps in the interpretation of revelation as a present relation between the divine and the human. Buber writes that "all revelation is summons and sending"; he could just as well have written that "all responsibility is summons and sending."[12] The two terms are mutually clarifying.

RESPONSIBLE TO AND RESPONSIBLE FOR

Responsibility in the life of the human being has two elements: listening and answering, or being *responsible to* and *responsible for*. The process of acting responsibly is a dialectical play between these elements. The first moment of responsibility is listening, that is, being responsible to someone or something. The second moment is replying: one is responsible for the action that follows upon listening. This dialectical exchange then issues in a third moment, namely, responding to what one has been responsible for.

This interplay continues throughout a person's lifetime. At any moment, I can be responsible only for what I am responsible to. But what I am responsible to is dependent on what I have previously been responsible for.[13] Thus, a person who is sensitive to the needs of the poor will act to relieve poverty; the action in turn will generate greater awareness and further action. In contrast, the person who acts out of ignorance is likely to become more ignorant of a moral demand and less compelled to act.

This interdependence of responsible to and responsible for may seem to doom the human being to a closed cycle of determined behavior. Can there be any moral progress if I am responsible for my actions only insofar as I am aware of responsibility, an awareness itself dependent on how moral I am? Human beings are, indeed, strongly conditioned by genetic makeup, early experiences, and the physical/social environment. It is easy to show that human beings are not free in the way that they often think they are. Much of evolutionary biology today seems ready to close the circle and exclude freedom.[14]

The human being would indeed be left to fate if the sense of responsible to were omitted or if it is underdeveloped. Freedom depends on attentiveness to what is happening and on a capacity to reflect on previous actions in a way that gradually widens the cycle of responsible to and responsible for.[15] A failing in responsibility often lies in what is not done because we are unaware that it should be done. The failure to attend—to be responsible to—is often at the base of moral fault. Ignorance can be culpable (morally even if not legally) when we could have known and should have known but we are selectively unaware.

Until the late nineteenth century, the word responsible was nearly always followed by *to*. The action of a person depended on to whom or to what it was a response. The first use in the *Oxford English Dictionary* refers to a legislature being responsible to the people.[16] Of course, it was assumed that responsibility *for* particular actions would follow, but the basic meaning of the word was answering to someone or something. The religious origin of the term was still implied in that usage.

Beginning about 1870, "responsible" took a decided shift. Responsible to became overshadowed by responsible for. Instead of expressing relational interdependence, the twentieth-century meaning of responsibility has often been a claim to radical independence. People are constantly told to be responsible for themselves. Being responsible for one's life is the proud claim of some people and an overwhelming burden for others.

The historical figure who is in the middle of this transition is Friedrich Nietzsche. He is the first writer to describe the human being as the "responsible animal."[17] Nietzsche was well aware that responsibility had been to something beyond the human. In his view, responsibility had taken a disastrous turn in the Jewish and Christian versions of responsiblility to a God who supports the weak. The responsible animal is overwhelmed with a guilt that has been imposed by priests.[18] And modern atheism, according to Nietzsche, is nothing but a pale form of theism. Beyond both theism and atheism, responsibility in Nietzsche's writings is for creating the new man, the man of the future.

A cruel joke lies at the heart of Nietzsche's work. The heavens are depopulated; man is no longer responsible to God. Whatever goes wrong now cannot be blamed on the creator God. Man is henceforth responsible for his own life. At the same time, Nietzsche is a precursor of Freud in exploring the subconscious or unconscious forces that influence human life. "The decisive value of an action is precisely that which is not intentional in it."[19] We think that a person is acting freely, but "it" acts beyond the awareness of the person.[20] While being given the summons to reinvent man, the human individual is revealed to be incapable of controlling the smallest action. Thus, one can read Nietzsche as either the greatest exponent of willing or else as the one who collapses the human will.[21] The twentieth century was caught between believing either that the individual is autonomous or that every individual is a pawn of circumstance and fate.

Responsible To

If the term responsibility is to be properly related to revelation, the first question is to whom and to what should one be responsible. The short but comprehensive answer is that one should listen to everyone and everything. Obviously that is not an efficient strategy. We need help to sort out the many voices in our heads and to interpret what we are summoned to. Nonetheless, the important word at a particular moment might be spoken by friend or stranger, young or old, living or dead, brilliant or slow witted, human or nonhuman. Responsible human listening cannot in principle be closed to wisdom coming from any source.

In practice, all of us adopt guides and guidelines in which we trust. A parent or a friend may be the chief guide when we are young. A scholar

or a school of thought may later gain our trust. A religious tradition is
such a guide for how to interpret the whole of reality. Jewish and Christian traditions say that God is more likely to speak here rather than there,
but listen carefully because it could be just the opposite. Those who
demand a premature certainty are likely to become attached to one set of
ideas that increasingly filter out much of the beauty and meaning in life.
The alternative to a system of fixed certainties is a gradual growth in certainty as one's life is lived in response to the best lights that one has at any
moment.

The Jewish and Christian idea of revelation as a present relation
offers a basis to think out to whom/what we are responsible. The first step
in a life of moral responsibility is the receptive phase. Morality begins not
with right, duty, law, or decision but with the readiness to receive. Paul
Tillich writes, "The usual question, 'What shall we do?' must be
answered with the unusual question 'Whence can we receive?' People
must understand again that one cannot do much without having received
much. Religion is, first, an open hand to receive a gift and, second, an
acting hand to distribute gifts."[22]

Giving and receiving are opposite ends of a single relation; there is no
giver without a receiver. In human exchanges, receiving is a form of
giving oneself; the giver therefore receives in giving.[23] Human gifts keep
moving until they return to the giver. If the circle is too small, the sense
of gift may get replaced by the calculation of self-interest. But if one
passes on the gift without calculating the return, the circle keeps expanding.

The mark of religious experience is a receptiveness that is sheer
acknowledgment of a gift. Revelation and responsibility begin at the same
place: gratitude for being, for life. This attitude has to be renewed each
day throughout the course of a lifetime. And, as Annie Dillard writes,
"the dying pray at the last not 'please' but 'thank you' in the same way
guests thank their hosts at the door."[24]

When this element of receptivity or acceptance is lacking, the discussion of ethics cannot go very far. Ethics is bounded by a set of categories: duty, law, right, and good. All of these have a legitimate place in
human life, but none of them is expansive enough to provide a basis for
what human life eventually requires. Since Aristotle's time, people have
looked for a rational system that would give order to life while leading to
the good or happiness. But suffering of various kinds remains intractable,
and death is the final puzzle in each life. Philosophers from Plato to Heidegger warn that mortality must be dealt with or else it will cause an
infection in every choice.

Jewish ethics begins not with the good but with the holy.[25] It first attends not to what is good for me but to the abundance of creation and the generosity of the creator. "To the philosopher the idea of the good is the most exalted idea. But to the Bible the idea of the good is penultimate; it cannot exist without the holy. . . . Things created in six days He considered good; the seventh day He made holy."[26] The Jews, in imitation of God, were bidden to become not just a good people but a holy people: "I am the Lord your God . . . be holy, for I am holy" (Lev. 11:44). The observance of Sabbath remains a central symbol of the holy. One "does nothing" so as to appreciate the gift of creation, which is expressed in the present revelation and anticipated as a final Sabbath.

Christianity adopted this symbol of Sabbath, changing the observance to Sunday. This day was called the first and the eighth day of the week because it represents both creation and the end of history. The Greek virtues that Christianity absorbed into itself can be useful instruments in the journey to holiness, but they can easily block a recognition that in biblical religion what comes first is the overflow of life.

That sense of life as gift was preserved in the mystical side of Jewish and Christian religions, aided by the Neoplatonic insight that there is a "beyond being" which is the source of all good. Plotinus derived his philosophy from Plato and Eastern sources,[27] but as to why there is a creation he could have agreed with Christian and Jewish belief. The rabbinic sages said, 'Why did God create the world? . . . God created it out of love. Why out of love? Because love is the only thing which has need of a partner, and therefore God created humankind in God's image.'"[28]

Throughout the centuries, this sense of gift—of joy, gratitude, and wonder before creation—has characterized the lives of many Christians and Jews. But the confessional manuals of the medieval church lost sight of morality's context. The Reformation restored some of the ecstatic at the heart of morality but generally resisted the mystical impulse. Despite the obstacles, Catholic, Protestant, and Jewish religions continue to produce saints or "holy ones." The secular world has also produced a kind of sainthood, people with a mystic's sense of humanity and the interdependence of all life.

The contemporary ecological movement sometimes shows an appreciation of the whole, the all, life, a reality greater than the human. This movement is hampered by the widespread assumption that something called "the Judeo-Christian tradition" is its opponent. Much of the writing in the ecological movement has not grappled with the actual Jewish tradition, its good points and its dangers, as well as the distinctively Christian influences in Western history. Some of the earlier classics in the environmental movement, such as Albert Schweitzer's *Ethics and Civilization* (1923), were not averse to drawing on Christian mysticism.[29] Aldo Leopold's environmental classic, *A Sand County Almanac* (1949), turned to the Hebrew prophets for spelling out the relation of humans to the land.[30]

If environmentalism is not a religion, it nonetheless has many devoted followers who act with the passion of religious intensity. Its message is often an apocalyptic warning: Unless there is a mass conversion, life on earth will cease to exist at some point in the near future. Like Christian and Jewish religions, environmentalism has to find a way to keep together its devotees of small victories and its apocalyptic messengers who are trying to arouse a complacent public. If environmental writers could get beyond belligerent opposition to Judaism and Christianity, they could learn a lot from these religions, not scientific answers but how to channel religious passions.[31]

One of the main currents in contemporary discussions of ethics is evolutionary biology. Much fascinating material on the relation of humans to nonhuman life has become part of the scientific record. But the language for discussing human ethics is cramped within narrow limits. Some people seem to wish to replace physics with biology as the final science, everything being subject to the ultimate explanation by genetic code. The ethical question that arises within this framework goes under the term altruism. Many authors define ethics/morality as altruism, seemingly unaware that morality/ethics has been discussed for thousands of years without the existence of "altruism," a word invented in the 1850s.[32]

In the nineteenth century many scientists assumed that human beings are "naturally selfish." Humans seek their own good and do whatever is necessary for survival. But some people seem to do good for others; they are said to act unselfishly. Thus, there arose the need to coin the term "altruism" as the opposite of selfishness. Altruistic activity, which appears to be unnatural, was given two possible explanations. The first is that the altruist is simply ignorant of his or her own good. The second and nearly opposite explanation is that the altruist is craftily trying to get added benefits by appearing to be unselfish but is always ultimately looking for a return on investment.[33]

The twentieth-century discussion of this question has been complicated by the introduction of genes and DNA.[34] In this context, ethical decision is often completely removed from the conscious human being. As one slogan says, "an organism is only DNA's way of making more DNA." The humans are protectors of the genes; it is the genes that look out for their own selfish good. Thus, what seems to be altruism within small units can be explained by the close genetic relation. The genes recognize that family or tribal survival means a future for them. The struggle is no longer I against the world; rather, it is this family of genes against the others.[35]

Cooperation, at least within small units, has returned to center stage in evolutionary theory. If cooperation is natural, in-built to our genes, there is room for hope. But can people be educated to extend that cooperative attitude to larger human units: the city, the nation, humanity?[36] Who would not hope that this project is possible? But at the heart of such education is a conflict that approaches self-contradiction. Altruism toward one's city or one's nation, toward humanity or strangers, is not dictated by one's genes. The humans can try to pull off the maneuver, but they will be acting "unnaturally." In the end the genes, if they are so smart, will not be outwitted.

In Jewish and Christian traditions, morality is not altruism. The Jewish basis of morality/ethics, which was restated by Jesus as the basis of Christianity, is twofold. The Christian and the Jew are not commanded to "love thy neighbor instead of thyself" but rather "love thy neighbor as thyself." And the more fundamental and comprehensive command is to love and worship God. The love of one's neighbor is a response to the love that has been shown by God. Instead of selflessly giving away what is one's rightful possession, the Jew and Christian are to share with one's neighbor what has been received as a gift. Human love is neither natural nor unnatural; it is personal which is a transforming of the natural.

The test of who is my neighbor was already conveyed in the Hebrew Bible by the question What will you do for the stranger who is in need? This understanding of the love of neighbor was beautifully illustrated in many of Jesus' parables, such as the story of the Good Samaritan. The person who is my neighbor is not always the person closest to me. The neighbor may be the one who is farthest from me.[37]

Within a Jewish or a Christian ethic, there are no altruists, but there are people who are good and saintly, who risk their lives for a stranger, who labor among the poor, who generously forgive those who have wronged them. They do not need to have mastered the intricacies of Aquinas or Calvin, or to have grasped the "benevolence of being" or the "agape of God." They do have to respond to what the creator and creation offer within the limits of their concrete situation. The former slave Frederick Douglass wrote in his autobiography that "at the age of nine years old I knew that to regard God as 'Our Father' condemned slavery as a crime."[38]

In modern thought, the myth of the social contract maintains that I should be responsible to society. This contract may be able to govern human actions in most situations, but it is not clear that it can withstand crises. In addition, the current concern with the environment is an indication that a *social* contract is not broad enough at the base. Much of modern ethics revolves around the duty of the individual to obey the nation state and the corresponding rights of the individual to be protected against the overbearing power of the state. For the long run of history and for comprehending all creatures, ethics has to be based on something more than rights.

In the last few years it has become common to refer to "rights and responsibilities."[39] I think that this is an unfortunate use of language. The problem with rights is how to ground them in history, politics, and philosophy. Placing responsibilities parallel to rights only clouds the problem. A better language, both theoretically and practically, is to connect rights with duties or obligations. We have rights as we carry out duties; we have duties arising from other people's rights. But the two together have to be grounded in responsibility—the responding to something greater than ourselves although not destructive of ourselves. The rights and duties of the individual first arose and continue to arise from within responsibility.

The Declaration of Independence in 1776 began with appeal to "Nature and Nature's God" before proposing the rights of life, liberty, and the pursuit of happiness. The United Nations' Universal Declaration of Human Rights in 1948 deliberately omitted any religious appeal because of disagreement among those who composed the document. The original intention was to establish a covenant among the nations, something that would have binding legal force. Because of disagreements, the only thing acceptable was a "declaration." The hope was to reach an accord on the covenant at a later time. In fact, there have been several U.N. covenants in the half century that followed, most importantly the Covenant on Civil and Political Rights and the Covenant on Economic, Social and Cultural Rights. Securing observance of these covenants has proved to be exceedingly difficult.[40]

The Universal Declaration, without attempting to secure a philosophical or religious basis, immediately proceeds to list thirty rights. Perhaps the United Nations was implicitly invoking a sense of humanity, hoping for a restraint of violence by exposing to shame those who do despicable acts. If that is the case, the list of rights seems disproportionate to the national responsibility that the United Nations could realistically assume. Perhaps the document, to be effective, should have stopped after its first few rights, namely, not to be killed, not to be tortured, not to be imprisoned without due process. These rights might then have been connected to basic rights of subsistence and security. The nations would have a fair chance of enforcing those rights.[41]

Governments have to be responsible to their own people, who in turn need to be responsible not only to their government but also to something greater than their respective governments. As far back as the Roman Empire a need for a law was seen that would go beyond the laws of the nations. Cicero called this law the *jus naturale* or natural law. This name is not very helpful except perhaps for Stoicism, which subordinated the human to an all-encompassing Nature.[42]

For Christians, nature was embodied in the uniquely personal so that morality could never simply be a submission to the natural. In the Middle Ages, when "natural" took its meaning from a contrast with "supernatural," the natural law became a shorthand for what could be known universally by the power of human reason. But in the seventeenth century "man" was seen as the conqueror of nature. Now an appeal to natural law appeared to be a call to submit human freedom to laws of objective nature. The term "natural law," however, did not disappear because many people rightly feared what could happen if law meant only what national statutes affirm.

The Nuremberg trials after World War II had to reach back for a law that goes beyond the legal code of any nation. That court found itself on shaky legal grounds appealing to a natural law or a law of humanity.[43] Some political theorists of the last half century have written at length about natural law. The language has also entered into ethical discussions by way of evolutionary biology. A new synthesis of Aristotle and Darwin seems ready to overcome the split between the natural and the ethical that has dominated ethics for the last two centuries.[44]

Despite the inadequacy of the language that is available, these developments hold out some promise for a reestablishing of the basis of "responsibility to." An ethic that simply implies that people should be responsible to the laws of their nation, or that responsibility should be to ethical obligation apart from bodily desires, is hopelessly inadequate to the human situation today. The moral responsibility for human actions has to be grounded in a responsibility to something or someone greater than the individual or the nation-state. That reality goes by names such as history or humanity, nature or life, doctrine or law, Yahweh or Allah.

Some of the flattened out meaning of responsibility in the twentieth century can be traced to an essay by Max Weber, "Politics as a Vocation" (1898).[45] Weber contrasted two ethics: one based on ultimate ends, the other on responsibility. With such an opposition, responsibility was totally cut off from its religious roots and any sense of responsibility to. For Weber, the Sermon on the Mount is an example of ultimate ends; it is therefore opposed to responsibility. "The Christian does rightly and leaves the result with the Lord" in contrast to the responsible person, "who has to give an account of the foreseeable results."[46] Thus, the Christian is by definition irresponsible; being responsible becomes identified with a sober calculation of pragmatic means to rational ends.

Weber's language has had profound repercussions, especially in international affairs, where it is the basis of the claim to a doctrine called "realism." Michael Joseph Smith writes that "Weber's dichotomy of realism and responsibility versus idealism and good intentions endures to the present day; and lucid discussions of the precise content of responsibility, of the values that compete to judge the consequences of policy, remains a rare commodity."[47] Smith notes that what emerges for Weber as the ulimate end of ethics is Germany's national interest.[48] Weber would have been totally opposed to Nazism, but Hitler's projected reign of a thousand years was a grotesque version of the apocalyptic side of revelation. The dismissal of ultimate ends from the meaning of responsibility creates a vacuum ready to be filled by dictators of nations.

Weber's language also made its way into the newly emerging field of Christian ethics. The World Council of Churches used Weber's meaning of responsibility in its 1950 document on "responsible society."[49] In subsequent meetings of the council, more radical-minded Christian groups attacked the idea of responsible society as bourgeois insensitivity to developing nations.[50] This conflict was unfortunate in the way that both sides used the term responsible.

In contrast, H. Richard Niebuhr's *The Responsible Self* in 1963 did not assume such a truncated meaning of responsibility. This gem of a book, which Niebuhr called an essay in Christian philosophy, has its roots in Niebuhr's 1941 work, *The Meaning of Revelation.*[51] Niebuhr's main question of responsibility is about the ultimate end: "to whom or what am I responsible and in what community of interaction am I myself?" Unfortunately, Niebuhr's brief work, published after his death, did not overcome the bias that had developed toward "responsible society," with its Weberian implication that being responsible means not being very Christian.

In summary, the meaning of "responsible to" should be as broad and as deep as is possible. In practice, breadth and depth stand in some tension. We have to look for the best combination of them. One friend's advice may be too little, but the advice of ten colleagues may be too much, especially if none of the advice comes from the depths of friendship. Ten historical documents are not more revealing than one document that speaks to the heart of the matter. There are no clear rules for how each of us combines a broad-based response and a response from the depths of the self. We are not certain of the best way to respond in a given situation, but we can surely be aware that a narrow and shallow response is not the way of divine revelation.

Responsible For

If we are responsible *to* in the best way that we know how, we will get a more precise understanding of what we are responsible *for*. A vague, narrow, or shallow understanding of what we are responsible to will lead to a distortion in what our responsibility is for. One such distortion takes the form of an aggressive seizing upon some activity as a quick resolution of life's problems. People "make decisions" to change careers, choose a marriage partner, lose fifty pounds, or quit school without attending to important voices outside themselves and without lining up support within their own bodies.

The extreme case of this distortion is the terrorist who "takes responsibility" for a bombing. All the terrorists in the world seem to speak the language of responsibility. I suspect that having been hectored to take responsibility for his life, the terrorist says, "You want me to take responsibility. Here it is."

The distortion of responsibility by a terrorist is easy to recognize, but there are many subtle distortions in relation to what we are responsible for. In this section, I look at how we are often mistaken in understanding our responsibility (1) for other people, (2) for our own life, and (3) for things.

1. *I am not responsible for other people, except when they cannot perform some needed act.* We are regularly urged to take responsibility for others. So widespread is the belief that we should be responsible for other people that the opposite is often judged to be morally reprehensible. The favorite phrase here is that I should be "my brother's keeper."[52] The assumption which accompanies the phrase is that the answer to Cain's question in Genesis, "Am I my brother's keeper?" is obviously yes. But in the Bible God does not answer the question. If God had answered, I think the reply might have been: "No, I did not ask you to be your brother's keeper. Brothers are neither for keeping nor for killing. I asked you to be your brother's brother."

One of the most insistent calls for taking responsibility for others is

by the twentieth-century philosopher Eugene Levinas. It is likely that
Levinas was reacting against what he saw as Heidegger's moral complacency. It is not enough to be "attuned to language" to fulfill human
responsibility; Levinas insists on action to relieve the suffering of others.[53]
Levinas is aware that responsibility does not originate in the human will;
it "comes from the hither side of my freedom, from a 'prior to every
memory.'"[54] Levinas also insists that responsibility does not wait upon
reciprocity. I should act responsibly in regard to others, whatever I get in
return. I may be caught in a situation that is not of my making or that
seems unfair, but I am responsible for the action demanded of me.[55]

Where I think Levinas overstates and undermines his case is in constantly saying that we are responsible for others. Although he cites the
Bible for support, the Bible also implies a respect for the freedom of the
other person. My first responsibility for actions in regard to others is to
be responsible *to* them. Then the action will be in the best interest of
what relates us: if a brother, love; if an enemy, reconciliation; if a stranger,
care for needs. When one assumes a world of isolated individuals, then
the question is, Should I be responsible for myself alone or should I also
be responsible for other people? But in a relational world, the question is:
Should I be responsible *for* other people or *to* other people? The latter is
the way that my responsibility respects the freedom of other people.

One of the finest essays on responsibility was written by Dietrich
Bonhoeffer. As someone who returned to Nazi Germany to fight Hitler
and was executed for his efforts, Bonhoeffer cannot be accused of lacking
in concern for others or being selfish. For Bonhoeffer, the sweep of
responsibility embraces the whole of reality. It is concerned not only with
good will but also with the good outcome of action, not only with the
motive but also with the object.[56]

Bonhoeffer combines this sweeping responsibility with a strong sensitivity to the freedom of the other. I am not responsible for another person because he or she is responsible for his or her own actions. I am often
responsible for actions that affect the health, welfare, and happiness of
other people. But that must always be distinguished from being responsible for them. "There can, therefore, never be an absolute responsibility,
a responsibility which is not essentially limited by the responsibility of the
other man."[57]

Professional people, such as politicians, physicians, or priests, need to
be regularly reminded that responsibility should not creep over into
paternalistic usurpation of the other's freedom. Hans Jonas describes
"non-reciprocal relations," in which the fate of others has come under my
control. "The captain is master of the ship and its passengers and bears

responsibility for them."[58] That is overstating the authority. The captain is responsible for his actions that bear on the safety of the ship and the comfort of the passengers. The passengers, however, are responsible for their own actions (sexual, eating, conversational, and so forth).

The exception in taking responsibility for other people is that each human being does have times when he or she cannot decide things for himself or herself. That is the case for all of us when we are very young; a one-year-old cannot prepare its dinner. The same case may be true for people who are very old and near death. The situation of an old person not able to decide for himself or herself has become increasingly the case. And throughout the life of each person, events may temporarily prevent a person from acting on his or her own behalf.

If a person's incapacity to act is temporary, someone else has to supply actions for as long as and to the extent that the person is incapacitated. Toward the end of life this incapacitated condition may be permanent, and someone may have to decide to discontinue mechanical means that are being used to keep a patient alive. Continuing to use a respirator or a feeding tube is a human decision just as much as is terminating its use.[59] When someone else has to be responsible for our actions, we hope it will be a close family member or a friend who has our best interests in mind. Lacking that, we can hope for an ethics committee in a hospital to defend our interests.

Any of us may become responsible for acting on behalf of a stranger. If I come upon a crime or an accident and a person needs medical help, I can be morally responsible for getting that assistance. The United States does not have a "good Samaritan law" that would hold the bystander legally responsible. Nevertheless, if I am the person on the scene, some action is morally called for, if only to dial 911.

2. *I am responsible for those actions over which I have sufficient control; I am not responsible for my life.* Each of us is the product of heredity, environment, and early nurturing that leave some of our behavior beyond a direct or immediate control. Some people have truly severe addictions that make their lives a mess. Each of us has impulses, drives, and attachments that are incomprehensible to ourselves. But except for extreme cases, people retain the ability to reflect on their behavior and to take a step away from their worst behavior.

Freedom consists mainly in the ability to say no. At times (in a prison, within an unhappy family, on a needed job), one cannot do any more than say no, but that ability can be the difference between retaining the dignity of a human being and sinking into an inhuman state. By repeatedly saying no and doing what is possible at any moment, a person may gradually widen the area of behavior over which he or she has moral responsibility.[60]

In acknowledging moral responsibility for actions over which I have sufficient control, the qualifier, "sufficient," is necessarily ambiguous. Sometimes I am certain of being morally responsible for an action; the action is thoroughly mine.[61] Sometimes I am uncertain if I am morally responsible because of external or internal pressures. If I sometimes cannot judge my own responsibility, all the more is it true that I cannot judge other people's moral responsibility.

While I should take responsibility for some actions, I think one should avoid the claim that "I take full responsibility." The person who makes that claim is usually caught within a complex set of circumstances. The person may have done some horrible deed and cannot understand his or her own motives. Or the person is a member of an organization that is involved in some serious wrongdoing. In both cases, the individual cannot take full responsibility because it is not there for the taking. If the person is famous, the news media demand that he or she come forth and take full responsibility. Then the ritual of the person saying that he or she does so is applauded.

Most often when people use this formula they go on to show that they have little grasp of why they did what they did and what they now have to do to correct the situation. President Bill Clinton, in a famous four-minute speech on August 17, 1998, spent the first minute taking full responsibility for what had happened in his sexual escapades. He then spent the other three minutes bitterly attacking the special prosecutor. When President Vladimir Putin finally faced the public after the disaster of the Russian submarine *Kursk,* he declared, "I feel a total sense of responsibility and guilt for this tragedy." It was unclear what he was guilty of or what taking full responsibility would entail as a consequence.[62]

The person who has a realistic understanding of responsibility has a grasp of the seriousness of his or her moral failing and is determined that it will not happen again. He or she is likely to say: I accept responsibility for my part in this wrongdoing. I do not fully understand how this happened. I am taking steps a, b, c, or d to prevent a recurrence. For example, I am going to a therapist, I am joining a support group, I am resigning from my job, I am reassigning a worker.

Throughout the course of life, responsibility is for an action. My life as a whole is not available. Saying to someone "take responsibility for your life" is not helpful and can be depressing. The person who receives such advice cannot get control of his or her life by a decision. Jewish, Christian, and Muslim teachings are very clear on this point. What a person can do is accept some responsibility for the action that he or she is about to perform. In taking that one responsible step the person might begin to reorient his or her life.

As a concluding decision of my life, I may be faced with accepting what my life has been. Elisabeth Kubler-Ross popularized a five-stage theory of dying: denial, anger, bargaining, depression, and acceptance.[63] A simpler version can reduce the stages to two: denial and acceptance. Throughout life we rightly deny death's hand. Even when one is diagnosed with a fatal disease, the nearly universal reaction is denial. Such denial is a healthy response which allows a person to marshall his or her strength. This denial, according to Kubler-Ross, is followed by partial acceptance.[64] After a period of going back and forth—"I'm dying/I refuse to die"—people may reach a stage of simple and final acceptance. At that point I might be able to grasp how the many plot details of my life have produced the story of my life. Only at that point might it make sense to say that I take or accept responsibility for my life.

3. *I am responsible for creatures who cannot decide things for themselves.* Human beings are responsible for the things of creation that are not responsible for themselves. The human response within revelation is spoken for all creatures that do not speak. Ironically, we often get this responsibility backward and assume that we are responsible for people but not for things. It is things that we are clearly responsible for. The things sometimes include nonhuman animals, but the ability of animals to decide many things for themselves should be respected. Vegetative life and nonliving things, as far as we can determine, cannot decide anything. Human beings need to accept responsibility for protecting the environment and caring for individual elements within the environment. Sometimes that means aggressive action on behalf of a river, a forest, or an oceanfront. Sometimes human responsibility is exercised by noninterference, leaving intact the cycle of living things.

This exercise of responsibility for the nonhuman world is to be distinguished from a utilitarian attitude that sees things only as "things for use."[65] The charge is unfairly made that Jewish and Christian traditions placed "man" on top of nature, with everything else reduced to being an instrument for man. Jewish and Christian traditions did not place man on top; they placed humans at the center. They did not claim that the world was made for the greater glory of man (as many nineteenth-century thinkers did). Creation was seen to be for the glory of the creator.

One cannot deny that Jewish, and especially Christian, religions helped prepare the way for our ecological problems. If there is not a mutuality among the humans, especially between men and women, then "man"—rational, calculating, manipulative, dominating man—can be a danger to everyone. When "man" defined everything else as "nature" and discovered ways to control forces in his environment, he came to see his vocation as the "conquest of nature." From his imagined perch above nature, "man" became beginning and end of all things. But if revelation is a divine–human relation, then the human is at the center of creation, exercising a priesthood for all creation in praise of the creator. The first religious response, wrote Max Scheler, is, "Thou All, I nothing." The second response is, "Thou All, I not quite nothing."[66] The humans are not quite nothing, which makes them like everything else in creation; but they are also God's representative through whom all creation praises God.

RESPONSIBILITY AS PERSONAL/CORPORATE

One of the distinctions that most hampers a discussion of responsibility is the assumed contrast between individual responsibility and social responsibility. The contrast is deeply ingrained in modern politics, economics, and ethics. It is also reflected in religious books, church pronouncements, and seminary courses. At the turn of the twentieth century, "social" became the shibboleth of left-wing politics (social welfare, social security, social medicine, social-ism). Although in the 1970s, the right wing decided to have its own social agenda: (being against homosexuality and abortion, being for school prayer and vouchers); social ethics and social responsibility remain the cries of the left.

There is a constant complaint that the church does well at individual ethics but not social ethics. There is constant preaching to the government and the business world that they should exercise social responsibility. Many business corporations candidly say that their responsibility is to their shareholders. Some businesses, either from conviction or for public relations purposes, try to be socially responsible by contributing to charity.[67]

The language of individual/social is not up to the task for which it is invoked. It does little to control the rapacious aspects of the economic system. Social responsibility cannot encompass the complicated organizations of today nor the human relation to the physical environment. Max Weber claimed that Catholic and Lutheran antipathy to capitalism "rests essentially on the repugnance of the impersonality of relations" preventing the church "from penetrating and transforming them along ethical lines."[68] He is right that neither individual ethics nor social ethics can get at these impersonal relations. But while no one can easily specify what moral responsibility demands in the complicated patterns of contemporary life, we need to address problems with a language that includes impersonal structures.

If responsibility is to everyone and everything, if responsibility is for things rather than other people, there is no reason why moral responsibility should exclude impersonal relations. For that to happen, however, one must start with a distinction that relates the personal and the impersonal, rather than with the dichotomy of social and individual. Responsibility is always personal/corporate, that is, every act of responsibility is both a personal action and within a corporate structure. At the center of response is the understanding and freedom of a personal being. And the context of every moral decision is corporate or bodily existence. The corporate begins with the physical organism and extends into innumerable bodily organizations.

The term personal carries connotations that "individual" lacks; the dialogical partner in divine revelation is a person rather than an individual. A person is an actor, one who plays a role in the drama of life. The word "person" means to speak through a mask; the person is always partly hidden but is present through speaking. While playing many scenes, the actor in life's drama may be unclear as to how that scene fits into the overall plot. The actor has to trust that, by playing each scene to the best of his or her ability, a unity of personal existence will emerge. The actor in life always has conflicts in reaching a coalescence of character.[69] No one is transparent to himself or herself; one's own motives are never entirely clear. Why did I do that? Should I have acted differently? Hannah Arendt wrote that only bad people have clear consciences. The rest of us live with moral ambiguity, aware of our failures and the need for forgiveness.[70]

The term "individual," in contrast, does not suggest a dialogue that is internal to the self. The individual is a unit in actuarial tables, economic forecasts, and scientific studies. The responsible person, however, is an actor who has to negotiate a decision with his or her bodily self, past as well as present. The lack of unity in a person is not best described as a conflict of body and spirit or as an opposition of reason and passion. In negotiations of speaking and listening, the choice is between a superficial reason and a deeper reason that includes passion.[71]

The choice can also be described as one between a centered self and a fragmented self. In morally irresponsible actions the center does not hold. But the self cannot simply issue orders; it has to gain support for what it decides. The current metaphor of "making decisions" suggests that life is an engineering project, that a person is constructing a building which includes making things called decisions. I suggest that freedom is better imagined as a movie director trying out various takes and at some point saying "cut" (de-cide).

The best cut by the director does not always come from the most number of takes. Human freedom is not necessarily improved by increasing the available choices: fifty kinds of soap powder or cereal rather than three. Human freedom disappears if there is only one choice. But human freedom can be most strikingly revealed when there is only one thing to which the person must say yes or no.[72] The paradox of human freedom is that the range of choice narrows as a person exercises moral responsibility. That is, it becomes increasingly impossible to consider choosing what is evil in one's life. Eventually, there may be almost no struggle in deciding to do the right thing or at least in avoiding what is evil. Morally good people do not have to agonize over every decision.

The strange thing is how this process of increasingly limited choice parallels the situation of the person who is criminal or morally sick. The person who commits evil acts is likely to say, "I cannot do other; a greater force than myself takes over and 'it' acts. I do not deserve blame for my actions." Similarly, the person of heroic goodness may say, "I cannot do other; my life is taken up by a power greater than myself. I do not deserve praise for my actions."

This claim always has to be questioned. Even a person of great intelligence and virtue can be deluded about his or her single-mindedness. One can genuinely conclude that no other choice is possible only after a long and patient process in which free choices have coalesced into a pattern of peace with one's whole self. Michael Polanyi captures the paradox in these words: "While compulsion by force or by neurotic obsession excludes responsibility, compulsion by universal intent establishes responsibility. . . . The freedom of the subjective person to do as he pleases is overruled by the freedom of the responsible person to do as he must."[73]

Most of us most of the time, being neither heroic saint nor sick addict, confront a range of possible choices. Each actual choice changes, if ever so slightly, the range of our future choices. We exercise freedom by evaluating what we have done in the past as a factor in present and future choices. The simple yes or no at the center of the self reverberates through bodily life, sometimes within the body in a way that is not externally visible, sometimes in ways that dramatically alter the environment. The exercise of freedom is always corporately expressed, at least in one's own body and usually as an actor in one or more corporate organizations.

A corporation is any organization or institution, any body that is visible in space and time. A human body is a corporation, as is the Boston

Celtics, the United States Senate, the city of Rome, the American Medical Association, or Exxon Oil. It may seem quixotic to attempt retrieving the term corporation from its nearly exclusive control by the business corporation. In support of such a project, I offer three points of evidence: First, there is no etymological reason why the business world has any more right to the term corporation than any other body. Second, other corporations have been recognized as legal persons for over a thousand years.[74] Third, many religious, political, and educational organizations today retain a share of the term corporation as nonprofit organizations. Exploring responsibility requires preserving and shoring up "corporation" as the name for dozens of settings in which people act each day.

There is not one set of ethical rules for business and a different set for actions elsewhere. The business corporation is continuous with other corporateness in human life. The business corporation has points of similarity with other organizations in devising ways for the exercise of its power. It also has to give protection and support to the exercise of responsibility by "natural persons" within the organization. The structure for decisions in a business or another kind of corporation must have a responsibility to its own members.

Among its moral concerns has to be the issue of violence. A religious or professional organization ought to be specially attentive to this issue. Political and business corporations might not be at the forefront of resisting violence, but they cannot dismiss the concern as outside their domain. Some government agencies are inextricably involved in violence, but even the police and military have to seek to lessen violence. The soldier may have to be trained to defend his country but not in such an atmosphere that the training spills over into spousal abuse.

Another concern of political and business corporations has to be truthfulness. A political leader may not be able to tell the truth as he or she knows it, but a leader who becomes known as a liar will no longer be able to lead. No one in the business world can tell the whole truth and nothing but the truth on all occasions. Nevertheless, the business world depends on trusting people not to lie. Corporate spokespersons who lie might succeed in making short-term profits, but they do so only by destroying the company's longevity.

Deception of one's competitors is part of the business world. It can be morally acceptable. There is also some inevitable deception of the buying public, indicated by the slogan "buyer beware." The responsibility of a business corporation does not substitute for responsibility on the part of clients and buyers. If someone thinks he can get twenty-five percent return on an investment that has no risk, he shares responsibility with the crook who runs off with his money. The government's responsibility here is to protect clients and buyers against deceptive practices that can maim and kill. The government cannot provide total protection against greed and stupidity.

Max Weber is correct in saying that modern capitalism makes it difficult to say who is responsible for what. The problem should not be exacerbated by a radical individualism that regards institutions as completely impersonal, that is, other than us. At the end of a book exploring the dark side of nature, Lyall Watson concludes, "The best we can hope for is to exercise our freedom to choose with the advantage of as much knowledge as may be available. But we mustn't expect any help from our institutions. . . . All we have left, it appears, is ourselves."[75] This dispiriting conclusion assumes that "our institutions" and "ourselves" are entirely separate realities. The one thing guaranteed by such an assumption is that the dark and dangerous side of institutions will get worse. Such a development then feeds the feeling of alienation and the need for the individual to rebel against all organization.

The alternative attitude is to listen and respond to the main corporate structures that are extensions of myself. These structures include family, neighborhood, workplace, church, school, social club. On extreme occasions responsibility can involve a total refusal to cooperate with one of the formative institutions of one's life. For example, one might responsibly resist if asked to fight in an immoral war or to sell a deadly product. One may have to leave the country, go to jail, quit one's job, blow the whistle on one's employer.

No such steps should be taken precipitously without exploring other possibilities and without measuring one's ability to bear the burden of heavy responsibility. Most of the time, less dramatic action is called for. In most jobs, one can exercise responsibility by responding to one's boss, letting him or her know if something is wrong. If that does not work, there should be other means available to handle such problems (and if there are no other means available, one's responsibility may include trying to develop them). Going to the local television reporter or to *Sixty Minutes* is a last resort and not a career-enhancing move.

No one has the luxury of thinking that he or she is uncontaminated by the ethical problems of today's business world. We are all responsible to that world and, depending on our roles, responsible for some part of that world. Our responsibility varies in an organization according to the position we occupy: customer, neighbor, employee, member, director, owner.[76] If I am a neighbor I usually have no responsibility for the company, although it probably has some responsibility for actions affecting my well-being. If I buy a product, I share responsibility—if only in a minuscule way—for the corporation's policies. If I am a member or employee I associate myself and my reputation with the ethics of the corporation. If I am a member of the governing board or executive council, I share a direct responsibility for the corporate decisions. I can be held legally responsible for crimes committed by the corporation.

It should be noted, however, that an employee or even an owner does not invest the whole of his or her personhood in the corporation. People invest themselves to varying degrees, according to the nature of the organization, as well as their personal inclinations. One would expect deeper investment in being a father, a citizen, or a church member than in following a business career or belonging to a club. The distinctions here are more complicated than is generally assumed, and we lack an adequate language to formulate questions.

The distinction between a private life and a public life is not so clear as was once thought. People refer to personal as opposed to professional, but professional role is one of the expressions of the personal. No individual exists separate from corporate roles; instead, one is a person precisely in acting through and in these roles. "To be a full-fledged human moral person is to find a place (or places) in the structure of corporate entities."[77]

RESPONSIBILITY AND TIME

In this last section, a reflection on time will highlight the relation between revelation and responsibility. I have maintained that revelation is a present relation, the activity of the divine met by the response of the human listener. I acknowledge the danger of misunderstanding this principle if one assumes the common image of time as a series of points, that is, the past as a series of points to the left of the present and the future a series to the right. In that image, the past disappears behind our backs, and the present (point) excludes the past. Only if the past is included in the depths of the present can a religious tradition be respected.

Responsibility as always both personal and corporate helps to fill in how the relation of past and present is constituted. A responsibility to everyone and everything includes a responsibility to the past. In principle, this responsibility to the past is clear. It means responsibility involves my listening to the voices of the past for guidance in the present. The hazier issue is whether and how someone is responsible for the past. Can a person today be held responsible for actions committed in the past?

I have argued that a person is morally responsible for actions over which he or she has a sufficient degree of control. I am responsible for such actions in the present. Can I be held responsible for actions that I performed yesterday, last year, or twenty years ago? Legal practice and moral philosophy say yes. I am a physical or corporate being continuous in space and time. Despite evidence that all the cells of the body change over the course of a few years, no one argues on that basis that the defendant is innocent of the crime committed ten years ago.

It is interesting, however, that the person's state of mind in the present is often considered relevant. If the person accepts responsibility for the past action and is thereby genuinely sorry, a court is likely to be more lenient. The person's responsibility is altered by listening to his or her past and taking appropriate action in the present. The present of the person includes the past, which is always waiting to be reinterpreted. Physical events in my past may be fixed forever, but the meaning of my past—my responsibility to and for the past—changes continuously.

A paradoxical twist on the reinterpretation of the past is provided by introducing the future. Heidegger and Rosenzweig contend that the sense of the future guides the interpretation of the "past present."[78] I construe a meaning for the past according to where I see my life going in the future. The one indubitable fact about the future—my own death—casts its shadow upon the past within the present. If I cannot face my mortality with equanimity I will be blocked from accepting the past.

The moral responsibility for my past goes back as far as my childhood. Can it go back farther? Is a Christian born in the twentieth century responsible for the persecution of Jews in fifteenth-century Toledo? Is a German born in 1947 responsible for Nazi atrocities? Is a white citizen in today's United States responsible for the horrors of slavery? To all these questions an answer other than no seems grossly unfair. Yet such questions do not go away. In discussions of these issues, someone typically says, "Of course I don't believe in collective guilt, but . . ." and then goes on to attribute a kind of collective guilt spreading back into the past.

The problem here is the dichotomy of individual and social responsibility. Neither category is a help in relating past and present. The individual clearly has no part in the activities of the past centuries. And social or collective bonds to the past seem to require something mystical, mythical, or primitive. If one starts with the personal in a matrix of corporate relations that extend beyond anyone's imagination, however, the question takes a different turn. The fact that a young German did not commit Nazi atrocities does not mean he or she is free of all forms of responsibility. "Germany," "Christian church," "United States" are not fictions, nor are they (social) collections of individuals. They are corporate realities, artificial persons, that are responsible for some actions. A member of one of these organizations shares in the corporate act to the degree he or she decides, praises, approves, accepts, silently rejects, quietly opposes, or publicly protests the actions of the body.

As a member of one of these organizations in the present, I am morally responsible for protesting against an immoral act. As a member of the organization at a later time in history, I am still responsible for protesting—in the form of present actions—something clearly immoral in the past. Adult voices in the United States were needed in 1945 to protest the progressively immoral bombings of Tokyo, Hiroshima, and Nagasaki; few voices were heard. There is still a need for protest, although it obviously takes a different form more than half a century later.[79]

As a United States citizen I am not responsible for those actions in the past, but I am responsible to those past actions, which will lead to being responsible for present actions. Nothing is gained by having people feel vaguely guilty for crimes they did not commit. The rest of the world does not expect the United States and its citizens to wallow in guilt for past transgressions. But other countries would like assurance that the United States is responsible to its past, the bad memories as well as the good, so as to learn some lessons. Responsible action in the present has to be grounded in such knowledge.

The responsibility becomes clearer in those cases where the sons and daughters are visited with the bounteous goods of their fathers and mothers. J. R. Lucas writes, "We cannot eat the fruits of their labors and wash our hands of the stains of their toil. At the very least we take on some civil liability to make reparation for what was done in the course of producing those benefits."[80] A person who shares in the economic wealth of the United States is also heir to the stain of slavery, the devastation of the natives, and the impoverishment of other countries on the continent. United States citizens have a duty to know the past and, when circumstances demand, to make reparations. Sometimes a sincere apology is more important than money, especially if it is tied to other actions for justice in the present.[81]

Acceptance of the past in the present is connected to how we view the future. In a strange way, the past (the meaning of our past) depends on the future (our present projection of a future). The common image of time as a series of points creates a false symmetry of past and future. The past exists in a way that the future does not. Our responsibility to the future is fundamentally different from our listening to the voices of the past because one cannot be responsible to voices not yet spoken. We also cannot be responsible for future actions because those actions have not yet been performed. Nevertheless, we still sense a responsibility regarding the future, even though the language of individual and social responsibility leaves any connection to the future inexplicable.

A personal/corporate responsibility reveals two definite connections to the future: corporations and children. As a member of a corporation my present actions can influence the future. One of the main differences between natural and artificial persons is that the former die but the latter can be chartered in perpetuity. My present responsibility is mediated to the future by political, religious, environmental, and business corporations. I am responsible to the future and for the future insofar as I act within a corporation that will outlive me.

There is some irony in this fact. In the thinking of liberal theoreticians, progress has been measured by the individual's freedom from control by institutions. And yet, our contribution to a better world depends on the extension of our corporate selves into the corporate structures of large organizations. Peter French writes, "The endurance of corporate persons, a prospect that terrorized the Enlightenment liberals, insures the projection of moral and cultural responsibilities in both temporal directions."[82]

The other link to the future, to a future that has already begun, is children. One can be responsible to and for the future by caring for children. Adults have a responsibility for children—to the degree that a child cannot be responsible for its own actions. The model for the relation of adult teacher and maturing child is divine revelation and human response. Parents have a special responsibility for their own children's actions. But the parent as teacher slowly relinquishes responsibility for the child's actions as the child gets older.

Schoolteachers also have a specific responsibility in the care of children. The schoolteacher has to limit responsibility to those areas which he or she should professionally control.[83] The main focus of the schoolteacher's responsibility is schoolteaching. A teacher's responsibility is to teach; a student's responsibility is to learn. With very young children, a schoolteacher is inevitably given some of the cares of the parent. But that responsibility should be clearly defined, and it should decrease as students mature.

The danger of well-meaning adults is that they substitute their decisions for the child's own responsibility. A child is responsible from the moment of birth, if not earlier. Adults have to provide a safe haven during the time that infants and young children try out their responsibility to their environment and their responsibility for what they can do by their own physical and mental powers. A child's moral responsibility is not something that arrives all at once or even in one year. Modern studies have not significantly changed the traditional view that children can exercise a moral sense by age five or six, but that a developed moral responsibility for one's actions is not present until the teenage years.

The aim of the adult ought to be to continuously increase the young person's own responsibility. If a young person commits crimes, the parents have to examine what went wrong. The parents quite possibly share some responsibility for the child's failure. But recent efforts in the United States to make parents legally responsible for actions by their sixteen- or eighteen-year-old children are unfair.[84]

Children, it is often said, are the promise of the future. The statement is true in the most literal sense. Both revelation and responsibility concern promise. As I noted in chapter 5, God's promise is not just a statement in a book. The promise is flesh and blood, the vitality of the earth and all of its creatures. For most religious groups, children are God's special representatives. In Christian history from Augustine to the Puritans, children were cast as vessels of sin in need of harsh discipline. In modern times, children are more often sentimentalized as the model of human innocence. Neither attitude does justice to children as the embodying of possibility, promise, and hope for the future.[85] In negotiations to end factional wars, no more important question can be asked than What about the children?

This reflection on responsibility and the future may throw some light on the irrepressible concern with the apocalyptic side of revelation. Our responsibility in the present starts from the future. We are aware of our own personal mortality and also the question of where the world is going. Our attempts to tend to the wounds of the present, which have been inflicted in the past, presuppose an idea of what a true and full healing would be. Our small attempts at what Jewish mysticism calls "to heal the world" intimate a much greater healing by forces beyond our imagination but not beyond our hopes.

The wish of millenarian groups to bring on a victorious new era is a human concern that cannot be suppressed. That desire has produced futurology with its rational and optimistic predictions of how to solve our human problems. The grounds for these predictions is almost as shaky as the grounds for the ecstatic visionaries who predict the violent end to all history. In either case, we are distracted from listening and answering in the present. We will continue to be obsessed with future predictions until we can integrate concern for the future into more adequate meanings of responsibility, revelation, and the present.

7

The Logic of Revelation

THE PREVIOUS CHAPTER'S DISCUSSION of responsibility to the past is a step toward solving a logical problem that Christians and Jews have. The idea of revelation seems to be locked into the distant past. I have argued, to the contrary, that "revelation" names a present relation that incorporates the past by being corporately related to one's ancestors. The clearest continuity of corporation may be based on biology, but artificial persons also provide a link over the centuries. A Jew who listens to the book of Exodus is addressed as one among the people who are "my people." While the Christian's relation to an ancient people is more tenuous than the Jew's, the church as " the gathered people of God" provides some continuity.

If one has faith in his or her tradition and its documents, the idea of revelation has some coherence and credibility. But this strengthening of one's own sense of community and tradition can heighten another problem, one that is perhaps the modern world's main objection to the idea of revelation. Is it not arrogant, intolerant, and dangerous to claim that God chose (chooses) my people to speak to? Jews, Christians, and Muslims have often battled each other, but to people outside these three traditions, the claims of Jews, Christians, and Muslims look remarkably similar: God is with us; God spoke (speaks) to us; God deals with the human race through us.

Many Christians and Jews would like to minimize a clash between their respective religious group and the supreme modern virtue of tolerance. Unfortunately, the attempts simply to soften the conflict by playing down the strong claims of the past may serve only to weaken the tradition while still being unconvincing to the outsider. That has been the problem with much of liberal reform in Judaism and Christianity. Conservative parts of Christianity and Judaism, and perhaps the main part of Islam, take some delight from being in conflict with modernity.

An alternative to both liberal reform and conservative defense is to grapple with a paradox inherent to religious speech. For understanding revelation one has to use a logic that differs from the logic that has dominated modern Western thinking. This chapter describes the paradox at issue in the claim to revelation.

One of the bad compromises that Christianity and Judaism made with modern science was to accept the logic of general and special revelations. This distinction easily fits within the logic of modern science. The meaning of the dichotomy is very clear: some truths are available to everyone, but for those so inclined to believe, additional truths are available in Jewish, Christian, and any number of other special revelations. The modern world has shown little opposition to this arrangement so long as Christians, Jews, and other claimants to a special revelation do not start trying to apply these truths outside their respective boundaries.

The logic to be described in this chapter is not based on either a general or a special revelation. Its focus is a universal revelation that is available, to whatever degree it can be grasped, in particular embodiments. This logic is familiar to an artist who concentrates on a painting or a sculpture that is born of concrete details in space and time but is capable of crossing all spatial and temporal divides. In contrast, the logic of the fundamentalist who looks only for true propositions does violence to the logic of revelation. Church documents or sermons that try to tell people the truth but neglect the artistic form of communication fail to use the proper logic, one in which the universal and the particular are on the same side.

UNIQUENESS

For elaborating the relation of particular and universal, I will explore a single word: unique. I will argue that revelation should be understood as a unique experience and is therefore particular/universal. Although "unique" is a frequently used term, it is also a confusing and ambiguous term. I might not have chosen this hook on which to hang my case, except that the term is common in both Christian and Jewish writing. The claim to uniqueness is rather recent, mostly a nineteenth- and twentieth-century invention. Its original purpose was in large part defensive. But it is possible that "unique" can be a positive way for Jewish and Christian religions to engage contemporary ideas.

My use of "unique" for describing realities within Judaism and Christianity is not dictated solely by internal pressures. The term has a prominence in the arts and also in modern biology, psychology, and anthropology. Christian and Jewish writers would do well to examine the uses of the term unique outside their respective religions before deciding whether and how to employ this term for purposes of a religious logic.[1]

In Jewish writing the most pointed and frequent use of the term unique has been in reference to the Holocaust. A continuous debate has gone on for several decades as to whether the Holocaust is unique.[2] Actually, there is less disagreement in this literature than the surface conflict suggests. Nearly all Jewish writers call attention to the importance of the Holocaust not only for Jews but for the whole world. Some writers think that the word unique captures exactly what they are affirming. For other writers, "unique" is either a banality or an absurdity.[3] The disagreement over unique does not derive from slightly differing interpretations of the term; the difference comes from an incomprehension on each side of what the other side is saying. What seldom appears in this literature is any sustained attempt to clarify the meaning of the term unique.

I have no intention of discussing Holocaust literature here.[4] But I doubt that "unique" would have shown up in this literature if it had not already found its way into a description of Jewish history and Jewish life. In *The Gates of Prayer*, the prayer book of the Reform movement, the Jew prays to God "who has set us apart from the other families of the earth, giving us a destiny unique among the nations."[5] The word unique may not have been in the ancient Hebrew prayer, but it seemed appropriate to the modern translator. Franz Rosenzweig wrote to his friend Eugen Rosenstock-Huessy that "the election of the Jews is something unique, because it is the election of 'one people.'"[6] The traditional claims of chosenness and election show up in the twentieth century as uniqueness. For some Jews, all of their history can be summed up in this word. Martin Buber writes, "The uniqueness of Israel signifies something which in its nature, its history and its vocation is so individual that it cannot be classified."[7]

This contention that Jewish experience cannot be classified is precisely what worries other Jews who are interested in historical and comparative studies. Jewish historians are likely to say that "the uniqueness of the Jews may be a cardinal principle of Jewish theology but in the study of Jewish communities it serves only to replace theoretical understanding with metaphysics and self-congratulation."[8] Similarly, David Hartmann begins *A Living Covenant* by saying that his discussion of Judaism "in no way pretends to show how Judaism or the Jewish people are unique or superior to other faith communities."[9]

Christianity, similar to Judaism, is based on a claim to be God's people. The claim to uniqueness, however, is given a more concentrated meaning in Christianity: Jesus Christ is unique. So omnipresent is this claim that one might think that all the traditional titles of Jesus have been replaced by this one claim to uniqueness. In Christian writing there is seldom any protest against this claim. Although a belief that Jesus Christ is unique is a recent formula, it is assumed to be central to Christian orthodoxy.[10] But as with Holocaust literature, it is difficult to find in Christology any lengthy reflection on the meaning of unique or a recognition that the claim of Jesus Christ's uniqueness is not clear. I return below to this Christian confession of uniqueness. First, I reflect on the meanings of unique.

TWO MEANINGS OF UNIQUE

"Unique" is a fascinating word, laden with ambiguity. It is one of those strange words that has almost opposite meanings. Even more peculiarly, unique is a word that never strictly applies. The *American Heritage Dictionary* has one of its longest editorial notes attached to the word. The panel of experts, who are asked to rule on problematic uses of a word, are obviously frustrated by the seemingly illogical way that "unique" is constantly used. Generations of grammar teachers have insisted that there can be no comparatives modifying "unique." Something cannot be very unique or more unique. A thing is either unique or it is not unique.[11] And yet, more often than not, people use qualifiers of comparison before "unique."

I think popular speech shows a realization of the strangeness of the claim to be unique. The usual way of speaking seems at first glance to be loose, sloppy, or illogical. But there is an insight in this popular use of "unique" that opens up the contrasting meanings of "unique." The root meaning of "unique" is to be different from others, to be not equal. While there is only one way to be equal or the same, there are literally endless ways to be unequal. In a spectrum of inequality, uniqueness puts no cap on the range of being different from. The unique is different from every other, different in all respects.

Does that simply mean that a unique thing is the only one of its class? Sometimes that is assumed to be the meaning of unique. But "unique" is not usually employed for that purpose. We simply say that something is one of a kind. People do not get confused or fight over that statement.

The claim of uniqueness does not stop with kind; it has no in-built restraints. It asserts different from all others in every way. Is that possible? Can an event, a thing, or a person be unique? If a thing is a thing at all, it shares a common note with other things; otherwise it would not be a thing. I think that people sense that fact when they say that something is "very unique," "more unique," or "most unique." What they mean is that the thing is extraordinarily different from other things to which it might be compared. The thing is different in so many ways and to such a degree as to approach (total) uniqueness. "More unique" means that something is more nearly unique. As the term is used in popular speech and in much scholarly writing, "unique" is about a process of increasing differentiation. Far from being a term that lacks comparativeness, it always implies comparison, sometimes to its own prior condition and usually to other things.

This first point about unique—to be different from others by a process of continuing but never finished differentiation—leads to a second point. The process of increasing differentiation can go in one of two directions: toward increasing exclusion or toward increasing inclusion. Something can be (more nearly) unique by having fewer and fewer notes in common with others. In the opposite direction, something can become (more nearly) unique by having more and more notes in common.

In the sequence wxyz, xyz, yz, z, the last element, z, can be called the most nearly unique in this set of four elements. It shares only the note z with the other three elements; it is the most different of the four. We cannot say it is simply or totally unique because there could be $z1, z2, z3, z4$. The element z changes over time and it is divisible further. Whatever has been claimed to be indivisible has turned out to be divisible into subunits. Electrons are more nearly unique than atoms.

In the opposite direction, a thing can become more nearly unique by a process of increasing inclusion. In the sequence a, ab, abc, abcd, the fourth element, abcd, can be called the most unique of the set. It is different from all the others by including all of them. Abc is more unique than a or ab, but abcd is still more nearly unique. However, abcd is not simply and totally unique. The sequence suggests the possibility of an abcde, abcdef, or abcdefg, the last being the most unique in the set. While human history continues, no thing could be completely unique, inclusive of every other thing.

I am not merely proposing a logical hypothesis of what "unique" could mean. I have examined thousands of examples in ordinary speech and scholarly writing for how the word is actually used. The examples break down fairly evenly between these two meanings. The first meaning may seem to be the obvious, logical, and the usual sense: uniqueness is simply a matter of excluding sameness. When human beings are the ref-

erence for the term, however, the second meaning of uniqueness is usually implied. The first meaning logically applies to a world of objects outside one another in space. Things are more nearly unique as they share
fewer commonalities. But the second meaning is needed to describe the
openness of the human being. People become more nearly unique as they
take in more and more of the world, as they become more inclusive of
their time, their place, their people.[12]

UNIQUE REVELATION

Using the paradox of uniqueness, I take up the term revelation and several associated terms, especially "covenant" in Jewish history and "Jesus
Christ" in Christian history. The use of unique is subject to misunderstanding, but that danger cannot be avoided in the challenge raised by
Jewish and Christian religions. At the beginning of the modern era, the
Jewish claim to revelation was thought by many to be embarrassing and
indefensible. "The very possibility of a unique revelation to a unique
Moses at a unique Sinai seems to have vanished with the advent of
modernity."[13]

The compromise that was worked out with the Enlightenment was a
special revelation to complement the general revelation open to all. The
(exclusively) special revelations of Judaism and Christianity stood
opposed to each other. Within each religion the liberals emphasized the
general revelation that can be found everywhere. The conservatives
defended the special revelation that can be found only within their religion. Paul Tillich describes this conflict within twentieth-century Christianity under the categories of humanist versus neo-orthodox: "The latter
group says that there is only *one* revelation, namely, that in Christ; to
which the former group answers that there are revelations everywhere and
none of them is ultimate."[14]

The unique revelation that I wish to describe would be able to affirm
some truth in both of these Christian positions. That is, although there
is only one revelation, it can also be said that revelation is everywhere.
Similarly, it is true that for Christians revelation is finally summed up in
Christ, but it is also true that no human articulation of revelation is final.
Neither Christians nor Jews can claim to possess the universal divine revelation. There is a Christian interpretation of revelation that need not be
pitted against the Jewish interpretation.

An accusation of idolatry by Christians against Jews or by Jews
against Christians should be avoided.[15] What each side sees as a claim to

ultimacy on the other side is simply the affirming of what is (most nearly) unique. A unique revelation is the affirmation of a truth that has been experienced, together with the affirmation that God is greater than anything humanly experienced.

The double meaning of "unique" allows the word to connect two things that may seem to be incompatible. On one side, Christian and Jewish origins are firmly set in a precise place at a precise time in history. There was a unique Moses at a unique Sinai. Likewise, a unique Jesus was born at the time of King Herod and in the town of Bethlehem. On the other side, the possible human recipient of revelation is not fixed in one time and one place. The words spoken at Sinai or from Calvary can resonate in human lives of any time and any place. The words *can be* of universal significance, but they do not automatically translate to every time and every place. The uniqueness of human receptivity is what makes the Bible's word *potentially* universal. The actual, living, human being always embodies both meanings of unique; that is, he or she is firmly set in space and time while he or she is also open to the whole universe.

When these two meanings of unique are not held together, revelation becomes either an object in the past or else an inner conviction in the present. Eventually, "revelation" that has the latter meaning is likely to be put aside for a word that has a more subjective meaning. Paul Tillich is quoted above as saying that the humanistic Christians accept many revelations. More likely, these people give up completely on "revelations" and talk about "faiths," a word that conveys inner conviction and an undefined reference to the outer world.

On the other side of the divide, in what Tillich refers to as neo-orthodoxy, Christian revelation or special revelation is taken to be God's special gift to the chosen few. God is imagined to have intervened in past history. Although there is much talk of history here, this view is antihistorical. It is the view that led Mircea Eliade to say that "Christianity entered into history in order to abolish it."[16] In this conception, the truth or truths of Christianity are suprahistorical and remain untouched by the present flow of history. This object, "the Christian revelation," has been given to only one group, who are to preserve it from attack and preach it to others.

The language of exclusivistic uniqueness is not a problem so long as Christians do not identify their Christian beliefs with a Christian revelation. The "gospel," for example, is unique to Christianity; no other religion competes for ownership of that term. So also, every Christian doctrine is unique in the sense of being exclusively Christian. Similarly, Jews use the word "Torah" in an exclusivistic way that is proper. A problem arises only if Torah and revelation are used interchangeably, because it then appears that revelation is being claimed for something that pertains only to Jews.

Jewish mysticism often captured the paradox of uniqueness. "Jewish mystics took the Torah as a unique reality whose every jot and tittle had cosmic significance. . . . The Hebrew letters, words and names possess the power of creation and more."[17] Jewish mysticism, by isolating every jot and tittle, carried the increasing exclusiveness of the unique to an extreme. But it is also in mysticism that one finds the increasing inclusiveness of the unique. For the mystic, a Hebrew letter becomes the basis for an opening to the whole universe. The Hebrew letter is not an object to be possessed but a spark that can illuminate the divine.

The two meanings of unique thus come together in the mystic's experience. It is in and through the highly exclusive Jewish material that the mystic is open to an increasing appreciation of all creation.[18] At its best, the apocalyptic element in Christian history also produces awareness that God is in the present, opening out to some unexpected future. The Christian mystic, like the Jewish mystic, is attached to the concrete reality of the scriptures and doctrine but has a sense of unity with the whole cosmos.

This strange combination of particular and universal suggests frustration for anyone who tries to get a general understanding of religion. The reality of the particular/universal, which is expressed in the paradox of unique/unique, cannot be translated into general terms. If one tries to bypass the exclusivistic elements of a religion and retain a universal outlook, one merely comes up with empty generalities.

Although a complete translation of religious experience is never possible, the recognition of this problem leads to two conclusions: (1) a religious group that does not intend to be intolerant should not be surprised when their intramural language is thought by outsiders to be intolerant; (2) some of those outsiders are secular groups who do not understand religious speech. Some of the outsiders, however, may be other religious groups who lay claim to the same intramural language. Every religious group today has to examine its language, statement by statement, word by word, to avoid claiming ownership of terms to which other groups have legitimate claim.

When two or more religious groups share a common heritage, the problem can be very sticky. Below I examine "covenant" and "Messiah" as two words of distinctively Jewish origin that were appropriated by Christianity. The term revelation has a different history. It has roots in Christian, Jewish, and Muslim religions. None of these three religions should use the term with an implied exclusiveness. Thus, "Torah is revelation" and "the gospel is revelation" are problematic statements. The seeming claim to possession can be offensive to other groups. This possible offensiveness to others is a symptom of the fact that "Torah is revelation" is also a misleading statement for Jews. Likewise, Christians saying that the gospel is revelation is not only offensive to Jews but misleading to Christians.

Good intentions are not sufficient to create a universal language. Neither do good intentions avoid offending people who do not wish to get included in someone else's attempt to speak universally. A person or a group can intend that a statement have no boundaries of space or time. For example, Christians may claim that in and through Christ, one can perceive God in all things. To that statement, which professes to be universal, the rocks, rivers and trees are not likely to raise any objection. Other human beings, however, whose perceptions differ from Christians, may have a lot to say about the concrete details of how and where God speaks. When that happens, the Christian can retreat from the conversation with good, but misunderstood, intentions. Or the Christian can engage in listening and responding, perhaps getting better insight into God's speaking and even a better formulation of Christian belief.

The exclusivistic language of a religious group is not only allowable but indispensable. It must, however, be set within the inclusive uniqueness of the human recipient. If the term revelation is to be a pointer to the ultimate relation of creator/creature and if "revelation" is shared by several religious traditions as such a pointer, then its most proper use is in relation to a uniqueness of increasing inclusiveness. Such a uniqueness cannot be conveyed by a thing or an object. The personal/corporate being as recipient and respondent has to be center stage.

A book is unique in an exclusive sense; a community listening to a reading from that book can be unique in an inclusive sense. Of course, nothing guarantees that a group calling itself a community will in fact be increasingly inclusive by reaching out beyond itself. But if the group truly is a community it will be interested in the good of humanity and the communion of all creatures. Powerful voices within Jewish and Christian communities have to keep reminding their people that the world is their mission, not mainly for converting others to their belief, but in acting justly, helping humans who are in need, and giving voice to rock and rivers, sun and stars.

This increasing inclusiveness of a unique revelation suggests an orientation to the future. The revelation is always situated in the present community with roots in the past. Its past and present are interpreted through its attitude toward the future. Christianity is not or need not be antihistorical. It is grounded in history while it continuously calls into question the image of history as a mere succession of events. Crucial events happened in the past that have broken through the isolation of unique (exclusive) events. The Christian church's desire has been to establish a human community capable of a uniqueness of increasing inclusivity. Up to the present, the results have been mixed. The future may hold something quite different from the past.

In Christian and Jewish liturgies, the past is not a sequence of historical events. The past exists in the memory of the community. "The historical events of the biblical period remain unique and irreversible. Psychologically, however, the events are experienced cyclically, repetitively, and to that extent, at least, atemporally."[19] Scholars have to do the hard work of delving into the complex historical record, but even a small child can grasp "why this night is different from every other night" in the context of the Seder meal. Similarly in Christian history, the study of scripture has produced elaborate and profound treatises. At the same time, scholars from Origen to Rahner praise the simplicity of a childlike openness to God's speaking through the scriptures.

Covenant

I cited above the term covenant as one that is complicated by being central to both Christian and Jewish traditions. An examination of "covenant" as unique will be helpful to an understanding of revelation as unique. Although the early Israelites adopted the term covenant from the Hittites, the religious meaning of covenant is derived from the Hebrew Bible.[20] But as "covenant" is used in the Bible, it clearly refers to a reality that goes beyond Jewish experience. It becomes a chief symbol for the divine–human relation. If another group besides Jews asserts its entry into the covenantal relation, the original users have nothing to complain about, so long as the new users respect the origin of the term and do not suppose that ownership is now theirs.

One of the most important questions of Jewish–Christian relations is whether there is one covenant or two covenants. The answer that I propose here is that insofar as covenant points to the ultimate relation of creator/creature, there can be only one covenant, uniquely open to all creation. That unique covenant finds partial embodiment in historical forms. There are not two forms but instead numerous forms of covenant.

When the Christian movement emerged as a reform party within Judaism, it inevitably involved the claim to be the true people of the covenant. This language would be the Jewish way to assert that the movement was genuine. Like reform movements in Jewish history before the common era, a renewing of the covenantal relation would be the heart of reform. But in the case of Christianity, the split between church and synagogue created a competition: Which of these two peoples is genuinely chosen by God to be the people of the covenant? By the second century, Christians had begun to speak of an old covenant and a new covenant. Actually, they more often used the word testament, a mistranslation of "covenant" when the Bible went from Hebrew to Greek.[21] The Christian use of old and new testaments softened and obscured the conflict. The Christians had two testaments and the Jews had one covenant, but the underlying conflict remained.

Many Christian writers in recent decades have tried to show that the New Testament itself does not lay claim to a "second covenant." That contention centers on St. Paul. In the past he had often been characterized as rejecting his Jewish heritage and announcing a new covenant.[22] A second covenant could not run parallel with the first; it would have to replace the first. Today it is argued that Paul remained proud of being a "Hebrew among the Hebrews," and a Pharisee (Phil 3:5). While Paul thought that Israel had "stumbled," he also thought they would be saved. "If their stumbling meant riches for the world, and if their defeat means riches for Gentiles, how much more will their full inclusion mean. . . . All Israel will be saved" (Rom. 11:12, 26).

Jews have not been enthralled by this new emphasis within the interpretation of Pauline writing, the contention that Paul was attacking not "the Jews" but "Judaizers" within the Christian community. Jews have been able to view Christianity as an estranged relative who is out doing things (perhaps some good things) in another part of the world. This recent writing on Paul would bring the estranged relatives back into the one household of the covenant. Whatever Paul may have envisioned, history provided a flood of estranged relatives who upset the original household. Many Jewish writers would prefer a Christianity that is largely the invention of Paul and that is discontinuous with Judaism.

If Jews and Christians lived on different planets, their respective claims could remain separate and parallel. But their languages, histories, and practical politics are too intertwined for that policy to be possible. Especially for Christians, an attitude to the Jews and an interpretation of Jewish scripture are at the heart of Christian belief and practice. Christian formulas are either pro-Jewish or anti-Jewish; they have never been and cannot be neutral. If only for self-protection, Jews have a stake in Christian doctrine. Beyond that, a Jewish–Christian conversation about covenant could be mutually enlightening.

One discussion of covenant that has been mostly intra-Jewish is a "two-covenant theory" identified with Franz Rosenzweig.[23] As I noted in chapter 5, Rosenzweig saw his attitude to Christianity as a reformulating of that of Judah ha-Levi, the twelfth-century poet and philosopher. The language of Judah ah-Levi is close to an upside-down Christianity in which the Christian church becomes a preparation for the Messiah. Summarizing Rosenzweig's position, a contemporary philosopher writes, "By attempting to move from the uniqueness of Judaism to the generality of the world it (liberal Judaism) inevitably loses itself in apologetics." Rosenzweig's solution is another unique people for Judaism's movement to the whole world.[24]

While the project is intelligible—two (nearly) unique peoples in conversation with each other and with the whole world—the language of two covenants undermines the proposal. Just as there is one creation, one revelation, one redemption, so also there is one covenant. The word covenant—on the basis of Jewish belief itself—includes all creation. There can be Jewish acknowledgment of a Christian share in living according to God's covenant with all creation. A healthy tension between Jewish and Christian expressions of covenant could replace either smooth continuity or destructive discontinuity in how the two religions are thought to be related.

Here is a place where Islam is a test of Jewish–Christian relations. Rosenzweig never got beyond the stereotype of Islam as the negative other. A two-covenant theory had no place for a third child of Abraham.[25] But Islam sees itself as a reform movement, one that is closer to the spirit of Judaism than is Christianity. Whatever deficiencies a Jew or a Christian may see in Islam, why cannot Islam be seen as a (nearly) unique people trying to be loyal to God's covenant as Muslims understand it?[26]

The assertion that there is only one covenant, which has numerous expressions, is consistent with the Tanakh/Old Testament. A confusing formula of "two covenants," however, has been used by some Christian interpreters of the Old Testament. There is actually much agreement between Christians and Jews on the interpretation of the Hebrew Bible, but a different emphasis creates a different story line.

The Jewish reading of the material is simpler than the Christian. Sinai provides a single focus for understanding the relation between God and his people. Modeled on the relation of a lord and serfs, God promises to be with the people; they in turn are required to be faithful. "Yahweh was not simply a witness to the covenant, but a party to it. The divine–human bond provided the basis of its unique social interest and concern."[27]

The covenant formed at Sinai is the centerpiece of Jewish thinking about covenant: "Now, therefore, if you will obey my voice and keep my covenant . . . you shall be to me a kingdom of priests and a holy nation" (Exod.19:5-6). This single Mosaic form of covenant was a lens to read the history that led to and from Moses. The promise to Abraham is seen as a foreshadowing of the Mosaic promises and the beginning of the people, Israel. Reading farther back, the Jews perceived an earlier covenantal experience in Noah. The story of Noah and the flood (Gen. 7–9) uses the term covenant seven times. The agreement with Noah is "an everlasting covenant between God and every living creature of all flesh that is on the earth" (Gen. 8:16). Through the covenant made with Noah and the commandments given to him, Jews see the inclusion of all peoples in God's plan of salvation.[28]

The final step in seeing the past included in the present was to tell the creation story at the beginning of Genesis as the first expression of covenant. The covenant with Noah was a renewal of God's covenant with Adam and Eve, a covenant that had been strained but never abandoned. Thus, the term covenant had arisen at one moment of history to describe one expression of one group. And yet, reflection on the idea widened and deepened inclusion until it was seen to embrace all past history.

The increasing inclusion by looking to the past was stimulated by looking to the future. The covenant involved a historical people so that the consent of each generation was needed. The covenant was regularly renewed in a liturgical ceremony. The text was read, witnesses were invoked, rewards and punishments were promised. At times of national crises, special covenantal reforms were called for. The most striking example of this renewal in the preexilic period was under King Josiah when the book of Deuteronomy appeared. The whole book is a kind of covenant renewal, not a second covenant but a reaffirmation of the one covenant.[29] "Not with our fathers did the Lord make this covenant, but with us, who are all of us here this day" (Deut. 5:3).

During the Babylonian exile renewals of covenant faced new problems. With the return from exile, the call for covenant renewal were heard again. Renewal of the covenant is prominent in Ezekiel, Jeremiah, and Second Isaiah. The struggle is not finished; all of history is needed to bring out the possibilities of the covenant. Similar to the increasing inclusiveness brought about as the past was deepened, so also the prophetic concern with the future opened the covenant invitation to all nations (Jer. 16:19; Isa. 56:7).

The Christian reading of covenant in the Old Testament is more complicated. For Christians, God makes a universal promise to Abraham.

It is narrowed in God's dealing with Moses but universalized in promises to David. Even when the kingdom of Israel falters and the Israelites are taken into exile, the hope of a new and greater king is kept alive (2 Sam. 7:16). In the process of looking to the future for redemption, more of the past is seen to be included in God's plan. The covenant is seen to begin with Adam and to find (nearly) unique realization in the movement from Abraham to David to Jesus, who is called the Second Adam and the Son of David.

Christians are especially attracted to those texts that refer to an interiorizing of the covenant. In religious reforms, interiorizing and universalizing usually go together. A complicated external code cannot be translated beyond a small group.[30] The more that the law can be simplified into a few maxims, the wider can be its application. When interiorizing is pushed to the exclusion of ordinary daily struggles, however, the result can be an escape to a private illusion of self-sufficiency. It is easy to believe that one's intentions are good and that one has embraced millions, but religion lives in the practices of charity and justice.

The interiorizing of the covenant is emphasized in the one Old Testament passage that actually refers to a new covenant: "I will make a new covenant with the house of Israel. . . . I will put my law within them, and I will write it on their hearts" (Jer. 31:31-33). Much of this sentiment is common in the prophets. If there is one covenant with endless expressions of renewal, then there is a new covenant every day in the hearts of the faithful.[31] Jews do not disagree with Christians on this point, but they see these moments of individual conversion within the whole of covenantal history. Jews fault Christians for seizing the Davidic promises without accepting the Mosaic discipline of Torah. The result of this lack of covenantal discipline is a premature and apocalyptic messianism.

Christian writing now sometimes refers to two covenants, not the Old and New Testaments, but the Davidic and Mosaic covenants in the Old Testament. This language can obscure the need to join these two forms of covenant: the promissory form of Sinai ("I will . . . you must") with the Davidic unconditional form ("I will do . . ."). What are called two covenants are not two objects but two ways of seeing human activity in response to divine initiative. God's unconditional promises do not exclude the need for human response. The promise of not being abandoned is not a cause for complacency. If you are a sinner, the presence of God might be worse to contemplate than God's absence (Deut. 28:14-22). The two forms of covenant are brought together in Psalm 89: "I will punish their transgressions with the rod, but I will not remove from him my steadfast love" (Ps. 89:33-34). By keeping these two aspects of covenant in tension, a Jewish–Christian conversation would be possible about the meaning of a unique covenant open to the whole world.

Messiah, Jesus, Christ

Christians draw a story line out of the Old Testament that differs from the Jewish reading of the Tanakh because Christians read the Old Testament through the New Testament. That does not mean Christians are wrong; all interpretation involves the perspective of the interpreter. In this case, the promise of a Messiah is given greater prominence by Christian interpretation leading up to Jesus of Nazareth, who is declared to be the Messiah. Do the Christians have a good case? The fathers of the church tried to show that Jesus was the expected one, but they had to acknowledge that he was not exactly what had been expected.[32] An examination of uniqueness is one way to bring out the fact that Jesus unites Judaism and Christianity, while belief in Christ is what divides the two religions.

For purposes of this discussion, one must distinguish between the terms Jesus and Christ. Jesus is indisputably the name of a first-century Jew, who is proclaimed in the gospel. "Christ" is a title, originally a translation of the Hebrew word Messiah, but one that quickly took on a complex philosophical meaning. Jews can have a conversation about Jesus if they are inclined to do so. Jews are not likely to discuss "Christ" either because they do not share the belief or because they do not know what is being discussed. The ambiguity in referring to "Jesus Christ" also causes confusion among Christians.

I do not think Christians should or will give up referring to "Jesus Christ" in their liturgy. In discussing a claim of uniqueness, however, there has to be a clear understanding that "Jesus Christ" is not the first and last name of someone. The question Is Jesus Christ unique? can only be answered by first breaking the question into two parts: Is Jesus unique? and Is Christ unique? Jesus is unique and Christ is unique, but they are unique in contrasting ways. Jesus is clearly a particular person; Christ is a claim to universality. Only after affirming both uniquenesses and recognizing the tension between the two of them should the two words "Jesus" and "Christ" be united. Then the statement "Jesus Christ is unique" can express a Christian belief about the continuing and future transformation of the universe.

Is Jesus unique? The answer is easy, perhaps too easy. For anyone who is aware that "unique" is an adjective that describes every human being, the answer is an impatient yes. A writer involved in Christian–Buddhist dialogue writes "that Jesus is unique is obvious even to Buddhists, just as a Christian would hardly question the uniqueness of Gautama. Is not each of us unique?"[33] The answer to the last question is yes, but uniqueness is not a simple fact of perception. The uniqueness of the personal/corporate being emerged slowly in history. Forces from Buddhism to Greek philosophy contributed to the uniqueness of the human person. By any measure, the Jews have made a big contribution to this emergence. Jesus of Nazareth is one of the most important individuals through whom the idea of unique person was established. On almost everyone's scale, Jesus of Nazareth is one of history's most unique persons.

Christians have a right and a duty to emphasize that Jesus was a very unique person. Some Christian writers try to downplay the claim to uniqueness because they see it as unecumenical.[34] I would say that Christians have not emphasized enough the uniqueness of Jesus. Most Christians cannot appreciate Jesus' uniqueness because they do not know Jewish history well enough. A person's uniqueness is formed out of all the circumstances of his or her life. One can affirm Jesus as very unique only as one appreciates the Jewish people, the land, and the time that formed the context of Jesus' life. Jesus arose out of a long tradition in ancient Israel. As was true of the great innovators before him, the presence of his person was the meeting place of past and future, the renewal of the covenant between God and his people. Jesus gathered up disparate strands of Jewish thought into a coherent whole; he was exorcist, charismatic healer, and prophet.[35]

Jesus was a Jew who was in dispute with Judaism. That stance was not unusual for a Jew of those times, nor indeed for a Jew of today. He argued with the Pharisees because his teaching was so similar to theirs.[36] He was perhaps at the liberal end of pharisaic opinion, arguing for the spirit of the law as more important than the performance of every letter of the law. Nearly all reformers try to interiorize morality, thereby simplifying external codes. But if one reads the Gospel through the lens of justice for the poor, then Jesus is seen not as a nineteenth-century liberal but as an apocalyptic reformer who warns that judgment is at hand.[37]

Is Christ unique? The answer to that question is more complicated than that of Jesus' uniqueness. Jesus is the name of someone who is obviously very unique. "Christ" is the name of something—a title, an ideal, an idea, a hope. "Christ" as a title is very unique in an exclusivistic sense; it is under Christian control. Somewhere on earth someone may be saying "I am Christ," but no major religious group competes with Christianity for ownership of the term. There is nothing wrong or surprising about this fact. Each religious group uses language uniquely its own to define who they are. "Christ is the unique way of salvation" is not a universal truth of philosophy. It is a confession of faith that defines a Christian. The statement is true for Christians, or at least it becomes true as they engage in acts of prayer and service. Outside of Christianity, the statement that "Christ is the unique way of salvation" lacks sufficient meaning to be either true or false.[38]

This exclusivistic uniqueness of "Christ" should not be offensive to others who do not speak this language. A problem only arises for both Christian and non-Christian when "Christ" is interchanged with "Jesus." From the earliest period of Christianity, there has been a danger that Jesus the Jew would be obscured by reference to Christ. Christianity then becomes a philosophical system built around the idea of Christ and things that of their nature are exclusive.

That danger is considerably increased by the strange phrase "Christ event" in twentieth-century Christian writing. Karl Barth constantly refers to revelation as a "unique event."[39] But it was Oscar Cullmann's *Christ and Time* that popularized the phrase "Christ event." The book had clarity and precision, but that was part of its problem: "Christ" became mathematically situated. In the book's second part, "The Unique Character of the Christ deed at the Midpoint," the author repeatedly refers to the "Christ event," which happened once and once for all.[40] In later editions of the book, Cullmann played down the location of the Christ event at the midpoint. But the bigger problem was that he laid out history as a series of points, and one of those points was where the Christ event was located. That image creates insuperable problems in trying to relate Christianity to the rest of human history. History after the Christ event becomes a "mopping up" operation after the war has been won.[41]

The illogical but dynamic-sounding Christ event spread throughout much of Christian writing. Wolfhart Pannenberg, while very critical of Cullmann, also uses the phrase Christ event. He, too, has to ask what happens "after Christ"?[42] There can be only one Christian answer to that question: nothing happens after Christ. For Christians, the revelation of God is summed up "in Christ," the unique revelation of God. That belief makes sense only if "Christ" can refer to a further realization of person and community in the future and not simply to an event in the past.

A deed, an action, or an event in the life of Jesus is unique in an exclusive sense. That is not a logical problem for Christianity so long as the person and the life of Jesus are not collapsed into Christ event. The Christ has to unite past and future in the present. That cannot happen with the category of Christian revelation. It can happen with a respect for past doctrines and an awareness of future judgment.

One test for a Christian understanding of the uniqueness of Christ is the relation of "Christ" to Jewish history both past and present. The meaning of the idea of Christ is in part shared with Judaism. The announcement that Jesus is the Messiah or the Christ would have made little sense outside of a Jewish context. But very quickly the term Christ went on a fascinating journey, absorbing into itself the meanings of *logos* from Greek philosophy. In contrast, the term Messiah remains to this day a mainly Jewish term.

Today the term Christ overlaps but is not coextensive with Messiah. That connection is enough for Christianity to be indissolubly tied to its Jewish roots. If it could be recognized that "Christians are right in asserting that Jesus is the Christ; and Jews are right in asserting that Jesus is not the Messiah," then a fruitful conversation might be possible.[43] Even within Christian language, it is possible to say that Jews are correct in awaiting a Messiah or messianic age still to come. If Christians would make this distinction between Christ and Messiah, it would allow Jews the chance to appreciate Jesus as one of their own, the rabbi from Nazareth.[44]

This conversation might also reorient Christian thinking to the Christ of the present and the hoped-for Christ of the future. From the beginning, Christians have tried to link Christ with the whole world. Their *idea* of Christ was intended to be open to all others by a process of inclusion.[45] But the actual realization of such inclusiveness depends on the proper linking of "Christ" with Jesus, with the Jewish people, and with the actions of the Christian church.

When Christians say that "Christ is unique," that should signify they intend to work toward a greater inclusiveness, a more genuine community, than the world has yet seen. The term Christ, without ceasing to be a title for a first-century Jew—indeed precisely as a title attached to that person in that community—foreshadows the concrete realization of a world of unique persons in peace with each other and with nonhuman life. The Christian church can lay claim to having brought about a partial embodiment of that human community. The Christian task is to get on with the realization of a greater uniqueness. Jesus as the Christ, or as the beginning of the fullness of Christ, embodies divine activity and human response. The exclusive uniqueness of the term Christ and the inclusive uniqueness of Jesus combine to form a liturgical formula that realistically acknowledges the limits of the church, together with its openness to the future.

Does the Christian belief that Jesus uniquely embodies the divine–human relation imply a claim of superiority to Judaism because a unique revelation presupposes one person? No doubt there is a sense in which each religious group sees itself as superior to others. But looking only at the logic of uniqueness, does Christianity complete the logic in a way that Judaism does not? Jews and Christians differ on how the divine is "incarnated," but their positions are not necessarily contradictory.[46]

Two points on the relation of person and community should be noted. (1) Salvation for the Jew is personal as well as corporate. Judaism, like Christianity, is interested in the salvation of the whole world. This salvation is made present in the lives of individual persons. "Why was only a single man created? To teach you that for him who destroys one man, it is regarded as if he had destroyed all men, and that for him who saves one man it is regarded as though he had saved all men."[47] (2) Salvation for the Christian is corporate as well as personal. Jesus is the Christ, Redeemer, Son of Man, and Son of God insofar as he is understood communally. At its best, the Christian focus on Jesus as unique is an affirmation of the whole human community. "Jesus experienced a relationship to God which he experienced as new and unique in comparison with other men, but which he nevertheless considered to be exemplary for other men in their relation to God."[48] Thus, in both Christianity and Judaism salvation applies to the person in the community.

A problem has arisen in Christianity when an individual called Christ is isolated and the exclusive focus becomes "Christ's death on the cross" as the one place of redemption. It has then happened that "traditional doctrines of 'The Incarnation' siphoned energy away from all bodies but one, that tortured, executed body whose resurrection was not enough."[49] The uniqueness of Christ becomes a denial of community, body, and time.

The confusion here lies in the nature of mediation. Is Jesus the sole mediator between God and the human race? Religious reformers usually claim that their opponents have inserted a mediator—a middle man—between the Nameless one and the people. Christians and Jews make mutual accusations on this point. Does Jesus, as Christians claim, do away with the intermediacy of law and create a new intimacy between divine and human? Or does Christianity, as Jews claim, interpose a mediator between God and humanity, while Jews go straight to God? Protestant and Catholic Christians similarly accuse each other of creating a go-between.[50]

The logic of personal/corporate uniqueness is needed to explain this strange confusion. Religious reformers often shoot down one middle man only to have another pop up in its place—very often the reformers themselves. The revolutionary vanguard takes power in the name of the people, but unless language, imagery, and communal relations are revolutionized, the system will produce a new mediator that siphons power from the people while it arrogates divine qualities to itself.

Human life does require mediation of one kind or another. Humans deal with others, indeed with themselves, only through the mediation of corporate expressions. The way to get rid of a single, exclusive mediator is to make everyone and everything potential participants in mediation. Where is God's grace to be found? Everywhere. What is revelatory of God? Every action and every word. How does God save? Even in the smallest gesture.

The genuine religious life of Jew, Catholic, Protestant, Muslim, and others has an immediacy that avoids any *thing* between divine and human. At the same time, each religion situates persons in corporate and communal structures that are not outside the divine–human relation, structures that mediate all reality to the personal center of understanding and choice. Christians and Jews agree that everything in the universe represents divine creativity and creaturely response. Living organisms express this relation and animals distinctively so. Human beings bring the relation to its (nearly) unique expression, a conscious and free response to divine activity.

Jews find the greatest expression of revelation in the life of the community. Christians find the process summed up in Jesus' life, death, and resurrection. That Christian belief gets obscured when Christ is said to be the unique mediator; "Christ" then functions as the impersonal instrument of divine truths given to authoritative agents. Instead, Jesus should be seen as the person who reveals personal uniqueness and keeps the Christ idea from becoming one more metaphysical abstraction. Jesus as the Christ is the relational reality that guarantees equal opportunity for all human beings, who are themselves representatives of nonhuman creation.

HUMAN UNIQUENESS

The uniqueness affirmed of Jesus, far from being exclusive, is intended to be an affirming of each human being. And the uniqueness of human beings is a way of affirming the goodness and relative autonomy of everything in creation.[51] This Christian doctrine is a variation on the Jewish idea of chosenness. The Jews as the chosen people are the representatives of humanity. The real chosen people are the humans; they represent all creation. Despite being a small and fragile species, the humans embody a dramatic demonstration of divine activity and creaturely response.

Both chosenness and uniqueness are characterized by receptivity,

which includes the capacity to suffer. Suffering does not first mean physical pain, although pain seems to be an inherent part of the humans' suffering of the world. Neither Jewish nor Christian religion glorifies pain;
the impulse is to reduce pain and give comfort to those who suffer it. But
both Jewish and Christian religions accept the fact that each person has a
choice of how to deal with life's inevitable pain. "No one can relieve him
of his suffering or suffer in his place. His unique opportunity lies in the
way he bears his burden."[52]

Human life, as I noted at the beginning of this chapter, is a peculiar
combination of the two kinds of uniqueness. The uniqueness of our ever-
increasing inclusiveness is based in our nature, but its actualization follows upon a psychological openness, a moral readiness, and a metaphysical courage. The humans' nature is to *have* no nature, but to be an
openness to all natures. Nonetheless, humans also have to deal with the
fact that, to the extent they are spatial beings, they are *things* of exclusive
uniqueness. Thus, their survival and secure existence is connected to
resisting intrusion, on getting away from control by competitors.[53]

A healthy and full human life depends on the person's exclusive
uniqueness being kept subordinate to the inclusive uniqueness. For
example, the territorial imperative to strike out at intruders to one's space
has to be restrained by listening, understanding, and compassion. Other
animals have inborn restraints in the form of instincts. The human breakthrough to inclusive uniqueness replaced instincts with a much greater
capacity for learning new things. The greater receptiveness also means
that restraints are not automatic. The humans are the great killers on
earth; they can kill millions of their own kind. Everything depends on
whether there is a receptive attitude to the other. Violent intrusion into a
human being is dehumanizing, while the received entrance of another
human within the boundaries of one's physical integrity can be the most
pleasurable and meaningful of human experiences.

Each human being is born unique; its vocation is to become more
unique. Human beings have to discover the paradox of power for the
development of inclusive uniqueness. That is, coercive, dominating, violent imposition can be impressive-looking power, but it is the human
temptation to evil. What is actually the humans' lasting strength first
appears as a weakness, namely, the ability to listen carefully and act com-
passionately. When it comes to accepting responsibility, the humans are
tempted by the lure of liberation: escape from their place, flight from
their bodies, refusal to sympathize with the other animals.

The humans' place is at the center of creation where Jewish and
Christian traditions located them: men and women in mutual relation.

In a logic of uniqueness, the choice is clear: either "man" is at the top as exploiter of everything that is weaker than man or else the human beings are at the center as nurturers of life. Man as user is not the measure of all things. Nonetheless, the measurer of all things is the human being as poet, as nurturer, as contemplator, as lover, as scientist, as athlete.[54]

In Jewish and Christian traditions, creation is a hierarchy of receptivity and responsibility. The main image is not a pyramid of power but concentric circles, "a wheel inside a wheel" (Ezek. 1:16). Until the twelfth century, "hierarchy" was philosophically conceived as concentric circles. When the term was translated into Latin as *ordo sacer* it quickly took on a bureaucratic image.[55] Our choice today is a hierarchy based on a pyramid or a hierarchy based on cycles of life. In a cyclical pattern, everything depends on everything else. Each kind plays its part; no kind can be disparaged and no kind should be destroyed. Each creature has its own unique form, with some creatures more unique than others.[56]

The humans can transform processes of nature, but the danger is that, because they cannot grasp the interconnection of all things, they can call progress what is in fact the destruction of a larger ecological process. Not everything that can be done by humans should be done by them.[57] Throughout the centuries religion has provided restraints. The last few centuries have seen an unprecedented break with those restraints. Exorbitant demands have been made upon the land, the forest, the rivers, and the ocean.

Jewish and Christian traditions continue to offer some restraint, but they also bear some responsibility for ecological problems. In their haste to affirm "the uniqueness of man," Jewish and, more so, Christian religions jumped over some of the concentric circles on the way to the center. An interest in the great feats of great men can undermine the genuine uniqueness of ordinary men and women, as well as the distinctive lives of nonhuman animals. The exclusivistic kind of uniqueness in the lives of great and powerful men leaves the other humans and the nonhuman animals gasping for breath.

The Darwinian revolution of the nineteenth century, according to one interpretation, glorified the most powerful individuals. But it can also be read as restoring a sense of the organic unity of creation. In the latter reading, the nineteenth century moved from one kind of uniqueness to another. The exclusivistic uniqueness that tried to separate "man" from beast (a development of the seventeenth and eighteenth centuries) was undermined. An inclusivistic uniqueness re-emerged with the unity of all life and with the humans as the workshop of all creation.[58]

One of the most interesting essays on uniqueness was written by

Peter Medawar.[59] The essay is in large part about skin grafting, the complexity of it in humans as compared to mice. Medawar argues that human uniqueness is not a difference of degree or a difference of kind, but a unique combination of endowments. "Every human being is genetically unique: the texture of human diversity is infinitely close woven."[60] Not surprisingly, human culture is deeply rooted in its biological and animal nature. Culture is humanly unique because it is open to contributions by all living organisms.[61]

One characteristic of all living things is that they die. The humans share in this characteristic, but the uniqueness of a human life gives a special meaning and pathos to dying. John Hick says that in relation to the other animals the human being is doubly unique: (1) The human being knows that he or she is going to die; and (2) in an important sense, he or she refuses to believe it.[62] Other animals cannot get long-range forecasts of their deaths and are therefore saved from denying their mortality. Human beings are pressed to deny death because to go on with daily life seems unbearable if all the struggles are in vain, if the joy as well as the sorrow ultimately counts for nothing.[63]

Elisabeth Kubler-Ross, in the final paragraph of *On Death and Dying*, captures the connection between a unique human life and the moment of death: "To be a therapist to a dying patient makes us aware of the uniqueness of each individual in the vast sea of humanity. . . . Few of us live beyond our three score and ten years and yet in that brief time most of us create and live a unique biography and weave ourselves into the fabric of human history."[64] Religions differ in the meaning they see in death and the life beyond this life, but there is consensus that death is not simply the last in a series of points. A person's dying is a unique moment of inclusiveness; to accept death is to affirm the life that has preceded it. Death is summation and transition; it is the revelation of life.

Karl Rahner has some of the most creative theological thinking on death.[65] According to Rahner, one's life moves either toward greater isolation or deeper communion, toward either exclusive or inclusive uniqueness. The act of dying reveals what might have been unclear during life's journey. Dying gives us a final chance to ratify or to reject our choices. Each of us can die alone or die with all humanity. In Christian terms, dying in communion with humanity is "dying in Christ." Jesus' life was summed up and ratified by his death. Each person's death is the most nearly unique experience that frees us from limited communion with our immediate environment for greater communion with all creation.

The Jewish and Christian term for affirming life in spite of death is resurrection.[66] Instead of describing another world, resurrection is a negative, or, more precisely, a double negative term. It affirms life by negating the negation of life. Resurrection negates those theories in which the human body is the temporary prison of an immortal spirit. Resurrection, according to Rahner, "only forbids in a *negative* sense the exclusion of particular elements of man from the outset as of no consequence for his final state."[67]

The Jewish and Christian doctrine of resurrection is a realistic affirmation of life and its inevitable accompaniment, death. We are given life, which is a kind of miracle. Human uniqueness is the experience that life has possibilities beyond anyone's imagination. For Christians, resurrection is a reference to the cosmos before it is a puzzling fact about Jesus. Resurrection is about living and dying and living, about doing your work the best that you can and loving those around you.

The announcement of Jesus' resurrection was to an audience already familiar with the term. Such a resurrection stood within the Jewish tradition, but with one big discrepancy: "If you had the faith of the Pharisees, his appearance would not have startled you, but it would have surprised you. You would have been stunned chiefly that he was alone."[68] The Christian formula that "Christ is risen" is somewhat premature. What the Christian gospel affirms is that Jesus was raised from the dead as the firstfruits or down payment of the resurrection of the whole Christ.[69] Jews and Christians can agree that the most unique revelation/apocalypse would be a final resurrection at the end of history.

PARTICULAR/UNIVERSAL REVELATION

I noted at the beginning of this chapter that the egalitarian attitude of the modern world has a problem with religions linked to particular people and definite places in far away times. Why is the divine not available on an equal opportunity basis? My response to that question has been to describe a logic of uniqueness. For human beings, located in space and time, but open to all reality, the greatest truth and ultimate goodness are mediated by the particular. A particular experience in the present is unique to the extent that it opens to the universal. The present experience can only approach universality to the extent that it is in touch with the voices of the past and the hopes of the human heart.

This way of grasping experience is more true of the arts than of modern science. The test of a great work of art is that it can be appreciated by people in different times and other places. Anyone might perceive a truth about his or her life by reading *King Lear*. If one were to try translating

King Lear into a series of general truths applicable everywhere, the power of the particular to be revelatory would be lost.[70] A universal truth cannot be stated, but a person can get closer to it the deeper that he or she penetrates the particular. "Whoever grasps this particular in a living way will simultaneously realize the universal, too, without even becoming aware of it—or realize it only later."[71]

The human race has found it impossible to construct a universal language. In the seventeenth century Gottfried Leibniz believed that he could accomplish this task, and that "this language will be very difficult to construct, but very easy to learn. It will be quickly accepted by everyone on account of its great utility and its surprising facility, and it will serve wonderfully in communication among various peoples."[72] Such has often been the belief of young, mathematically oriented minds. The sad little joke about (supposed) universal languages, writes Mary Midgley, is that almost no one speaks them.[73] In contrast to the clear but flat meaning of artificial languages, poetry requires us to stop, reflect, and catch a glimpse of a truth that we cannot fully articulate.

The lasting significance of human action does not depend on the size of the army, the riches of the nation, or the sophistication of the technology. Size, power, and complexity hover over every human endeavor. Jewish and Christian traditions challenge the assumption that might makes right and that divine creativity is might writ large. God might be revealed in a gentle wind as much as in the hurricane, in the lives of illiterate people as well as in scholarly research, in the extending of a caring hand as much as in the preaching to millions. Thomas Aquinas was quoted in chapter 3 as saying that God is appropriately revealed in realities that have low stature in human judgment.

The Torah or Jesus is revelatory today as each is remembered in a community. The process for Jew and Christian is very similar, even though the focus of interpretation differs. Both religions are universal by being particular.[74] Christian writing often assumes that Jewish religion is particular (meaning that only Jews are allowed in) in contrast to Christianity's message, which is said to be universal. In Jewish writing, the reverse is often said: Judaism affirms a universal ethic for the salvation of all; but Christianity is particular, allowing in only those who accept its savior.[75] Both of these characterizations are unfair and untrue; they subvert the very logic that both religions are built on. Christianity's (potential) universality is rooted in the particularity of Jewish history.[76] A message cannot be universal unless it is embodied in community and place. Furthermore, Christianity cannot judge who is saved; only God knows that. Judaism also excludes no one from salvation, but Judaism's (potential) universality needs more support than it can receive from the commandments given to Noah or the ethical reasoning of modern philosophy or secular Zionism. Jewish universalism needs a vibrant Jewish community in the present, which as Rosenzweig suggested, could be enhanced by a link to the particularity of Christianity.[77]

Jews and Christians are in danger of misunderstanding their own internal logic when they mischaracterize each other. They ought to join forces in presenting a logic of uniqueness, in which the particular and the universal go together. God may be revealed in a very unique way through one people, one person, one moment. Jewish belief that God is most fully revealed in the life of the Jewish people is not an absurd belief; neither is the Christian belief that revelation is focused in a single life.

For both Christians and Jews, their policy should be to share the truth as they have experienced it. That experience has universal relevance, even though every formulation of experience is particular.[78] By engaging in dialogue both with each other and with people who have experienced other truths, a more unique experience might become available for the human race.

8

Revelation as Teaching–Learning

I HAVE DESCRIBED the approach in this book as educational, a word that usually has a positive but ambiguous meaning. By an educational approach, I mean that education understood as a lifelong process of maturing is a context for revelation. And within that context, the more specific relation of teaching–learning offers a fruitful metaphor for understanding the idea of revelation. But teaching–learning has to be explored in its richness and fullness before it can serve as the metaphor for the relation of divine revelation and human receptivity.

TO TEACH

As in the previous two chapters, I single out one word, "teach," that exemplifies a needed reform of language. Just as an understanding of revelation can be grasped in the idea of moral responsibility and in the logic of uniqueness, so revelation might be understood with the metaphor of teaching–learning. Before teaching is used to describe divine activity, however, it must be rescued from its professional captivity of the past century.

In chapter 3, I cited a comment of Karl Barth that at the beginning of the Reformed church stands a schoolmaster. This fact, Barth says, shows both the strength and the weakness of the Reformation. Barth faults John Calvin for the fact that he not only proclaimed Christianity but that he also expounded it.[1] Barth is saying that to imagine God as a schoolmaster is an inadequate metaphor, and I would agree. But what is the alternative? Why is schoolmaster inadequate and how do we improve on it? What metaphor is to be assumed for imagery and language when we speak about God's relation to the universe or the divine–human relation?

I do not think that Barth offers an explicit answer to this question, but like everyone who addresses religious questions, and certainly like every Christian theologian, Barth has to assume a primary or governing metaphor. His principle that "only God can speak of God" does not provide a way out. The question is not what God is imagined to say but how God is imagined saying it. On this point, Barth assumes what most Christian theology does, namely, that God preaches. Whatever God says, the words are delivered in a form analogous to the act of preaching. I think this assumption comes through in the contrast cited above that Calvin's fault is he did not merely proclaim Christianity but he expounded it.

From the beginning of the Christian religion, its members have been urged to proclaim, to herald, to gospel. One could not remove this activity without distorting Christianity. But can proclaim bear the whole burden? Why should it not be acceptable both to proclaim and to expound? I think the reason is that with the invention of "Christian revelation" in the sixteenth century, God is presupposed as a proclaimer before Christian theology begins. Given that presumption, the problem with "proclaim and expound" is that if God does the proclaiming and we do the expounding, then most likely we will only mess up things. But suppose God is not (mainly) a preacher?

I think that preacher and schoolmaster are admirable vocations; the activities of preaching and schoolteaching can be understood as modest embodiments of God's creating, revealing, redeeming. Instead of opposing preaching and schoolteaching, I would argue that they are complementary forms of the act of teaching. I think Barth's problem with Calvin is not that he was a teacher but that he was a schoolteacher. Or the problem is that Calvin confused teaching and schoolteaching. Such an accusation might be unfair to Calvin, but it is safe to say that in the last century and a half, teaching and schoolteaching have regularly been conflated.

Ambiguity and conflict regarding "to teach" go back millennia. Most of Plato and much of Aristotle can be read as reflection on the act of teaching. If "to teach" means to tell people what to think, the teacher is faced with justifying such authority. But "to teach" can have other meanings, as Socrates showed and every religious tradition demonstrates. Religious communities teach by exemplifying a way of life, practicing a discipline, and using strange ways of speaking. Great religious teachers, such as Gautama and Jesus, used provocative sayings and stories but very little rational explanation.

In every religious tradition, to teach means to show someone how to live. Since to live includes dying, to teach means most comprehensively to show someone how to live and how to die. And since religions see

death not as a last moment in a series of points but as an attitude formative of one's life, religious teaching often starts with dying.[2] A modern
flight from religion has been accompanied, not surprisingly, by a flight
from death.

The Enlightenment attack on religion was also an attack on teaching.
Immanuel Kant's description of enlightenment as "overthrowing one's
tutelage" aptly applies to both religion and teaching.[3] Since Kant's time,
teaching has been defined in opposition to rational adulthood. Teaching
is allowed to be done to people who have a capacity for rational activity
but who must be told how to exercise it. It is believed that as soon as the
pupil can think for himself or herself teaching should cease.

Since psychology took over educational language at the turn of the
twentieth century, learning has been praised at length, but teaching is
always suspect. The worst assumption that dominates educational literature is that teaching and learning have no real connection. Early in the
century endless research tried to establish which behaviors of the teacher
would necessarily cause learning by the student. The researchers could
not find any.[4] The failure to identify any behaviors of the teacher that
would cause learning meant that at most a teacher could try to promote
learning or perhaps motivate learners. Just as often, the teacher could be
accused of interrupting learning.

These studies on the effectiveness of teaching were framed around
classroom instruction. The assumption is that teaching belongs to a small
group of people who perform this activity in a special room on willing or
unwilling recipients of a certain age. But a study of the activity of teaching should begin with the assumption that it is an act that every human
being—at least every *human* being—performs each day. What the etymology of "teach" conveys and what most uses of the term outside professional education literature affirm is that teaching means showing
someone how to do something. And learning is the response to being
taught.

Teaching and learning are not causally related. Teach-learn is a single
activity seen from either end, as philosophers from Aristotle to Dewey
have said.[5] Teaching–learning is especially important to human beings
who are born open to great possibilities but who start with few, if any,
instincts. Like the word "responsible," "teaching–learning" can be applied
beyond the human world. Clearly, a (nonhuman) animal can be taught,
and animals teach their young. How far we extend the language of teach–
learn is ours to choose. The religious belief that the universe and every
creature in it can teach us is not a wild inflation of language.

In a relational world, the test of teaching is learning; if there is no learning, there is no teaching. Conversely, the test of learning is teaching; no teaching, no learning. A person at the front of a classroom who is gesturing, writing on the blackboard, and reading from notes is trying to teach. Success depends on someone learning what is being taught. People learn what they are taught, although what is taught is often not what the person designated as teacher is intending to teach. David Elkind comments that "a slow learner is quick to learn that he is slow."[6] It is important to note that the "slow learner" learns that lesson through being taught that he is slow. He is taught by the rewards of the system and perhaps by the conscious or subconscious signals of the person at the front of the room. If someone is judged to be a slow learner, the problem might not be a psychological deficiency. Teaching-learning is a social and political activity. Teaching can be improved by finding out who and what is teaching a student and asking how that might be modified.

Teaching is badly misconceived when treated as an aspect of adult-child relations. Teaching by human beings is best understood when primarily seen as a relation between adults. Peter Elbow says that teaching, like sex, should only be performed between consenting adults.[7] I do not think Elbow would wish to exclude children totally, but children would be treated much better if they were introduced into a teaching–learning relation that already exists between adults. Teaching is a gift that is offered to family member, friend, colleague, teammate, stranger.

Classroom instructors have a very limited environment in which to teach. They are constantly being told that they are responsible for the students' learning. The burden is insupportable and unfair; it leads to moral conflict and discouragement. The teacher is not responsible for the students' learning; the teacher is responsible for teaching. The student is responsible *for* learning; the teacher and the student are responsible *to* each other.

Teaching–learning begins with the student acting. The would-be human teacher has to contemplate the activity and show the student how the activity could be done better. Then the student has to try out the suggestion and decide if the proposed change is an improvement. "Good teachers are almost infinitely responsive. Boys and girls become good students for teachers who provide, often for the first time, a response to what they feel most deeply."[8]

Showing someone how to do something embodies a metaphor that is visual (show) but also oral and tactile (how to do). Teaching begins in silence and ends in silence. Great works of art teach, according to what senses they appeal to. A work of literature teaches in and through its words. A painting by Vermeer or Van Gogh can teach simply by how it portrays sunlight. Karl Barth says that Mozart teaches us because he does not try to teach but simply plays, and it is as such that "he teaches us that creation praises its Master."[9]

For teaching a physical skill, several forms of speech are directed at some physical movement. For example, you cannot teach a person to swim either by explaining swimming or showing a picture of a swimmer. The teacher and the student have to get into the water. The teacher's hands indicate the body's movements. The student has to practice coordinating several kinds of movement. The teacher's speech may range from comforting the learner's fears, to issuing precise commands, to evaluating a session's progress. The teacher and the student succeed together or they fail together. That is evident in teaching bodily skills, such as swimming, riding a bicycle, or tying a shoelace. No parent announces, "I taught Jimmy to ride the bicycle but he didn't learn."

The Bible and Teaching

This relation of teach–learn offers a comprehensive metaphor for what Christians and Jews came to call revelation, especially when this visual metaphor is joined with the metaphor of word of God. The language of teach–learn does not conflict with other traditional images used for the divine–human relation.

The Bible tells of an encounter with the divine that found expression in the image of covenant. By using the term for a Hittite suzerainty treaty, the Israelites thereby described a relation between lord and serfs. The language of "the Lord and his servants" can still be heard in today's church and synagogue. In time, covenant absorbed other relations into its meaning, such as the marriage covenant and a covenant between nations. A more mutual relation could therefore be implied by covenant, but the metaphor is still limited.

The image of God as lover and the human being as the beloved has roots in the Hebrew Bible. The prophet Hosea is often cited here, although the relation described in the book of Hosea is a man and his unfaithful wife, which is analogous to God and the faithless nation. One has to look to the Song of Songs as a more direct precedent to later Christian mysticism in which God is lover and the soul is the beloved.[10]

One of the great breakthroughs in Jewish history was the emergence of God as loving Father. We are especially indebted to the pharisaic movement for this development. Jesus in the New Testament made special use of this metaphor. People are generally more comfortable with the image of father than with God as a great warrior or king. But even the best of metaphors have limitations. The image of father implies that God is like a parent and humans are like children, but humans grow up. Although they remain children before God, they have to find a religious life that is childlike but not childish. In addition, the Bible, with its customary concreteness, does not call God a parent. God is "our Father who art in heaven." There are a number of maternal images in the Bible, for example, God imagined as a mother bear defending her cubs (Hos. 13:9). But Jesus' God is "father" rather than either parent or mother. That gender limitation deserves to be pointed out, but it should not exclude the positive image of a father who lovingly cares for his children.

The metaphor of teacher-learner and the activity of teaching–learning can embrace all the biblical images and in addition can include the movement of understanding. God is Lord of all, and humans are not in the same class; nonetheless, humans try to understand God's commands and respond intelligently. God is like a parent but of children that grow up and look for the understanding of adult children. God is lover but the love is not reducible to sentimental feelings. One has to discover the quiet depths of love in human relations as the basis for an image of God. The word of God has to be listened to daily so that in the course of a lifetime one's understanding becomes disciplined (taught).

In Jewish tradition, teaching–learning is praised as intrinsic to life with God.[11] The family is the first school of conduct in which the parent teaches the law to children through ritual, example, and verbal instruction (Deut. 6:4-9). The whole prophetic tradition is a learning experience with the prophet's words and actions at the center of the teaching. The structure of the covenant renewal is one of recalling the past, demanding a response in the present, and warning about the future.

Torah is a term that first means not law but instruction, as in the instruction given by a mother or father (Prov. 1:8; 4:1). Torah comes to mean the whole Bible and oral teaching as well. Torah is the speech that wisdom teaches (Prov. 7:2) and the word of the prophets (Isa. 8:16; 30:9). Torah is regularly associated with learning. "When man is led for judgment, he is asked . . . did you fix time for learning."[12] The Talmud says three times that the non-Jew who concerns himself with the teaching of God is made equal to the high priest in Israel. "Greater is learning than priesthood and royalty, for royalty is acquired by thirty stages, priesthood by twenty-four, but the Torah is acquired by forty-eight things—by study, by diligent attention, by proper speech, by an understanding heart. . . ."[13] Learning comes about by all forty-eight activities. "Man is not asked how much he knows but how much he learns. The unique attitude of the Jew is not the love of knowledge but the love of studying."[14]

The New Testament does not refer directly to studying, but it continues the tradition going back to Moses that the law is our teacher. The individual religious leader teaches, backed by the authority that tradition, community, and law provide. St. Paul refers to the law as a pedagogue (Gal. 3:24). Paul seems to say that the pedagogue or teacher has been replaced. In Paul's time, however, the pedagogue was the slave who brought the boy to the teacher (the RSV translates the word as "custodian" instead of the King James Version's "schoolmaster").[15] Paul is not dismissing the need for teaching and teachers. In his imagery the law brings us to Christ, who is the law's end in the sense of meaning and purpose. God's teaching remains. For the Jew it is expressed in the Mosaic law, and for the Christian it is summarized in Christ.

In the Gospels, Jesus is presented as a teacher, one who wished to fulfill every letter of the law (Matt. 5:11). Jaroslav Pelikan, in discussing the images of Jesus, says that "teacher" (rabbi) was the most universal and least controversial title attributed to Jesus. By the second century, however, the title was embarrassing and by the third century obscure.[16] Why did this happen? Once the split had occurred between church and synagogue, the title of rabbi was not one that the church wished to emphasize. Jesus is called rabbi fourteen times in the Gospels. He is also called *didaskalos* forty-two times, a word that could be translated "teacher" but more often was translated as "master."

While rabbi or teacher came into prominence in modern Judaism, Christianity had an ambivalent attitude to teaching and to calling Jesus the great teacher. As the title Christ overshadowed the name Jesus, teacher took second place. An unfortunate opposition developed which seemed to offer the following choices: Jesus as teacher versus Christ as savior; epistemology versus ontology; knowledge versus salvation.[17]

No such dichotomies need appear if the relation of teaching–learning is understood at a profound level. Teaching–learning is not simply providing and acquiring knowledge as a step prior to acting. Teaching is showing someone how to do something; most comprehensively, it is showing someone how to live and how to die. Learning is a response to being shown how. Most profoundly, that means responding to how we should live and die with understanding, gratitude, and acceptance. If teaching–learning is understood this way, then revelation and redemption are not entirely discrete processes. Such an understanding of revelation and redemption is crucial for how Christian ministers see their role and for the entire pattern of Christian church life.

Clement of Alexandria

The Greek fathers of the church were not hesitant to use "education" for divine providence and "teacher" for Jesus as the Christ. They adopted the classical term for education (*paideia*) and its rich cultural connotations. Christians were encouraged to study classical literature as part of their "Christian education."[18] They took over Plato's principle that God is the teacher of the universe, and they saw Christianity as fulfilling what Plato had begun describing.[19]

The early Christian writer who most thoroughly developed the language of education and teaching was Clement of Alexandria. "The life of Christians, in which we are now trained, is a system of reasonable actions—that is, of those things taught by the Word—an unfailing energy which we have called faith."[20] Clement makes a direct connection between the Christ as teacher and Paul's use of revelation. "The divine teacher shows us how we are to know ourselves and reveals the father of the universe, as far as human nature can comprehend."[21] The last phrase indicates that while a divine teacher shows us how to live, there also has to be a learner who receives the teaching. "Playing at ball not only depends on one's throwing the ball skillfully, but it requires besides, one to catch it dexterously. . . . [T]he teaching is reliable when faith on the part of those who hear . . . contributes to the process of learning."[22]

This teaching or instruction is always of a practical kind: to improve the soul. Its aim is to train the moral not the intellectual life. "Those who are diseased in soul require a pedagogue to cure our maladies and then a teacher to train and guide the soul to all requisite knowledge when it is made able to admit the revelation of the Word."[23] Here the teacher comes after healing; and revelation, being closely associated with teaching, is subsequent to healing. In this pattern, revelation is not a speculative category acquirable prior to Christian living. Saying that the Word first exhorts, then trains, and finally teaches, Clement assumes the need for moral training before one can understand the teaching of revelation.

Clement also plays on the fact that "pedagogue" contains the word child.[24] Pedagogy is the training of children, and we are all children before God. With children, training in practical activities comes before theoretical knowledge. The child comes to know with simplicity and innocence. Christianity is both a *gnosis,* a complicated and profound system of knowledge, and at the same time a teaching accessible to simple and unlettered believers. The child plays the mediating role between these two ends of Christianity; the child is open to all knowledge but is actually capable of grasping as knowledge only a very little of what is available. God speaks to us "as if lisping with children." The classical schools of philosophy cannot compete with the word of God. "Wherefore these things which have been concealed from the wise and the prudent of the present world have been revealed to babes."[25]

Augustine

As the towering figure at the origin of Western Christianity, Augustine presents an emphasis different from Clement and the other Greek fathers of the church. Augustine readily uses the term teacher for God, but he tries to exclude human participation in the term. He argues that teaching–learning is a single process, but he internalizes the activity within the soul. What is said by someone who is called teacher jogs the memory where teaching–learning actually occurs.

Augustine here follows Plato in the belief that knowledge is innate, but he does not agree with Plato on the prior existence of the soul. Although Augustine insists that "God alone, who teaches truth, holds the teacher's chair in heaven," he is not entirely consistent in excluding human participation.[26] Having been influenced by the great rhetoricians, especially Quintilian and Cicero, Augustine cannot give up on teaching as a great human activity. He cites approvingly Cicero's "to be eloquent you should speak 'so as to teach, to delight, to sway.'"[27]

Augustine's treatise *The Teacher* was written early in his career (389 c.e.) But he commented on it toward the end of his life: "I wrote a work entitled *The Teacher.* There it is debated, sought and found that there is no teacher giving knowledge to man other than God. This is also in accordance with what is written by the Evangelist: 'You have one master (teacher), the Christ' (Matt. 23:10)."[28] Augustine relies heavily on this passage of the New Testament that reflects the opposition between the early church and the synagogue. Jesus is warning his disciples not to glory in the honorific titles of father and teacher in imitation of the contemporary Jewish leaders. In denying that human beings can be teachers, Augustine, one might say, deduced a metaphysics from a political conflict over titles.[29]

Augustine begins *The Teacher* with an exchange in which all speaking is said to be teaching or learning. Even when we ask questions, Augustine says, we are teaching someone what we want to learn. After a brilliant start, Augustine quickly undermines the exaltation of (human) teaching by encapsulating the process in "closed chambers" or "the inner recesses of the mind." God is to be "sought and entreated in the hidden parts of the rational soul."[30] Despite the fact that most of the treatise is valuable material about the nature of language, the end of the treatise dismisses the human teacher. "Who is so foolishly curious as to send his son to school to learn what the teacher thinks? When the teachers have explained by means of words all the disciplines they profess to teach, even the disciplines of virtue and wisdom, then those who are called 'students' consider within themselves whether truths have been stated. They do so looking upon the Inner Truth."[31]

Augustine has a legitimate warning here for any human being who claims the title of teacher. Every teacher has to respond to the question: Who appointed you as teacher. One who claims to teach truth, virtue, or wisdom has to appeal to a reality that goes beyond the teacher-student relation. Augustine is also helpful in his reminder that the student is not an empty bucket waiting to be filled but an active participant in the process. The teacher shows how, but the learner has to judge whether the teaching improves the activity of the learner in the concrete circumstances of his or her life.

Augustine's words unfortunately go beyond a caution of humility on the part of teachers. He removes the function of teaching altogether from human beings and others on earth. Although he is less severe in other writing, especially *The Teaching of Christianity*, his undercutting of creaturely participation in the act of teaching set a bad direction for Christianity. The process of teaching–learning is set outside the give and take of bodily, political life.

There is an amazingly short jump from Augustine to twentieth-century writing on learning that disparages teaching. Augustine's God has been replaced by psychological development that similarly excludes the human teacher. Maria Montessori contributed to this movement by denying that the mother teaches the child to speak.[32] In his scholarly study of language, Steven Pinker ridicules the idea that a mother is a teacher of language: "First, let us do away with the folklore that parents teach their children language."[33] Pinker's object of attack is the special use of language called "motherese," but the statement dismisses teaching. Carl Rogers's influential book *Freedom to Learn* is a sustained attack on the assumption that anyone can teach anything.

One of Augustine's contributions to education was to see an educational pattern to history.[34] The "ages of man"—infancy, childhood, adolescence, manhood, old age—are intimated by Augustine, connecting him to modern developmental psychology, which has its beginnings with Comenius and Rousseau.[35] For Augustine, education has to reinforce qualities that are necessary to the creation of a "new man." Revelation includes awareness of human sinfulness and the need for divine grace. Augustine's concern with sin sets him against most of modern educational theory. Interestingly, a secular commentator, who is intent on defending the Enlightenment, has to admit in referring to Augustine that there is "far more evidence extant in favor of the Christian doctrine of Original Sin than Rousseau's doctrine of Original Virtue."[36]

Thomas Aquinas

The views of Thomas Aquinas on education and teaching are similar to those of Augustine, except for one crucial difference. While Aquinas agrees with Augustine that God is teacher, he disagrees on how this relates to humans as teachers. Aquinas's philosophy of participation holds that creatures participate in God's act of being. If God's teaching is inseparable from God's being, each creature participates in teaching as well. The human being, as the one who can hear God's word and can question all being, has a preeminence among teaching and teachable beings.[37]

Aquinas's explicit treatment of "the teacher" is surprisingly brief, found mainly in his treatise *On Truth*. To the first question, "whether a man or only God can be called a teacher," Aquinas replies in the affirmative. Yes, a man truly has the power to teach because "denying secondary causes derogates from the order of the universe." Aquinas then lists eighteen objections to man as teacher, several of those objections from Augustine. Aquinas proceeds to reaffirm that a human being can be called teacher, but instead of admitting that he is contradicting Augustine, Aquinas smooths over their differences: "When Augustine proves that only God teaches, he does not intend to exclude man from teaching exteriorly."[38]

Their disagreement is not whether God is teacher but how to interpret "only Christ is your master." As I pointed out in the previous chapter, Christian use of "Christ" can be either exclusive uniqueness or inclusive uniqueness. For Augustine, Christ as unique teacher means that no one else is teacher. For Aquinas, Christ as unique teacher means that everyone else is teacher, too. To sustain this latter meaning, "Christ" has to be the name of a present and future reality, not simply a way of referring to a teacher in the past.

Aquinas is intent on taking an educational approach to the whole of *sacra doctrina* (teaching). In the foreword to the *Summa Theologiae*, he contrasts two methods: one that follows the order of history, the other that is according to education. Since the *Summa* is intended, in his words, "for the education of beginners," he proceeds according to the order of education. *Sacra doctrina* includes more than theology. Besides dealing with "science" as theology does, *sacra doctrina* includes practice, affective knowledge, and imagery.[39]

On one side of the relation, Aquinas describes God's activity as his being. His revealing is therefore his presence in his people.[40] Creation is not an act in the past; it is the continuous overflow of God's goodness. On the other side of the relation, Aquinas describes the humans as "knowing God implicitly in everything they know."[41] The human mind is actively, not passively, potential. By its own inner forces, aided by the teaching of another person, the mind can reach what has been unknown. The combination of God's continuous activity and the humans' active receptivity suggests an understanding of revelation as a present relation of teacher and student.

Aquinas does not draw that conclusion. Two obstacles prevented his using "revelation" in that way. First, there is the connotation of revelation as the exposing of a secret. We do not have secrets revealed each day. Aquinas contrasts the progress in knowledge on the part of the teacher and the student. The teacher learns what has not been known before by a process of discovery (*inventio*). The student gathers knowledge that in *sacra doctrina* is to be found in the scriptures and the writings of the fathers. The activity is one of memory, the gathering up (re-collection) of the past.[42]

The second reason why revelation is not seen as teaching–learning is that Aquinas plays down the apocalyptic side of revelation. Although he refers to a Christ of the present and the future, especially in his sacramental theology, "Christ" is more often a name for someone in the past. Christians believe that there is no revelation beyond Christ or after Christ. The principle that revelation is a present relation that impels activity toward future redemption can be orthodox belief only if "Christ" refers to the present and the future, as well as to the past. In Christian terms, all teaching–learning is "in Christ" because all creation operates under this sign.

Similar to Augustine, Aquinas has a caution of humility for all human teachers. While there is a necessary connection between teaching and learning, no guarantee exists that one's *intention* to teach will result in the student's learning. A human teacher speaks words and makes gestures, but these do not cause learning in another. The one called teacher cannot take credit for what the student has learned, nor should he or she be depressed by the failure of the student to learn. The would-be teacher has to discover what is already teaching the student and then try to reshape that relation.[43]

Human teaching thus has a mystical side to it, in which we must "renounce the fruits of our actions." But since as Augustine said, we can have spiritual goods only by giving them away, the impulse to teach others is one of the humans' greatest ambitions.[44] According to Aquinas, the wisdom given to any of us is given "as on a loan"; it is not our possession. We teach as we share in God's wisdom, sometimes despite what we are trying to teach.[45]

Contemporary writing can find no causal connection between the intention of the (school)teacher and the learning of the student. Aquinas's philosophy agrees with that. But instead of declaring teaching and learning to be separate processes, Aquinas recognizes teaching as going beyond intention, beyond words, and beyond humans. If teaching is disconnected from learning, the temptation is to look for more coercive means that will get results. In Aquinas's framework of teaching–learning, one can never give up on teaching, even if we are often stymied in how to go about it. Teachers, especially schoolteachers, need faith, hope, and love to continue at teaching when no productive result is assured.

Martin Buber

For developing the theme of God as teacher and the humans as learners, modern times offers an array of Christian and secular thinkers. The reformers Martin Luther, John Calvin, and George Fox are obvious examples. Immanuel Kant, Friedrich Schiller, and Gotthold Lessing are less obvious choices, but they bring in modern notions of the schoolteacher and the developing student. Friedrich Schleiermacher, Søren Kierkegaard, and Friedrich von Hügel wrestle with the sensitivities of the modern believer. Theorists of religious education such as Horace Bushnell, George Albert Coe, or even John Dewey reflect on revelation as an educational category.[46]

Although these and dozens of other writers could supply my final example, I have chosen to finish this second part of the book in the same way as I did the first part, that is, with a Jewish thinker. The general reason is the same: the need of Christianity for Judaism as a dialogical partner in thinking through revelation. But here the reason is more specific. The metaphor of teaching–learning for revelation is much better developed in Judaism than in Christianity. I noted above that Christianity has a tension between Jesus as teacher and Christ as redeemer. Jesus the teacher or rabbi tends to get overshadowed. The Jews did not have that problem. The Torah is the name for God's teaching. And the leader of the Jewish congregation is called rabbi or teacher.

Just as with Christianity, Jews have a tendency to identify revelation with an ancient text, understood only by experts. But just as Christianity corrects that tendency by taking seriously the liturgy and morality of today's Christians, so the Jewish prayer book insists that God teaches today. And the response to God's revealing action is human action for justice.

Several Jewish thinkers provide the possibility of illustrating the meaning of revelation as teaching–learning. Franz Rosenzweig, Abraham Heschel, Abraham Kook, or Eugene Levinas would be candidates. I take Martin Buber as my main example for two reasons: (1) his insistence on the present for the encounter of revelation; and (2) his use of "responsibility" and "uniqueness" in ways that connect him to the themes in the second part of this book.

Martin Buber approaches the issue of revelation from philosophy, theology, and education. His most famous work, *I and Thou*, provides the philosophical framework. But that I-Thou relation was filled in by his writing on the Hasidic masters, on the Bible, and on various themes of education. He does not allow philosophy to rule everything else; "in a great act of philosophizing even the finger-tips think—but they no longer feel."[47] It is only in the religious act that we are open to the divine with fingertips that feel.

The word that is spoken by the great teacher is not a clear body of knowledge. "The relation is wrapped in a cloud but reveals itself, it lacks but creates language. We hear no Thou and yet feel addressed."[48] For the Jew the Torah is the clearest expression of divine instruction, but specific laws cannot be identified as revelation. "The Torah of God is understood as God's instruction in His way, and therefore not as a separate *objectivum*. . . . A vestige of the actual speaking always adheres to the commanding word, the directing voice is always present or at least its voice is heard fading away."[49]

Revelation is thus the teaching of God who is present and the learning of the human community which comes into existence by responding. "The present exists only insofar as presentness, encounter and relation exist. Only as the Thou becomes present does presence come into being."[50] The human as learner is necessary for revelation to occur. The reception is not a passive filling up. Like any good student, "the man who is 'mouth' is precisely that and not a mouthpiece—not an instrument but an organ, an autonomous, sounding organ; and to sound means to modify sound."[51]

The human response is not mainly in the form of knowledge or beliefs; "consciousness is the first violin but not the conductor."[52] The Jew is encouraged to express belief through action. "The key to the truth is the next deed, and this key opens the door, if the deed is so done, that the meaning of the act finds its fulfillment here."[53] Meaning is found through engagement of one's person. "It only reveals itself as one takes part in its revelation."[54]

The divine teacher uses the whole of creation as the means of teaching. "Natural events are the carriers of revelation, and revelation occurs when he who witnesses the event and sustains it experiences the revelation it contains."[55] Education includes the ways that our response is developed. "The world, that is the whole environment, nature and society, 'educates' the human being."[56]

Responsibility is central to Buber's idea of revelation and his concerns with education. "Responsibility presupposes one who addresses me primarily, that is, from a realm independent of myself, and to whom I am answerable. . . . He who ceases to make a response ceases to hear the Word."[57] His essay on education was done for a conference on the theme of "the development of the creative powers in the child," a phrase that was a problem for him. The popular notion of "creative powers," he claims, is exclusively concerned with the originative instinct to make or achieve but "what teaches us the saying of Thou is not the originative instinct but the instinct for communion."[58] Humans are not creators; they are responders.

This idea of responsibility within a community is directly related to his idea of uniqueness. By being responsible we move from the uniqueness we are born with as humans to the uniqueness of a life in communion. Buber describes conscience as "the individual's awareness of what he is 'in truth,' of what in his unique and non-repeatable created existence he is intended to be."[59] The uniqueness of the responsible person is not the "solitary one" but a life of increasing inclusivity. Only in relation to the divine teacher can the conflict between a uniqueness of exclusivity and a uniqueness of increasing inclusivity be resolved.

LANGUAGES OF TEACHING

One way that the church tried to exercise a control of teaching was by limiting it to a follow-up operation. In New Testament times, teaching was placed second to announcing, preaching, or proclaiming. The apostles, it is written, went out and "preached Jesus," announcing the good news of salvation. Those who accepted Jesus and were converted were then taught some of the moral and doctrinal implications of their belief. Thus, "to preach" and "to teach" were taken to be successive moments in the life of the Christian.[60] Although this sequence makes sense in the intramural language of the church, it is a problem when that language interacts with other religions and with modern secular speech.

The verb "to teach" has much broader possibilities than a follow-up to preaching. Church people sometimes dismiss teach and teachers as equivalent to dry instruction and academic instructors. For example, one regularly hears in Roman Catholic discussions that "a catechist is not a mere teacher." What is presumably meant is that a catechist's work in a liturgical setting differs from the work of a schoolteacher. Instead of giving up the words teach and teacher to the classroom, church ministers need to reclaim a legitimate share of teaching.

Both church ministers and classroom instructors need a richer meaning of teaching than one that is equated with the classroom instruction of children. Reflection on teaching could helpfully begin with the way a mother and infant interact and go on to the many ways we teach every day as part of some community of teaching. Most of our teaching is nonverbal. We show others how to live and die, whether or not we intend to do so. The so-called corporal works of mercy are a central teaching in the New Testament. The clearest statement of how God judges a human life uses these works as the criteria: feed the hungry, give drink to the thirsty, shelter the homeless. In much of history, this kind of teaching—acts of quiet and compassionate help—has been done by women. If women had been able to have their fair share of writing on teaching, the meaning of teaching probably would not have been narrowed down to one of telling, explaining, and transmitting knowledge.[61]

An educational approach to revelation and a metaphor of teach–learn for understanding revelation have the danger of turning God into a schoolmaster and revelation into a lecture. Education is not equivalent to school; neither is teaching equivalent to classroom instruction. Revelation is not a reasonable explanation or a fifty-minute monologue.

The eighteenth century was only too eager to turn revelation into an educational experience in which "revealed religion" is a teaching aid for reason. Gotthold Lessing, in "Education of the Human Race," writes, "What education is to the individual man, revelation is to the whole human race. Education is revelation coming to the individual man; and revelation is education which has come, and is still coming, to the human race." Within the education still coming to the human race, revelation is an early step on the road to reason. "Revelation gives nothing to the human race which human reason could not arrive at on its own; only it has given, and still gives to it, the most important of those things sooner."[62]

The academic imprisonment of "teach" is not healthy either for teaching or for academic institutions. The kind of teaching which the church calls preaching is one in a range of languages that are appropriate to various educational settings. Most educational settings require a mixture of teaching languages. For example, a parent in the home uses numerous languages of teaching with a child: praising, encouraging, warning, asking, criticizing, forgiving, and many more. If parents are not recognized as teachers, it is because they are not usually giving rational explanations of subject matter.

The languages of teaching can be grouped into three families: rhetorical, therapeutic, and dialogical. Each of these families contains many languages; I will use three examples to explore each family. The first two families are opposites; the third draws on the relation between the first two families.

Rhetorical Languages

Rhetorical languages assume a goal to be reached. Either a physical skill is desired by the potential student or a community belief is at issue for a learner within that community. Language is used to try to move the hearer from here to there. The term rhetorical, despite recent attempts to retrieve a richer meaning, might still suggest moralistic, trivial, or mechanical rules.[63] At its origin in Greece, the word referred to artful persuasion by speech. Some of the mistrust in the word is unavoidable. Is not anyone suspect who tries to persuade me to act in the right way? Should not each person decide for himself or herself what is right? Who gives anyone the right to tell someone else what the truth is? Or whether anything is true?

The beginning context for rhetorical speech should be the performance of bodily activities. Showing someone how to perform an action that they have asked to learn (swim, ski, cook) involves simple, precise commands. This use of language involves no inherent moral conflict. The learner by presenting his or her own body for instruction signifies a willingness to be instructed. A problem arises only when rhetorical language is separated from immediate, bodily activity. Then the question "by what authority" becomes inevitable.

This problem is muffled when the learner is a child. At least from society's standpoint parents, schoolteachers, and a few other groups have the right to tell children: Do this; don't do that. From the child's standpoint, especially as the child moves closer to young adulthood, the justification of the adult's rhetoric is nowhere near so obvious. Even a very young child may think that there is a better way than what has been commanded. Rhetorical speech needs complementing with the other families of languages so as not to become corrupted.

Three examples of rhetorical speech are *storytelling, lecturing,* and *preaching.* The moral persuasion becomes more direct as one moves from the first to the third. Good stories, that is, stories with rich, human texture that endure for generations, do not have an obvious moral. They show a slice of life from which we might learn a lesson. They do not tell us what to do. Even a story for a child should respect the child's intellect and not simply moralize. The test of a good children's story is that it also engages adults.

Narrative makes a character come alive. Paul Ricoeur describes the revelatory power of such speech: "Here truth no longer means verification but manifestation, that is, letting what shows itself to be. What shows is in each instance a proposed world, a world I may inhabit and wherein I can project my own possibilities."[64] Any good teacher uses stories of one kind or another. The great teachers in history use crafted gems, such as those that are found in the parables of Jesus, "stories which shatter the deep structures of our accepted world. . . . They remove our defenses and make us vulnerable to God."[65] If God is the great teacher, then stories have to be one of the main languages of divine teaching.

Lecturing is a narrower form of speech with a more explicit claim to truth. The word lecture started by meaning "to read." A text exists that is read aloud. By the Middle Ages, lecturing had the sense of explication, an interpreting of the text. In that interpretation, the reader has questions put to him or her by the text. The lecture in the medieval university was a prologue to disputation, which was to resolve problems in the text.[66]

In the nineteenth century, audiences came to lectures in order to learn from authoritative pronouncements by the lecturer.[67] The speaker and the audience still accepted a standard of truth that provided the authority to deliver a lecture. Perhaps most lectures today seem boring and pointless because the presupposition of the lecture form is usually missing. Lecturing can still have a place but only when the audience and lecturer accept the limitations of a fixed text and rational interpretations of the text. A State-of-the-Union speech, with all of its appropriate formality, is an example of a lecture that can make sense.

What followed lecturing and disputation in the medieval setting was preaching.[68] True mastery of *sacra doctrina* called for preaching. Here was the most pointed moral demand and therefore the most problematic rhetoric. The Christian church invented preaching as an art form, although its roots are in the Hebrew prophets' exhorting the people to be faithful to the promises they have made.[69] The early church also took over a form of writing called *parenesis*, a letter of moral exhortation, illustrated by Paul's First Letter to the Thessalonians.[70]

The direct object after the verb "to preach" is "message." The text having been read and interpreted, the preacher exhorts the congregation to go out and improve the world. A precise set of conditions is necessary for preaching to be a legitimate and effective language of teaching. The preacher has to be designated by a community; the community's beliefs have to be embodied in a text; the preacher has to awaken a response with a controlled use of emotion. According to the cliché, one should not preach to the converted, but that is exactly who should be preached to, namely, those who are ready to hear and are prepared to draw moral conclusions from the interpretation of the text.

Since television advertising uses a corrupt form of preaching ("buy this antacid and all your suffering will be ended"), it is difficult for any preacher today to avoid sounding like a pitchman for his product. Instead of increasing the decibels and playing into the stereotype of preacher, today's preacher has to be straightforward in the task, neither apologetic for the activity when conditions are appropriate nor excessive in the burden placed on preaching.

The sixteenth-century Reformation restored preaching to a central place in Christian worship. The Protestant minister should be credited with keeping alive a rhetorical form of speech that is used also by parents, politicians, and business leaders. But preaching needs a context of other languages or else it becomes overbearing. For its own good, preaching has to be neither an addition to teaching nor the whole of teaching.[71] Usually in Protestant churches the sermon is carefully prepared and solemnly delivered, but often too much is asked of it in shaping the lives of church members. And for addressing the nonchurch world, preaching is of little value unless preceded by the example of Christian lives and accompanied by the willingness of a community to listen as well as to preach.

If God is a great teacher, then God is a preacher, reminding us who we are and what our response should be to the gift of life. God's commandments are central to Jewish and Christian traditions, but God does not hector or nag. "The commandment of God permits man to be man before God. It allows the flood of life to flow freely. It lets man eat, drink, sleep, work, rest and play. It does not interrupt him."[72] God as preacher knows when to speak and when to be silent.

Therapeutic Languages

The second family of languages is called therapeutic. These languages are appropriate when there is no moral end in view. Their purpose is not to move the will but to heal the organism and thus make willing possible. This family stands in contrast to the rhetorical family, but it also complements rhetoric. Before someone can be exhorted to do the right thing, he or she may need calming, comforting, or consoling. A person overcome with sorrow or fear is not a good candidate for a sermon. Therapeutic languages do not presuppose a well-knit community. It is the brokenness of life or at least the incompleteness of community that calls for therapy.

Three examples of therapeutic speech are *thank/welcome, confess/forgive*, and *mourn/comfort*. They are best stated as interlocking pairs. Whereas rhetorical speech moves almost completely in one direction, therapy always involves some mutuality. Healing occurs in the flow of life between two parties. In therapeutic speech, teacher and student often switch places, sometimes without realizing it. Just as rhetoric arises from simple bodily commands (push the pedal, raise your arm), so therapeutic speech can be as simple as "uh-huh" or "I'm sorry."[73] At other times, more elaborate speech is needed but within a ritual setting.

Religion, rather than science or philosophy, has usually been the main carrier of ritual. But ritual has not fared well in post-Reformation Christianity, especially in the United States. The abuse of ritual in the medieval church produced a strong reaction in the Calvinist part of the Reformation. The Puritans tried to strip their religion of ritual, something that proved to be impossible. While Western Christianity still struggles with the place of ritual, the contemporary world is nonetheless indebted to religion for preserving therapeutic languages as a part of teaching.

The first therapeutic language is thanking, and its correlative, welcoming. It is a positive attitude that grounds all creaturely life, illustrated by the simple ritual of saying "thank you/you're welcome." I noted in chapter 6 that responsibility begins with the response of gratitude. The vocation of the humans is to say amen. The first religious gesture is to sing praise to God. Humans can never say to God: now we're even.[74]

Thanking is not for the purpose of reaching a goal; it is simply acknowledging life and its accompanying gifts. Heidegger played with the etymological connection between thinking and thanking. Our thoughts begin in thanking, although in Heidegger's case it is not clear to whom he was thankful. Francis of Assisi, in G. K. Chesterton's description, did not have that problem. "The great painter boasted that he mixed all his colours with brains, and the great saint may be said to mix all his thoughts with thanks."[75] Revelation as teaching–learning includes the creator's gift of all creatures and the response of gratitude by the morally responsible creature at the center.

The second therapeutic language is confess/forgive. When the bonds of community have been broken, confession of failure and forgiveness of the one who failed are prerequisite to other activities of the group. The confession of sin to the priest was one of the main rituals that the Protestant Reformation opposed.[76] The practice of this sacrament was filled with abuses and badly in need of reforms. The Roman Catholic Church initiated some reform and continued to demand sacramental confession. By the time of Vatican II, the practice was obviously in need of other reforms. The opportune moment seems to have been lost, and the sacrament is no longer a part of most Catholics' lives.

Confession, however, has not likely ceased in the lives of Catholics, Protestants, Jews, and others. The impulse to externalize the burden of guilt seems built into the human soul. The problem is to find a ritual setting that is appropriate. The psychotherapist replaced the priest for a small part of the population. For a different part of the population the radio call-in, the television talk show, the advice columnist, and the Internet chat room provide forums for confession. Critics look down on such confessions, but people use whatever means are available.

Confessing one's sins to a television audience, however, is not likely to have the desired effect. A person or a small group of people has to offer a stable bridge to reconciliation with oneself, one's neighbor, and God. The voice from the soul of the penitent needs to hear a responding voice of forgiveness.[77] Ideally, the one who accepts a confession is the one who has been wronged. Then the word of forgiveness can immediately heal the bond that has been broken. When the wronged person or persons cannot receive the confession, a representative of the wronged community can begin the reconciliation. Sometimes, the fault is such that an apology is rendered but is not accepted. That does not mean that the confession has been futile. It may simply mean that the magnitude of the fault has not yet been fully appreciated and more time is needed before there can be complete healing.[78]

Recent times have seen the development of truth commissions in recognition of the fact that although justice can never be fully achieved, the revelation of truth can be a positive move toward justice. The South African government's Truth and Reconciliation Commission was an admirable experiment in recognizing the danger of recrimination together with the need for the guilty to confess their crimes. The panel would not have been so effective without the presence of Archbishop Desmond Tutu, who, with Nelson Mandela, provided an anchor for the power of reconciliation.[79]

Religious people wish to confess their sins to God, who alone forgives sin. But the belief in many religions, a belief explicit in Jewish and Christian traditions, is that confessing/forgiving within the human community is both preparation for and living embodiment of reconciliation with God. Jesus highlighted this teaching of the Hebrew Bible in his parables. Christians pray daily, "forgive us our debts as we forgive our debtors." The interlocking of confessing and forgiving means that we cannot be forgiven unless we forgive. Given the fact that all human beings falter in their commitments, a person is penitent today and confessor tomorrow.

The third therapeutic language is mourn/comfort. Its most evident need is when a loved one dies and the communal bond is stretched to the breaking point. But mourning and comforting have to be learned throughout life; they do not suddenly appear in integral form at times of death. Even more than for other therapeutic languages, mourn/comfort needs a ritual for healthy expression. As in all rituals, the actual spoken words may be few and are likely to have a formulaic quality. Sometimes people avoid funerals because they do not know what to say. Their bodily presence is the most crucial word that is spoken; whatever further is said to the mourner will most likely be appreciated.[80]

People have to learn how to mourn the small deaths that occur throughout life. A teenager mourns the death of childhood, even while eagerly looking forward to young adulthood. A middle-aged man mourns the death of his youth while trying to find the way to act mature. Men and women may have to mourn the death of a marriage, or the last child leaving home, or the crippling disease of a parent. Thomas Aquinas makes the intriguing comment that those whose vocation is to extend the boundaries of knowledge are especially in need of mourning.[81] There is no end to sorrow on earth and therefore no limit to the need for mourning and comforting.

Each particular act of mourning, however, should have limits. Religious rituals of mourning are wisely designed to express what needs expression but within the context of life's triumph over death. In Jewish tradition, if a wedding and a funeral meet, the wedding takes precedence. One should mourn the dead, but it does neither the dead nor the living any good to go to excess. The control of mourning within traditional gestures shows respect for the one who has died, while avoiding obsession with death.

For how long should one mourn? The usual answer today is that every person is different and, therefore, there are no rules. As a result, the distraught person may have no guidelines, no markers provided by a comforting community. Each person is indeed unique, but that means he or she can learn from the experience of the whole human race. Religious rituals of mourning and comforting were worked out over centuries of time and may embody a wisdom that is lacking in today's popular psychology.[82]

As in all the therapeutic languages, teacher and student can easily reverse roles. Each of us faces many occasions of mourning a loss and a comparable number of times when we are called upon to comfort. The best preparation for comforting is learning how to mourn. Every great loss stokes memory of previous losses so that we cry at funerals for all of those whom we have buried. A mourner at a funeral frequently ends by comforting those who have come to offer comfort. If the mourning is genuine, no one keeps score or finds it strange that teaching–learning goes both ways.

Religious rituals, despite curtailment and deficiencies, have kept alive the sense of therapeutic speech as a language of teaching–learning. Jewish and Christian traditions have not found it difficult to imagine God as a great therapist. God seems to be engaged in a grand healing effort, putting together the shards of a broken world. The doctrine of hell seems incompatible with a skilled therapist who never quits.[83] But the great therapist's salvation or redemption is not without our efforts, which include listening intently and acting as welcomer, forgiver, and comforter as well as thanker, penitent, and mourner.

Dialogical Languages

The third family of languages is the dialogical. Of course, in one sense all teaching–learning is a dialogue. The process does not go on without an exchange that for human completeness involves speech. In this third family, the dialogue involves consciousness of the language being used, a reflection on rhetorical and therapeutic speech. The task is not to reach a higher level of abstraction but instead to go more deeply into the words. What are the presuppositions of an explanation or argument? What are the meanings of words and how far can those meanings change?

This family of languages places the student into a dialogue of language with itself. This dialogue has to maintain a tension between the rhetorical family in which the end of the teaching is in view and the therapeutic family which has no end. If either of these families completely dominates, teaching is in trouble. If lecturing or preaching is equated with teaching, we get oppressive attempts to transmit knowledge from the enlightened to the benighted. If therapy takes over, teaching is reduced to leading discussions in which everyone feels better but little knowledge is gained. Both forms of the reduction of teaching are evident in our era. Dialogical forms of speech are paradoxical reminders that the truth is possessed by no one, but that a search for the truth is the human vocation.

The first example of dialogical speech is dramatic performance. It is similar to rhetorical speech in having some kind of narrative with an end in view. It is similar to therapeutic speech in that the words are an expression of bodily emotions. But unlike either of those forms of speech, dramatic performance self-consciously reflects on the words that it uses. The actors play a role; the whole performance is called a play.[84] The performed play is not real, according to ordinary standards of real. The playwright speaks to the actors, the actors speak to each other, the play speaks to the audience. If there is no audience to receive the words, the pretending of the play collapses.

The line between ordinary reality and the staged play is a fragile one. The audience needs some distance to hear the dialogue within an imagined world. Too great a distance turns the play into a mere object for entertainment, criticism, or boredom. Some twentieth-century experiments in theater have moved the line separating play and audience, either by having the actors reflect on themselves as actors within a play, or else by drawing members of the audience into being part of the play. When done well by a Samuel Beckett or Tom Stoppard, the experiments release the world-shaking possibilities of the theater.[85] When poorly done, such experiments turn the play into preaching, therapy, or both.

God as playwright or director is a metaphor compatible with Christian and Jewish traditions. The divine creator's script invites audience participation and ad-libbing by the actors. We try out various roles before settling into one or a few that are comfortable. The eighteenth century was opposed to "hypocrisy"—trying on many roles—and favored sincerity, meaning single-minded.[86] That bias is still with us. A premature sincerity might not be a virtue when we are in a play of our lives whose general direction we sense but whose outcome is beyond our view.

A second dialogical language is dialectical discussion. Sometimes debate is merely an exercise in trying to score points against an opponent.

But when debaters respect their opponents there is implicit acknowledgment that the truth lies beyond what either party can currently articulate. The medieval principle that truth is an *adaequatio* between words and things is thought to be a simplistic assumption that the mind replicates the external world. But equality would be rendered by the word *aequatio;* in contrast, the word *adaequatio* indicates that at most our words are ad-equate, that is, are an approach to truth but not equal to reality.[87] Every formulation of the truth can be improved upon.

It can be a wonderful experience for a young person to hear two mature people engage each other's arguments. But thinking of oneself as a philosopher or dialectician too early in life can be illusory. For Plato, Aristotle, and Aquinas, philosophy is reserved for the mature. Regarding the young, Plato warned that "the study of dialectic accustoms him to criticize all prevailing opinions, so that he easily falls into anarchy and lawlessness."[88]

In a school, the faculty should give an example of fair-minded and intelligent debate, within their disciplines and across disciplines. Each faculty member should also be in conversation with other colleagues in his or her field beyond the school. Today's media make realistic a conversation across the country or across continents. In the medieval *disputatio*, one could not answer an objection until one repeated what the objector had said to the satisfaction of the objector.[89] The philosophers, said Cicero, in contrast to orators, speak "about subjects which are calm, with no trace of turmoil. . . . They speak to teach not to overwhelm."[90]

In religious discussions, especially within Christianity, the acceptance of this calm philosophical exchange is sometimes considered scandalous. The theological disputations at the University of Paris in the thirteenth century were looked upon with great reservation by many church officials.[91] I noted in chapter 4 that in the Luther–Erasmus conflict, Erasmus wanted to have a dialectical discussion, but Luther, unfortunately, would have no part of it. There is a time for preaching a message; there is also a time for acknowledging the ambiguity of all language and the need to debate the formulation of any message.

Early in its history, Christianity laid down formulas as the test of orthodoxy. This procedure had the advantage of taking words seriously, but at the possible cost of squelching creative thinking which might be helpful in the future. Doctrinal formulas most often have been intended to set limits to orthodoxy without closing down thought. At the First Vatican Council, the Roman Catholic Church condemned both a rationalistic and an irrationalistic approach to faith. The implied invitation was to think more profoundly about faith. Unfortunately, the invitation was generally neglected by church officials and theologians who found "definitions" of faith in the council's pronouncements. The Second Vatican Council wisely avoided easy-to-misuse formulas of belief.

Jewish tradition has generally had a better record in admitting dialectical discussion. The Mishnah records an incident that concluded a three-year debate between the schools of Hillel and Shammai. "A heavenly voice was heard: The opinions of these and the opinions of those are both the words of the living God."[92] In this case, the decision went to Hillel, but Judaism recognized a place for minority opinion. In Judaism, there are very few points of orthodoxy (correct opinion) and more concern with orthopraxis (correct activity).

Is God a dialectician? Since Christians and Jews believe that God's word is absolute, the final standard of truth, it might seem impossible to adopt this aspect of teaching–learning. However, we never encounter the word of God except mixed with human words. Some ambiguity always remains in determining the divine voice.[93]

Jews have never hesitated to argue with God. From the time of Abraham down to post-Holocaust literature, there have been questions, complaints, and debate directed toward God. Jews have gone so far as to put God on trial to explain the suffering of his people. "God has never stopped talking to his people, and his people have never stopped answering back. The Bible is part one of the argument, and the Talmud is part two; even more argumentative than its predecessors."[94] Christianity has had less of this element. But Thomas Aquinas, in saying whether Job should have been arguing with God, gives the very Jewish answer: "Truth does not change because of the high dignity of him to whom it is addressed. He who speaks the truth cannot be overcome, no matter with whom he disputes."[95]

Academic criticism, as the final language in the final family of teaching languages, is a comprehensive form of teaching but in a paradoxical way. It depends for its content on rhetorical and therapeutic languages, as well as dramatic performance and dialectical discussion. Academic criticism, because it lacks its own substance, can either be utterly vacuous or else the most powerful of teaching languages. Here every word's meaning is in question as well as the meaning of meaning itself. There are not two sides to every question but innumerable sides. The conversation is with the human race, and the main topic of the conversation is the nature of conversation.

Academic criticism occurs in few places except classrooms. The schoolteacher, like the actor, is regularly accused of not living in the real world. Something described as "merely academic" is a way of dismissing any real significance to the point at hand. Sometimes schoolteachers are in fact unrealistic and out of touch. Often, however, the dismissal of concerns as academic is a defense against criticism that can undermine the certainties of generals, politicians, CEOs, and stereotyped thinking. The schoolmaster's questioning of every orthodoxy is actually an explosive instrument that needs to be handled with care and humility.

If religion has a difficult time accepting dialectical discussion, it often seems in total conflict with academic criticism. The classroom is not a place for affirming beliefs; it can be a place that exposes every belief to comparison and contrast. No student's beliefs, however, should be mocked or ridiculed, especially when he or she is young and vulnerable. Theodore Sizer, in his fine studies of the public school, shows an unusual sensitivity to religious speech. He finds nothing wrong with a student saying she is going to be a teacher because "Jesus told me." Eventually, she will have to examine for herself what these words mean, but an outsider should show some respect for that as a statement of motive.[96]

Despite the danger that religious belief can be undermined by academic criticism, an adult religious life has to find its way through an academic testing. In today's world of interacting religions, we cannot avoid comparison. Dialogue within a controlled academic setting hardly ever leads to conversion to another religion. In Christian–Jewish dialogue, the usual outcome is that the Jews become more Jewish, the Christians become more Christian. In religious study, similar to the study of languages, we come to appreciate and understand our own by comparing it to others. Religion comes within the principle stated by John Stuart Mill: "What Cicero practiced as the means of forensic success requires to be imitated by all who study any subject in order to arrive at the truth. He who only knows his side of the case, knows little of that."[97]

Is God an academician? I have put this characteristic last in my treatment of revelation as teaching–learning, but I would not exclude an academic aspect from the relation. The main image here is not God as schoolmaster drilling in the subjunctive, but God as player with words. What I have described as academic criticism may sound reserved for graduate students. Actually, five-year-olds are sometimes better at this game than Ph.D. candidates who have been drugged on leaden prose. The Jewish, Christian, and Muslim premise that God speaks is audacious. The evidence is ambiguous, but it starts with the young child saying: What does that word mean? What's the word for that?

Conclusion

THE LAST THREE CHAPTERS have suggested ways that "revelation" is related to practical and theoretical issues of the present. The historical material can now be given a more pointed summary when seen through the lens of these systematic concerns. Although the first five chapters could only sketch out some historical highlights, the following points form a consistent record of the past and a realistic proposal for the present and future.

"Revelation" is an infrequent but influential term that runs throughout the history of the Christian era. There are two extreme opinions about the history of this term. Some authors have no problem in finding revelation in the Old Testament, the New Testament, and all of the church fathers. It is assumed to be the building block for Christian theology. Other writers maintain that revelation did not begin to be discussed until the seventeenth and eighteenth centuries. It is claimed that revelation is a modern construct that could perhaps be eliminated from Christian theology.

A survey of the actual uses of the term comes out at a place in between these two opinions, with room for debating which direction to emphasize. If one looks only for the word revelation, then most Christian writers would be surprised to find how infrequent is the use of the term. One could argue that it is barely, if at all, in the Old Testament; it is in the New Testament but not so prominently as to jump out at the reader. It is hardly more common in the Greek fathers of the church or in the early Latin writers. It has a more central role in medieval writers and in the Reformation period. Thus, to say that the term is not important until modern times is a useful but overstated corrective to the more common assumption that revelation is the central idea of the Bible and all of Christian theology.

Where there is room for debate is how far to distinguish the word itself from the idea that we think the word conveys. It is important to stay close to the word itself while also being attentive to terms that are closely related in meaning. In English today, the word "manifestation," or the more ordinary "discovery," can sometimes be a synonym for "revelation." But one should not neglect subtle differences in root meanings. Since the verb "reveal" and, more so, the noun "revelation," came to have a special place in Christian thinking, it is important to pay attention to the words.

USE IN THE BIBLE

The Greek word for revelation (*apokalypsis*) came into the Septuagint translation of the Old Testament. It was used in the New Testament as a term referring to secret knowledge and truth. The metaphorical root of the term is visual. It indicates that a veil has been removed so that what was once in darkness has now come into the light. What is revealed has been made visible; the revealed is something that can now be seen. This emphasis on the truth as what is visible stands in considerable tension with the Hebrew Bible's use of metaphors that are oral/aural in nature: the truth is what is heard. Perhaps it is possible to use both visual and oral metaphors in understanding truth, but one of them is likely to be subordinate to the other.

The Christian use of "revelation" could simply be the result of Greek being the language available for the composition of the New Testament. But one could also argue that Christianity took on certain characteristics or emphases because of its cultural origins, including the Greek language. The Pauline Epistles speak of God's plan that once was hidden but now is revealed. The Fourth Gospel speaks of God's Word who has appeared and has been seen. This language became the basis for statements of Christian piety that we have "seen" God, a somewhat puzzling claim. The belief that one has seen the final and absolute truth can be illusory for oneself and dangerous to others.

The word revelation is used only once in the last book of the New Testament, but it seems hardly an accident that the book itself is known as the Revelation of John or simply, Revelation. Since the word means an unveiling of secrets, then a book that purports to unveil the conclusion to all of history was appropriately named Revelation. From the second century to the present, the Christian church has had to resist a reading of the last book that makes superfluous most of what precedes it in the

Bible. The people who want to see how the story ends seize on the final book where one gets a picture of how things will stand in the end.

LATIN SPLIT

The Latin church attempted to control revelation by using two different words, thereby isolating the Revelation of John and similar literature that came to be called "apocalyptic." Most of the time when the New Testament uses "revelation," the Vulgate translation uses the classical word *revelatio*. But in the verse at the beginning of the last book, and occasionally elsewhere, the Latin word *apocalypsis* was used; the origin of this term is in the second century. The English word apocalypse is in continuity with the Latin word; it today has the connotation of a violent end to everything. When writers say that "revelation" was not an important category until modern times, they are presumably referring to *revelatio*. It is indicative of the success of the Latin church that "apocalypse" is not discussed at all in this context.

The attempt of the Latin church to suppress the future-oriented side of revelation, that is, apocalypse, was never entirely successful. Despite the efforts of rational-minded scholars and authority-conscious bishops, an intense concern with the final, complete unveiling of history never disappeared. Church leaders should not have been surprised. Apocalyptic groups, who prepare for the end of the world and the triumph of God's anointed ones, are following out the meaning of "revelation." The early church not only included the book of Revelation in the Bible, they placed it at the end of the biblical story which already had a beginning and a high point in the past. What else is one to make of the last book but a conclusion to the time line?

A split has existed in Christianity from its earliest centuries that can be described by the contrasting connotations of *revelatio* and *apocalypsis*. An educated upper class looks to truths that have been revealed in the past. This body of material has been preserved by appointed teachers whose job is to safeguard and to explain the revelation. The picture of God and the universe that is contained in this revelation seems comfortable and reasonable to many people. For other people, however, this picture is deadening and smug, cut off from the harsh reality of death. Their picture of God is one of a severe judge whose mind cannot be fathomed by reason. One's only hope is to discover the secret key that unlocks the future. In this context, the term revelation can refer either to the secret code for interpreting the Bible or to the inner light that trumps human reason with a blinding vision of the judgment to come.

TIME

For trying to overcome this split within Christianity, we need to examine the nature of time. In our everyday image of time, especially in modern Western cultures, time is a line consisting of points. Christianity is often said to imagine time as a straight line pointing forward. The assumed alternative to a line pointing forward is a circle in which there is no hope for a better future; time moves eternally in the same groove. Time as a line pointing forward has been the image thought to be compatible with the modern idea of progress.

When revelation is placed on this line, the result is disappointingly limited, whether the focus is the past, the present, or the future. All three segments of time have the same character. If revelation is primarily past, it is thought to have happened at particular points of history. Scholarly research is needed to gather up the results of these past events. Revelation in the present is much harder to pin down. The present event is already past before one can discuss it. A present revelation is likely to mean a judgment about where the arrow of time is pointing. Revelation as a future event would seem impossible because it suggests that revelation has not happened yet. But that problem has not stopped Christian writers from talking at length about revelation as future. What is usually meant is that something has already happened that lets us know what is to come in the future. Past, present, and future revelations turn out to be more similar than different. Wherever the point of entry is, revelation tends to be information about the direction of the line.

The alternative to a straight line of progress need not be a closed circle. Indeed, straight lines and circles are variations on the same image, namely, a line consisting of points. If one tries to get a better image of time, one at least needs a three-dimensional image. The traditional religions that Christian writers have sometime disparaged were less concerned with circles than spheres. In the context of a spherical image, the cyclic aspects of time do not imply a vicious circle. The past is not so much behind us as beneath us and within us. The future might best be sought by "digging down" into the past. No single visual drawing can capture the whole mystery of time, but there are better images than that of time imagined as points along a line.

ALL THE SENSES

Time cannot be comprehended even with a three-dimensional image because a visual object is biased toward a single aspect of understanding.

No matter how complex the image may be, the past, the present, and the future will be imagined as divisible objects, things that can be placed before the eyes. But a fuller human experience of time includes awareness that we live in a present whose boundaries are never clear. We can live superficially in the present with little regard for either past or future. Or we can live profoundly in the present, touching the past with memory, aware of other beings in the present, and knowing that a future depends in part on our present actions.

In this experience of the present, we know that most of the past's influence on us is beyond whatever we could discover. But preceding generations have left us traces of understanding to keep alive human memory. The phrase "standing on the shoulders of the past" is literally true. Whatever good might be done in the future depends on a reshaping of the past. Humans who think they can "create" a future that does not depend on the past mistake themselves for gods. The humans have to try to reshape what the future will be even as they are aware that their fragile bodies and their limited intellects will cause the future to differ from every human projection.

The present needs to be experienced with the body and all of its senses for contacting the past and for situating a concern for the future. Especially in modern times, the visual has tended to overwhelm the other senses, but a bias in that direction precedes the modern era. It was not the seventeenth-century scientists but Aristotle who first described time as a series of points measured as to before and after. The Greek metaphor for intellectual understanding as the seeing of truth helped to shape the Christian New Testament and subsequent church understanding. Revelation as a coming into the light is biased toward the visual. A present that has depth and can appreciate the past on its own terms has to begin with hearing rather than seeing.

SPEAKING AND LISTENING

The Hebrew emphasis is on hearing God rather than on seeing God. The predominance of aural/oral metaphors does not exclude the visual. But giving special attention to conversation, to listening and answering, has reverberations in every aspect of life. For knowing an object visually, one stands back to get a better look; the knower is in control of the knowing. In speaking and listening, the parties lean toward each other, aware of being in a process that is beyond either party's control of the outcome. There is an interactive aspect to the relation in which the physical integrity of the organism is at issue. Conversation exists, as far as human beings are aware, only when at least one of the parties is human. The other party might be living or dead, an animal or a spirit. The more varied the conversation is, the richer is the present in its appreciation of the past and its care for the future.

The three Abrahamic religions—Judaism, Christianity, and Islam—adopted the term revelation even though each of these religions gives a primacy to words. In each of the three religions, the visual element has been attractive as the means of interpretation. That is, each has given special status to enlightened men (seldom women) who explain the sacred words. But at the origins of each of these three religions, the metaphors are oral and aural more than visual.

God as the one who addresses, calls, commands, promises, forgives, judges . . . is the central metaphor of Jewish and Christian Bibles and the Qur'an. This fact is signified by the Bible and the Qur'an not insofar as they are written documents (visible objects) but as language that is spoken, heard, memorized, recited, meditated upon, celebrated. As a literary object, neither the Bible nor the Qur'an is "the word of God." But when a person hears or reads the biblical or quranic words in the openness of faith, then the metaphor of "word of God" becomes appropriate.

A homily on a scriptural passage may help the believer to understand God's workings in history, but the application of the phrase "word of God" to church sermons is presumptuous. The word of God can extend to words outside the inspired scriptures, but the function of scripture and tradition is to indicate how to keep extending the application of the metaphor without trivializing it. The metaphor of word of God can be coordinated with the metaphor of revelation. Neither of them is a simple fact; both are ways of speaking about the relation of the divine and the human.

<hr>

PRACTICAL RESPONSE

God's word can be said to confront every person, not in a timeless, eternal moment but in the concrete circumstances of his or her life. The circumstances of today do not necessarily imply progress beyond the eras when the Bible and the Qur'an were composed. God remains almost totally incomprehensible to human understanding, but there is a knowing deeper than reason which responds to the "hidden but not unknown God."

Both "revelation" and "word of God" are better understood as practical rather than as speculative categories, but neither term immediately suggests practicality. "Revelation" has often been identified with doctrines and dogmas that have only a tenuous relation to action. Theology appears to say that the truth, which was once hidden, is now revealed; the case is closed; there is nothing more to do. The word of God can suffer a similar fate when the metaphor is translated into statements of fact (propositions) that God has produced for our enlightenment. For a practical orientation, the revelation/word of God has to be a personal and communal address so that God is understood to be speaking to "my people," a belief that makes my response unavoidable.

If the word of God is spoken within the personal, historical, and political circumstances of one's life, then the response has bodily and political ramifications. Christian and Jewish religions begin with the fact of a wounded world. Why the world is the way it is goes beyond anyone's explanation. What we do know is that we can either add to the woundedness or we can try to heal the world. Listening and responding to the word of God means working at the task of healing until the world-to-come. How one works at this task will vary according to one's interpretation of end: both one's own death and the end of the world.

The human participation in the revelational relation of divine speaking and human answering is "responsibility." Like every ethical or moral category, responsibility can become flattened out in meaning. In the second half of the twentieth century, calls for responsibility were often hollow. Still, the etymology and history of the term provide a basis to build on. "Responsibility" originated in the "apocalyptic era" in which Christianity and modern Judaism arose. Thus, responsibility and revelation are historically and logically joined.

The ability to answer a voice that has been spoken can be at least the anonymous beginning of a religious life. Does God's voice sound in the cries of children starving in Africa? Does God speak in the falling timber of the Amazon rain forest? Is it God's word when someone who has been brutalized says, I forgive you? Jewish and Christian traditions bring interpretive tools to the ambiguities of the human situation, but the person who responds to great suffering with utmost care and who answers hatred with love cannot be far from the kingdom of God.

PARTICULAR AND UNIVERSAL

This receptivity on the part of the human being (responsible to) and the result in the form of concrete action (responsible for) are part of a logic of particular and universal. There may be absolute or universal truths, but none of them can be stated in human language. Human speech, like human life, is concrete and particular. The human temptation is "contempt for the particular" which takes the form of rising above actual human beings and their mundane lives to find what is eternal and beyond limitations. The desire to find the source of glimpsed beauty and smudged perfection is an impulse of human beings that cannot be denied. The question is how to take the journey and where does it end?

In the richest prophetic, mystical, and sacramental strands we are encouraged to hallow the ordinary. Contrary to our first instincts that God is the most high and that we must ascend above matter, the journey starts by going down: toward the center of the soul, the center of the earth, the center of time's depths. Only from the still point at the center of all bodily life can a resurrection begin. In the subsequent rising, ascent becomes a legitimate direction, and "most high" can be one of the numerous names of the creator-revealer-redeemer.

Abstracting from individual cases to arrive at general laws in mathematical form can be a fruitful enterprise. The great scientific revolution has revealed secrets of the universe and brought practical benefit to part of the human race. But understanding the truth through individual cases and general laws is only one mode of human experience.

The paradoxical term "unique" is a way to capture the relation of particular and universal. In a two-dimensional, flattened-out world, particular and universal would occupy extreme endpoints. But in a world where the present has depth, each particular reality followed to its deepest aspect points to the universal.

In ordinary English, "unique" suggests this paradox: what is most particular can be most nearly universal. The unique is what is most exclusively particular and what is most inclusively universal. Where receptivity is greatest, the two meanings of unique can be closest. In its receptivity, the human being is the most nearly unique being we encounter, one that is open from its birth to all being and has a vocation to become still more unique. The great artists among us produce works which, while startling in their particularity, awake in an attentive listener the sense of a truth and a beauty beyond human words. The unique God would therefore be one of infinite receptivity.

DIALOGUE WITHIN REVELATION

In Christianity's attempt to make peace with the seventeenth-century scientific revolution, it absorbed the logic of individual cases and general principles instead of the logic of particular and universal. The result is that Christianity is burdened with an unworkable language. The distinction between natural religion and revealed religion was novel in the sixteenth century. It led to a logical-sounding distinction between general revelation and special revelations. The assumption in most books on religion, including those of Christian theology, is that Christian revelation is one of those special revelations. Thus, the existence of God is thought to be part of the general revelation, while believing God is three persons in one nature is the puzzling addition that Christianity's special revelation supplies.

The term "Christian revelation" was invented in modern times. "Christian revelation" is unknown to the New Testament, the church fathers, medieval theology, and the Reformation period. Christian revelation may seem to be an acknowledgment by Christians that they share the term "revelation" with Jews and Muslims. Unfortunately, the term does the opposite by setting up a competition. Who has the true revelation? All three claims cannot be equally valid. The way to get tolerance and perhaps some genuine cooperation is to retrieve the traditional language: one God, one revelation. Not general plus special revelations, but one universal revelation that has particular expressions. Christians have a right and a duty to argue for their interpretation of God's revelation/ word. Their interpretation can never be definitive and exhaustive, but it will surely be less deficient if it is aware of Jewish interpretations. The language used by Isaiah and Daniel, or John and Paul, or Aquinas and Eckhart, or Luther and Calvin still has great power. The language of Herbert, Locke, Butler, Voltaire, and Rousseau is dead weight in today's theology books.

The exposition of Jewish, Christian, and Muslim interpretations of revelation, each done in relation to the other two, is still a task for the future. Only occasionally in this book, when it did not seen arrogant and presumptuous, have I referred to Jewish and Muslim histories. The references have more often been to Judaism since the origin of Christianity and the meaning of Christian doctrines are unintelligible without Judaism.

In modern times, Christians and Jews (less so Muslims) were affected by Western enlightenment. Judaism and Christianity did not present a united front in the seventeenth century. Instead of a common opponent, Jews and Christians were set against one another with their special revelations. A Jewish-Christian-Muslim alliance may still be a dream of the future, but the beginning of that alliance is a conversation of Christians, Muslims, and Jews under the rubric of revelation/word of God. That conversation cannot occur while Christians continue to refer to the "Christian revelation."

TEACHING—LEARNING

The key to Christianity's formation of its own members, to dialogue with other religions, and to criticism of secular society is education, including but not restricted to academic instruction. In both Christianity and Judaism, education is often equated with trying to instill answers into children's minds. If revelation is assumed to be written data from the past, then only a few people can and will be trained to read the revealed truth. The rest of the people are told what to think. But if revelation/word of God is understood as a teaching–learning relation, then human teaching is a participation in divine teaching and a person learns by responding to all of God's creatures.

The activity of teaching can be understood in one of two ways. In the first way, a teacher is one who explains something or provides information. On the receiving end, the potential learner may or may not learn. This meaning of teaching has ancient roots, but it is especially prominent in modern times: a teacher is an adult who enlightens children until they can overcome their subservience.

The alternative meaning of teaching is that of showing someone how to do something; most comprehensively, showing someone how to live and how to die. Here there is no teaching without learning, no learning without teaching. Any thing, any event, any animal can be a teacher, although the human community is especially suited for teaching. The human individual is the preeminently teachable animal who can respond freely and intelligently to what is taught.

Revelation is divine teaching that exists only with a human response. Most of God's showing how is in silence and in beauty. When words emerge from the silence and enhance the beauty, there are numerous forms of divine speech. But God does not seem especially concerned with explanations. Mostly the word of God gets expressed in stories wherein the main plot line is discernible while many subplots need filling in. The word of God also takes the form of commands. The central commands are obviously for our own good while lesser commands involve debatable details.

The human's verbal response begins with "amen," and it ends with the same word. In between, the humans are to use all their resources to praise and to thank, to forgive and to be forgiven, to mourn and to comfort. If revelation is the present relation between a God who speaks and a human who responds with all of his or her being, then a multifaceted education of each person is called for: a formation of good habits, an appreciation of art and science, a training for one's work and for political engagement, an assistance in personal and communal prayer.

Notes

Abbreviations of Series
CCSL: Corpus christianorum: Series latina (Turnholt: Brepols, 1954–).
PG: Patrologiae cursus completus. Series graeca (Paris: Garnier, 1857–91).
PL: Patrologiae cursus completus. Series latina (Paris: J.P. Migne, 1844–82).

NOTES TO CHAPTER I

1. *The Concise Oxford Dictionary of the Christian Church*, ed. E. A. Livingstone (London: Oxford University Press, 1977), 438.

2. Michael Barkun, "Politics and Apocalypticism," in *Encyclopedia of Apocalypticism*, ed. Stephen Stein (New York: Crossroad, 1998), 3.442.

3. Some recent titles are Eugen Weber, *Apocalypses* (Cambridge: Harvard University Press, 1999); Alex Heard, *Apocalypse Pretty Soon* (New York: Norton, 1999); Catherine Keller, *Apocalypse Now and Then* (Boston: Beacon Press, 1996); Charles Strozier, *Apocalypse* (Boston: Beacon Press, 1994); Stephen O'Leary, *Arguing the Apocalypse* (New York: Oxford University Press, 1994); one of the best selling books of the last thirty years is Hal Lindsey, *The Late Great Planet Earth* (Grand Rapids: Zondervan, 1977); and a series of eight best sellers on the apocalypse, including Tim La Haye and Jerry Jenkins, *The Indwelling:The Beast Takes Possession (Left Behind, 7)* (New York: Tyndale House, 2000); *The Mark* (New York: Tyndale House, 2000).

4. John Collins, *The Apocalyptic Imagination* (New York: Crossroad, 1984), 1–4; idem, "From Prophecy to Apocalypticism: The Expectation of the End," *Encyclopedia of Apocalypticism*, ed. John Collins (New York: Crossroad, 1998), 129–61.

5. J. L. Austin, *Philosophical Papers* (Oxford: Clarendon Press, 1961), 149.

6. Jacques Maritain, *The Rights of Man and Natural Law* (London: Geoffrey Bles, 1958), 31: "The choice of words in the practical domain is determined not by philosophers, but by the usage of men and by the common consciousness. And what matters above all is rediscovering the genuine meaning and value of words charged with great human hopes, and the tone given to their utterance by a conviction based on truth."

7. Hans-Georg Gadamer, *Truth and Method* (New York: Crossroad, 1989), 415–16: "Every word breaks forth as if from a center and is related to a whole, through which alone it is a word. Every word causes the whole of the language to which it belongs to resonate and the whole view of the world which lies behind it to appear."

8. Friedrich von Hügel, *The Mystical Element in Religion*, 4th ed. (London: James Clark, 1961); for the same point in Judaism, Gershom Scholem, *Major Trends in Jewish Mysticism* (New York: Schocken Books, 1961), 9.

9. Edward Hall, *Beyond Culture* (Garden City: Doubleday, 1976), 16.

10. I think that the constant use of "unique" in Christian theology is reflective of this claim. I examine the peculiar term "unique" in chapter seven.

11. George Mavrodes, *Revelation and Religious Belief* (Philadelphia: Temple University Press, 1988), 91: "So it is not uncommon now that modern theologians favor the view that in revelation God reveals Himself, while earlier theologians are said generally to have held the view that God reveals a set of truths, propositions, or doctrines."

12. Kendrik Grobel, "Revelation and Resurrection," in *Theology as History*, ed. James Robinson and John Cobb (New York: Harper and Row, 1967), 164: "Must we not say that a person *can* only reveal himself by revealing something other than himself, something *about* himself, *pertaining* to himself, but not identical with himself?"

13. For the meaning of God speaking, see Nicholas Wolterstorff, *Divine Discourse* (Cambridge: Cambridge University Press, 1995).

14. Probably the best summary of this debate is Kendrik Grobel, "Revelation as Word and as History," in *Theology as History*, ed. James Robinson and John Cobb, 1–100.

15. Barth's views on revelation are scattered throughout his *Church Dogmatics* (Edinburgh: T&T Clark, 1956); a helpful summary can be found in his essay "The Christian Understanding of Revelation," in *Against the Stream* (New York: Philosophical Library, 1954), 203–40.

16. Karl Barth, *Church Dogmatics*, I/1, 137.

17. Karl Barth, *Against the Stream*, 220, 225.

18. Ibid., 216.

19. Karl Barth, *Church Dogmatics,* on promise: I/1, 107–8; on command: I/1, 90; for the New Testament on this issue, see Ronald Thiemann, *Revelation and Theology: The Gospel as Narrated Promise* (Notre Dame: University of Notre Dame, 1985).

20. Bernard McGinn (*Visions of the End* [New York: Columbia University Press, 1979], 32) takes issue with the image of apocalypticism as a movement from below. He is especially concerned with the false equation of apocalypticism and violent uprisings by peasants. He points out that movements in the Middle Ages were often led by educated people. While keeping his point in mind, I think there is still sufficient reason to use the image of upper and lower paths for the split embodied in the words revelation/apocalypse.

21. Richard Landes, "The Apocalyptic Year 1000: Millennial Fever and the

Origins of the Modern West," in *The Year 2000: Essays on the End* (New York: New York University Press, 1997), 24: "We should acknowledge such impulses as a fundamental part of our world and seek ways to help those 'ridden' by these passions to reenter 'normal time' with irenic contributions to civil society, rather than with the savage violence of suicidal destruction."

NOTES TO CHAPTER 2

1. Pierre Benoit, "Révélation et Inspiration," *Revue Biblique* 70 (1963): 321–70; James Barr, "Basic Thoughts about Biblical Inspiration and Authority," *Escaping from Fundamentalism* (London: SCM Press, 1984), 1–7.

2. Quoted in Lee McDonald, *The Formation of the Christian Biblical Canon* (Nashville: Abingdon Press, 1988), 158.

3. Hans von Campenhausen, *The Formation of the Christian Bible* (Philadelphia: Fortress Press, 1972), 332.

4. Origen, *On First Principles* (New York: Harper Torch, 1966), preface (PG 11:115). For Origen's principles of biblical interpretation, see chapter 3.

5. F. D. Maurice, *The Kingdom of Christ* (London, 1883), 193: "Inspiration is not a strange anomalous fact; it is the proper law and order of the world; no man ought to write, or speak, or think except under the acknowledgment of an inspiration. . . . The question therefore is not really, Were these men who wrote the Scriptures inspired by God? But were they in a certain position and appointed to a certain work?"

6. Emil Fackenheim, *What Is Judaism?* (New York: Collier Books, 1987), 28. Similar sentiments are expressed in regard to the Qur'an by Aziz Lahbabi: "Not the text in itself is the revelation but that which the believer discovers every time afresh while reading it"; see Annemarie Schimmel, *Deciphering the Signs of God* (Albany: State University of New York Press, 1994), 165.

7. This was especially the case in the nineteenth century; see chapter 5.

8. Hayim Perelmuter, *Siblings: Rabbinic Judaism and Early Christianity at Their Beginnings* (New York: Paulist Press, 1989), 19.

9. I use the traditional Christian term "Old Testament" for the Christian reading of this part of their Bible rather than any recently attempted substitution. The problems associated with "Old Testament" cannot be solved by simply replacing the term. James Sanders ("First Testament and Second," *Biblical Theology Bulletin* 17 [1987]: 47–49) proposes what may be an improved language of first/second to replace old/new. Aside from the fact that the replacement is not likely to be widely accepted, replacing the term "Old Testament" may create the impression that Christianity's problematic relation to Jewish religion has been resolved. When referring to the text apart from either Jewish or Christian interpretation I sometimes use "Hebrew Scripture," which is the best compromise available. The larger pattern of change that the problem calls for is addressed in chapter 7.

10. Justin Martyr, *Dialogue with Trypho*, chapter 29 (PG 6:537). John Calvin, *Institutes of the Christian Religion* (Philadelphia: Presbyterian Board of Christian Education, 1936), I, 8, 10, cites Augustine as saying that the Jews are the librarians of the Christian church, because they have furnished us with a book of which they themselves make no sense.

11. An example would be the word "homosexual," which was invented in the 1870s. It is assumed by many Christian bodies that homosexuality or homosexual practice is condemned in the Bible. The Bible has nothing directly to say on the issue. In 1998, the Anglican Bishops at the Lambeth Conference agonized over what to say about the "practicing homosexual," a notion unknown to the author of Leviticus or Paul in his Letter to the Romans (the two texts usually cited). The most relevant text in the Bible might be "love one another." If St. Paul were to be transported to Greenwich Village today he might (after a period of adjustment) see the value in stable homosexual relations. He would still condemn some cases of sex between men, as for example, in our prisons where nearly always it is not homosexual practice but heterosexual rape.

12. Rolf Rendtorff, "The Concept of Revelation in Ancient Israel," in *Revelation as History*, 23–54.

13. Thorlief Boman, *Hebrew Thought Compared with Greek* (New York: W. W. Norton, 1960), 146–47; Heinrich Graetz, *The Structure of Jewish History* (New York: Ktav Publishing House, 1975), 68: "Paganism sees its god. Judaism hears Him; that is, he hears the commandments of His will."

14. Martin Hengel, *Judaism and Hellenism: Studies in Their Encounter during the Early Hellenistic Period*, 2 vols. (Philadelphia: Fortress Press, 1974).

15. Eusebius, *Ecclesiastical History* 5.8.11–14 (PG 19:449).

16. Sidney Jellicoe, *The Septuagint and Modern Study* (Oxford: Clarendon Press, 1968), 76–83.

17. Morton Smith, "On the History of *Apokcalypto* and *Apokalypsis*," in *Apocalypticism in the Mediterranean World and the Near East*, ed. David Hellholm (Tübingen: Mohr, 1983), 10.

18. Martin Jay, "In the Empire of the Gaze: Foucault and the Denigration of Vision in Twentieth-Century French Thought," in *Foucault: A Critical Reader*, ed. David Hoy (New York: Blackwell, 1986), 175–204.

19. F. Gerald Downing, *Has Christianity a Revelation?* (London: SCM Press, 1964), 21–33.

20. Lionel Blue, *To Heaven with Scribes and Pharisees* (London: Oxford University Press, 1976), 63.

21. The phrase "clear and present danger" is from Justice Holmes in Schenck vs. United States, 249 U.S. 47 (1919); the principle was enunciated by John Stuart Mill, *On Liberty* (New York: Norton, 1975), 53.

22. Nicholas Wolterstorff, *Divine Discourse,* 33–37.

23. Emmanuel Levinas, *Difficult Freedom* (Baltimore: Johns Hopkins University Press, 1990), 114.

24. Mary Carruthers, *The Book of Memory* (Cambridge: Cambridge University Press, 1990).

25. On oral tradition and the Pharisees, see Ellis Rifkin, *The Shaping of Jewish History* (New York: Charles Scribner's Sons, 1971).

26. Yves Congar, *The Meaning of Tradition* (New York: Hawthorn Books, 1964); Gershom Scholem, "Revelation and Tradition as Religious Categories in Judaism," *The Messianic Idea in Judaism* (New York: Schocken, 1971), 282–304.

27. Wolfhart Pannenberg uses a seeming redundancy to capture the paradox of tradition as a revolutionary force. He speaks of "the history of the transmission of tradition" to indicate that tradition is transformed in the very act of its being transmitted (or traditioned); see "Response," *Theology as History*, 258. For tradition as central to ethics, see Terry Nardin and David Mapel, *Traditions of International Ethics* (Cambridge: Cambridge University Press, 1992).

28. Gershom Scholem, *Major Trends in Jewish Mysticism* (New York: Schocken Books, 1941), 1–39.

29. John Collins, *Encyclopedia of Apocalypticism*, 1.129; M. Black, *The Book of Enoch or I Enoch* (Leiden: E. J. Brill, 1985).

30. John Collins, *Encyclopedia of Apocalypticism*, 1.134–40.

31. Louis Hartman, *The Book of Daniel* (New York: Doubleday, 1978).

32. See Charles Hill, *Regnum Caelorum* (Oxford: Clarendon Press, 1992), 41.

33. See John Collins, *Encyclopedia of Apocalypticism*, 1.159; Bernard McGinn, *Encyclopedia of Apocalypticism*, 2.103.

34. Jonathan Bishop, *The Covenant: A Reading* (Springfield: Templegate, 1983); Franz Rosenzweig, *Star of Redemption* (New York: Holt, Rinehart and Winston, 1970).

35. Emil Schürer, *A History of the Jewish People in the Age of Jesus Christ*, rev. ed. (New York: Schocken Books), 1973.

36. Thorlief Boman, *Hebrew Thought Compared with Greek,* 201; Hans Jonas, *The Phenomenon of Life* (New York: Dell, 1966), 236; Harry Wolfson, *Foundations of Religious Philosophy in Judaism, Christianity and Islam*, 3rd rev. ed. (Cambridge: Harvard University Press, 1962).

37. Philo's name does not appear in Talmudic literature.

38. Especially Origen; see chapter 3.

39. Philo, *On Drunkenness* (Loeb Classic Library 82; Cambridge: Harvard University Press, 1935), 3.359.

40. Philo, *On Flight and Finding* (Loeb Classic Library 208; Cambridge: Harvard University Press, 1935), 5.123.

41. There was an attempt to integrate the Gospels by Tatian (c. 160–c. 170). It was called the *Diatessaron* and was used in Syrian churches until the fifth century. See Eusebius, *Ecclesiastical History* 3.25.1 (PG 20:401).

42. Hans von Campenhausen, *Formation of the Christian Bible*, 62–63. On the significance of this point, see Robert Pattison, *On Literacy* (New York: Oxford University Press, 1982).

43. Norman Perrin, *The New Testament*, 2nd ed. (New York: Harcourt, Brace, Jovanovich, 1982), especially on Mark's Gospel, 144–45; 162–65.

44. Dale Allison, "The Eschatology of Jesus," in *Encyclopedia of Apocalypticism*, 1.276.

45. Ibid., 267.

46. Johannes Weiss, *Jesus' Proclamation of the Kingdom of God* (Chico, Calif.: Scholars Press, 1985 [1892]).

47. Albert Schweitzer, *The Quest of the Historical Jesus* (New York: Macmillan, 1950 [1906]).

48. Gerd Theissen, *Social Reality and the Early Christians* (Philadelphia: Fortress Press, 1992).

49. John Gager, *Kingdom and Community: The Social World of Early Christianity* (Englewood Cliffs: Prentice Hall, 1975).

50. Morton Smith, "On the History of *Apokalypto* and *Apokalypsis*," 17.

51. Harold Bloom, *Omens of the Millennium* (New York: Riverhead Books, 1996), 30.

52. F. Gerald Downing, *Has Christianity a Revelation*, 72–87.

53. Krister Stendahl, *Paul among Jews and Gentiles* (Philadelphia: Fortress Press, 1976), 7–23.

54. Morton Smith, "On the History of *Apokalypto* and *Apokalypsis*," 15.

55. Plato, *The Republic* 509–13; E. R. Dodds, *Pagan and Christian in an Age of Anxiety* (Cambridge: Cambridge University Press, 1990), 120.

56. John Ziesler, *Pauline Christianity* (New York: Oxford University Press, 1983), 71; Ulrich Wilkens, "The Understanding of Revelation within the History of Primitive Christianity," *Revelation as History*, 87–88.

57. Paul Tillich, *Systematic Theology* (Chicago: University of Chicago Press, 1951), 1.121: "What is essentially mysterious can't lose its mysteriousness when revealed"; see also Karl Barth, *Church Dogmatics*, 1/1, 188.

58. Richard Bauckham, *The Theology of the Book of Revelation* (Cambridge: Cambridge University Press, 1993).

59. Alan Culpepper, *The Gospel and Letters of John* (Nashville: Abingdon Press, 1998).

60. See Raymond Brown, *Community of the Beloved Disciple* (New York: Paulist Press, 1979); Ulrich Wilkens, "The Understanding of Revelation within the History of Primitive Christianity" in *Revelation as History*, 111.

61. Friedrich Nietzsche, *Beyond Good and Evil* (London: Penguin Books, 1973), 80.

62. Friedrich Nietzsche, *The Birth of Tragedy* and *Genealogy of Morals* (Garden City: Anchor Books, 1956), 182.

63. Other examples are *1 Enoch, 4 Ezra,* and *2 Baruch.*

64. Catherine Keller, *Apocalypse Now and Then* (Boston: Beacon Press, 1996), 43–44.

65. See Mary Carruthers, *The Book of Memory.*

66. Eusebius, *Ecclesiastical History* 3.25.1 (PG 19:267), where Eusebius reports that Dionysius accepted the book of Revelation but rejected the authorship of John.

67. Colin Roberts and T. C. Skeat, *The Birth of the Codex* (London: Oxford University Press, 1987).

68. Catherine Keller, *Apocalypse Now and Then*, 87.

69. Adela Yarbo Collins, *Crisis and Catharsis: The Power of the Apocalypse* (Philadelphia: Westminster Press, 1984), 156. See also Elisabeth Schüssler-Fiorenza, *The Book of Revelation: Justice and Judgment* (Philadelphia: Fortress Press, 1985), 199.

70. Diana Eck, *Encountering God* (Boston: Beacon Press, 1993), 96.

71. George Dardess, 'When a Christian Chants the Qur'an," *Commonweal* (Jan. 13, 1995): 17–20; Wilfred Cantwell Smith, "Is the Qur'an the Word of God?" in *On Understanding Islam* (The Hague: Mouton, 1981), 291.

NOTES TO CHAPTER 3

1. Ernst Käsemann, in R. W. Funk, ed., *Apocalypticism* (New York: Herder and Herder, 1969), 40.

2. Norman Cohn (*The Pursuit of the Millennium* [New York: Oxford University Press, 1957]) was very influential in the generalized use of millennial or millenarian for a great variety of social movements in medieval and modern times; Yonina Talmon, "Millenarianism," in *International Encyclopedia of the Social Sciences*, ed. David Sills (New York: Macmillan, 1968), 10.349: "The term is now used not in its specific and limited historical sense but typologically, to characterize religious movements that expect imminent, total, ultimate, this-worldly, collective salvation."

3. John Gager, *Kingdom and Community*, 20–65, for how the term millenarian does and does not apply to the early church.

4. Charles Hill, *Regnum Caeolrum*, 156, 193.

5. Tertullian, *Apology* 39.2 (CCSL 1:150).

6. Tertullian, *Against Marcion* 4.5.2 (PL 2:366): "Habemus et Johannis alumnas ecclesias. Nam etsi Apocalypsim ejus Marcion respuit, ordo tamen episcoporum ad originem recensus in Johannem stabit auctorem."

7. Ovid, *The Fasti* (London: Macmillan, 1929), 340 (book 6, line 619).

8. The one exception is 1 Corinthians 14:26: "apocalypsim habet."

9. Irenaeus, *Against the Heretics* 5.33.4 (PG 7:1210); Eusebius, *Ecclesiastical History* 3.39.11 (PG 20:296). Eusebius calls Papias's millenarianism "bizarre" and "mythological."

10. *Shepherd of Hermas*, 1.5 (PG 2:903).

11. *Shepherd of Hermas*, 3.9 1.1 (PG 2:982).

12. Tertullian, *On Spectacles* 30.1 (PL 1: 660).

13. Tertullian, *Against Marcion* 3.24 (PL 2: 355).

14. Polycarp, *Letter to the Philippians* 7.1 (PG 5:1011).

15. Leslie Barnard, *Justin Martyr: His Life and Thought* (Cambridge: Cambridge University Press, 1967), 158: "His eschatological language varies accord-

ing to circumstances, as with the New Testament writers, and this is the cause of his apparent contradictions."

16. Justin, *1 Apology* 52 (PG 6: 404–5).

17. Justin, *Dialogue with Trypho* 32, 49 (PG 6: 544, 581).

18. Ibid., 81 (PG: 6:668).

19. J. T. Nielsen, *Adam and Christ in the Theology of Irenaeus of Lyons* (Assen: Van Gorcum, 1968), 93.

20. Irenaeus, *Against the Heretics* 5.28.3 (PG 7:1200).

21. Ibid., 5.36.3 (PG 7:1224).

22. Ibid., 5.35.1 (PG 7:1218).

23. Ibid., 5.35.1, 2 (PG 7:1218–21).

24. Lactantius, *Divine Institutes* 7.14 (PL 6:779).

25. Ibid., 7.17, 19 (PL 6:793, 795); the first complete summary of belief in an antichrist is Hippolytus, *Treatise on Christ and the Antichrist*, written near the year 200 (PG 10: 725–88).

26. St. Irenaeus of Lyons, *Against the Heresies* (New York: Paulist, 1992), 11–15.

27. J. N. D. Kelly, *Early Christian Doctrines*, rev. ed. (New York: Harper and Row, 1978). René Latourelle, *The Theology of Revelation* (Staten Island: Alba House, 1966), 145: "The theme of revelation is to be found everywhere. There is no contesting the fact that the theme of revelation is in the foreground of all Christian awareness in the first three centuries." Latourelle may find the *theme* of revelation everywhere, but the *word* revelation is in fact quite infrequent.

28. Justin, *Dialogue with Trypho* 90.2 (PG 6:689); 94.4 (PG 6:700); 100.2 (PG 6:709); 103.3; (PG 6:716); as a noun, 62.4 (PG 6:617).

29. Clement of Alexandria, *Stromata* 5.14 (PG 9:129); *Paedagogus* 2.11 (PG 8:537–40); 1.6 (PG 8:280).

30. Ignatius, *Letter to the Magnesians* 8.2 (PG 5:661).

31. Justin, *Hortatory Address to the Greeks*, chap. 28 (PG 6:292).

32. Justin, *Dialogue with Trypho* 41 (PG 6:564); *I Apology*, 65 (PG 6: 428).

33. Justin, *1 Apology*, 53.3 (PG 6:405).

34. Irenaeus, *Against the Heretics* 1.10.1 (PG 7:549); 3.2.2 (PG 7:847).

35. Ibid., 3.4 (PG 7:855); see also Clement, *Stromata* 1.1(PG 8:686). Irenaeus is the first to unequivocally use "New Testament" and the first to list the four Gospels as canonical; see Hans von Campenhausen, *The Formation of the Christian Bible*, 171–72.

36. Irenaeus is an example of the way René Latourelle (*Theology of Revelation*) attributes a use of "revelation" to the fathers of the church (note 26). Latourelle (p. 103) refers to what Irenaeus says of "the very revelation of the New Testament" or that "the church hands down the revealed truth." In the passages Latourelle cites, Irenaeus refers to tradition, faith, doctrine, and scripture, but not revelation.

37. Irenaeus, *Against the Heretics* 4.6.3 (PG 7:987–88). The parallel text of Matthew 11:25 is Luke 10:21.

38. Franz Jozef Van Beeck, "Divine Revelation: Intervention or Self-Communication," *Theological Studies* 52 (June, 1991): 52.

39. Origen, *First Principles* 2.11 (PG 11:240).

40. Ibid., 2.2.2–3 (PG 11: 187–192).

41. Ibid., 1.6.6 (PG 11:165).

42. Ibid., preface (PG 11:115).

43. Ibid., 2.11.12 (PG 11:240); *Against Celsus* 4.50 (PG 11:1109).

44. Origen, *Commentary on John* 1.38 (PG 14:89); *Against Celsus* 2.71 (PG 11:908).

45. Origen, *First Principles* 4.1.6 (PG 11:352).

46. Ibid., 4.3.8 (PG 11:390), even while he cites Romans 3:2 that "to them was entrusted oracles of God."

47. Ibid., 4.1.1 (PG 11:341).

48. Origen, *Against Celsus* 4.71 (PG 11:1140).

49. Origen, *First Principles* 2.9.4 (PG 11:228).

50. Ibid., 1.1.2 (PG 11:121).

51. Ibid., 3.1.7 (PG 11:260).

52. Werner Jaeger, *Early Christianity and Greek Paideia* (Cambridge: Harvard University Press, 1965), 93.

53. C. Northrop Frye, *The Great Code* (New York: Harcourt, Brace, Jovanovich, 1982), 65.

54. Werner Jaeger, *Early Christianity and Greek Paideia*, 49.

55. See, however, Garry Wills's helpful defense of Augustine on this point (*St. Augustine* [New York: Penguin Books, 1999], 135): Wills points out that Augustine did not harp on sex; his preaching was directed against greed, violence, and deception.

56. Jerome, *Commentary on the Book of Daniel* (PL 25:534); quoted in Robert Lerner, "The Medieval Return to the Thousand Year Sabbath," in *Apocalypse in the Middle Ages*, ed. Richard Emerson and Bernard McGinn (Ithaca, N.Y.: Cornell University Press, 1989), 51.

57. Augustine, *The City of God* 20.7 (CCSL 708).

58. Ibid., 20.17 (CCSL 728).

59. Ibid., 20.9 (CCSL 715).

60. Ibid., 20.8 (CCSL 712).

61. The idea of a time between the Messiah and the general resurrection had been introduced into Judaism in 2 Esdras.

62. *The City of God* 10.14 (CCSL 47:288).

63. Ibid., 20.7 (CCSL 48:708).

64. Augustine, *De doctrina christiana (Teaching Christianity)* (Hyde Park, N.Y.: New City Press, 1996), 3.36 (CCSL 32:111).

65. Erika Rummel, *The Humanist-Scholastic Debate in the Renaissance and Reformation* (Cambridge: Harvard University Press, 1995), 29.

66. *De doctrina christiana* 3. 6 (CCSL 32:83).

67. Brian Stock, *Augustine the Reader* (Cambridge: Harvard University Press, 1996).

68. *De doctrina christiana* 2. 6 (CCSL 32:35); on the need for illumination by the Holy Spirit, *De Gratia Christi* 1.14.15 (PL 44:368).

69. Ibid., 4.7 (CCSL 32:123).

70. Ibid., 1.36 (CCSL 32:29).

71. Ibid., 3.28 (CCSL 32:100).

72. I am indebted in this section to Kathy Eden, *Hermeneutics and the Rhetorical Tradition* (New Haven: Yale University Press, 1997).

73. *De doctrina christiana* 3.21 (CCSL 32:95).

74. Ibid., 3.5 (CCSL 32:82).

75. See Jean Leclercq, *The Love of Learning and the Desire for God* (New York: Fordham University Press, 1974).

76. John Rist, *Augustine* (Cambridge: Cambridge University Press, 1996), 291.

77. There is a famous passage in book 6 of the *Confessions* (New York: Penguin Books, 1961), 114 (CCSL 27:75), where Augustine describes his teacher Ambrose reading without moving his lips. Silent reading was relatively rare, although there are references to it in the centuries before Augustine.

78. *De doctrina christiana* 4.15 (CCSL 32:138).

79. Gerald Bruns, *Inventions: Writing, Textuality and Understanding in Literary History* (New Haven: Yale University Press, 1982), 36.

80. C. Swearigen, *Rhetoric and Irony: Western Literacy and Western Lies* (New York: Oxford University Press, 1991), 204.

81. Phillip Cary, *Augustine's Invention of the Inner Self: The Legacy of a Christian Platonist* (New York: Oxford University Press, 2000).

82. A main theme of the *Confessions* is that God was "deeper in me than I am in me" *(interior intimo meo,* 3:11) (CCSL 27:37). Obviously, Augustine is using inner/outer as metaphorical because he can say, "you were inside me, I outside me" *(intus eras et ego foris,* 10:39) (CCSL 27:190).

83. As an example, see the otherwise superb treatment of Augustine in Charles Taylor, *Sources of the Self* (Cambridge: Harvard University Press, 1989), 127–42.

84. Frank Kermode, *The Sense of an Ending* (New York: Oxford University Press, 1967), 25. Kermode is referring to Rudolf Bultmann's writing, but the principle applies to much of Christian history. For Bultmann, see chapter 5.

85. See Philippe Ariès, *The Hour of Our Death* (New York: Knopf, 1981), for examples of the iconography. Ariès takes the early medieval art as apocalyptic. The interpretation is disputed by Yves Christe; see Bernard McGinn, *The Calabrian Abbot: Joachim of Fiore in the History of Western Thought* (New York: Macmillan, 1985), 85.

86. John the Deacon, *The Life of Gregory the Great* (PL 75:214B); translation in Bernard McGinn, *Visions of the End,* 64.

87. Bernard McGinn, *Visions of the End,* 299 (PL 75:214B).

88. René Dubos, on the Benedictine Order, in *A God Within* (New York: Charles Scribner's Sons, 1991).

89. For Byzantine apocalyptic, see David Olster, "Byzantine Apocalypses," in *Encyclopedia of Apocalypticism*, 2.48–73.

90. Paul Rorem, "The Uplifting Sprituality of Pseudo-Dionysius," *Christian Spirituality I: Origins to the Twelfth Century*, ed. Bernard McGinn and John Meyendorff (New York: Crossroad, 1985), 147–48.

91. John Rist, *Plotinus: The Road to Reality* (Cambridge: Cambridge University Press, 1967), 197; Plotinus, *Enneads* (London: Faber and Faber, 1969), 6.9.10; for a summary of the oral and tactile metaphors in Plotinus, see Gabriel Moran, *No Ladder to the Sky* (San Francisco: Harper, 1989), 54–56.

92. Pseudo-Dionysius, *Mystical Theology* (PG 3:997), cited in Denys Turner, *The Darkness of God: Negativity in Christian Mysticism* (Cambridge: Cambridge University Press, 1995), 22.

93. On the significance of the icon, see Jaroslav Pelikan, *Jesus through the Centuries* (New Haven: Yale University Press, 1985), 90.

94. Paul J. Alexander, "Medieval Apocalypses as Historical Sources," *American Historical Review* 73 (1968): 1997–2018.

95. Arthur J. Arberry, *Revelation and Reason in Islam* (New York: Macmillan, 1957).

96. S. H. Nasr, *Ideals and Realities of Islam* (Boston: Beacon Press, 1975), 53.

97. Mohammad Iqbal, *The Reconstruction of Religious Thought in Islam* (Lahore: Institute of Islamic Culture, 1986), 181; Annemarie Schimmel, *Deciphering the Signs of God* (Albany: State University of New York Press, 1984), 165.

98. Qur'an, 50:16.

99. Bernard McGinn, *Visions of the End*, 70–72; David Olster, "Byzantine Apocalypses," in *Encyclopedia of Apocalypticism*, 2.48–73.

100. M. D. Chenu, *Nature, Man and Society in the Twelfth Century* (Toronto: University of Toronto Press, 1997), 89; one of the Neoplatonic works, *Liber de Causis*, was attributed to Aristotle.

101. Peter Brown, "Society and the Supernatural," *Daedalus* 104 (Spring, 1975): 133–51.

102. Hastings Rashdall, *The Universities of Europe in the Middle Ages* (London: Oxford University Press, 1936), 1.269–583; Alfred Crosby, *The Measure of Reality: Quantification and Western Society 1200–1600* (New York: Cambridge University Press, 1966), 59.

103. Bernard McGinn (*The Calabrian Abbot*, 26) traces a connection between Joachim and the crusades through a meeting with King Richard the Lionhearted in 1191.

104. Joachim of Fiore, *Enchiridion Super Apocalypsim* (Toronto: Pontifical Institute of Medieval Studies, 1986); Bernard McGinn, "John's Apocalypse," in *Apocalypse in the Middle Ages*, 19.

105. He was condemned by the pope in 1255.

106. Frank Kermode, *The Sense of an Ending*, 28.

107. See Eric Voegelin, *New Science of Politics* (Chicago: University of Chicago Press, 1952), 119.

108. Marjorie Reeves, *Joachim of Fiore* (New York: Harper Torchbook, 1977), 7.

109. L. Festinger, H. W. Riecken, and S. Schachter, *When Prophecy Fails: A Social and Psychological Study of a Modern Group that Predicted the Destruction of the World* (New York: Harper and Row, 1956).

110. Marjorie Reeves, *Joachim of Fiore*, 48–49; Norman Cohn, *Pursuit of the Millennium*, 129; David Burr, "Mendicant Readings of the Apocalypse" in *The Apocalypse in the Middle Ages*, 89–102.

111. George Ovitt, *The Restoration of Perfection* (New Brunswick, N.J.: Rutgers University Press, 1986), 187–93; Friedrich Heer, *The Medieval World 1100–1350* (Cleveland: World Publishing, 1962).

112. Bernard McGinn, *Apocalyptic Spirituality* (New York: Paulist Press, 1979), 100: "Joachim did not put himself forward as prophet of a new revelation but as exegete to whom God had granted understanding of the truth revealed but hidden in the Bible."

113. Introduction to *Expositio in Apocalypsim*; in McGinn *The Calabrian Abbot*, 128. The other two ways of God speaking are "historically" and "simple truth."

114. Cited in McGinn, *The Calabrian Abbot,* 146.

115. See M. D. Chenu, *Nature, Man and Society in the Twelfth Century;* Charles Radding, *A World Made by Man: Cognition and Society 400–1200* (Chapel Hill: University of North Carolina Press, 1985); A. N. Whitehead, *Science and the Modern World* (New York: Free Press, 1967), 17.

116. Bernard McGinn, *The Calabrian Abbot*, 209.

117. Ibid., 207.

118. Carl Becker, *The Heavenly City of the Eighteenth-Century Philosophers* (New Haven: Yale University Press, 1932), 20.

119. Peter Coates, *Nature: Western Attitudes Since Ancient Times* (Berkeley: University of California Press, 1998), 50: "[Aquinas] made it quite clear that the 'book of nature' (natural theology) was subordinate and essentially supplementary to the 'book of God' (revealed theology)." What is clear is that this language bears little resemblance to the language of Aquinas.

120. Etienne Gilson, *Reason and Revelation in the Middle Ages* (New York: Charles Scribner's Sons, 1966), 21, 22, 28; 76: "revealed theology"; 64: "revealed religion."

121. Etienne Gilson, Proposition 175 condemns the proposition "Quid lex Christiana impedit addiscere." *Chartularian Universitatis Parisiensis,* ed. Henricus Denifle (Brussels: Culture and Civilisation, 1964), 1.553.

122. Aristotle, *Physics* 202b.

123. Thomas Aquinas, *Summa Theologiae* (New York: McGraw Hill, 1964), 1.1.8; John Jenkins, *Knowledge and Faith in Thomas Aquinas* (Cambridge: Cambridge University Press, 1997), 58.

124. George Lindbeck (*The Nature of Doctrine* [Louisville: Westminster/John Knox, 1984], 123) says that Aquinas is only an "apparent propositionalist" because of the intratextual character of his writing; Alister McGrath, *Genesis of*

Doctrine: A Study in the Foundations of Doctrinal Criticism (Oxford: Blackwell, 1990).

125. Thomas Aquinas, *Summa Theologiae* 1.1.10.

126. Thomas Aquinas, *Sentences of Peter Lombard* (Toronto: Pontifical Institute, 1997), 1.24.1.3.

127. Josef Pieper, *Guide to Thomas Aquinas* (Princeton: Princeton University Press, 1962), 101–2.

128. Karl Rahner, *Spirit in the World* (New York: Herder and Herder, 1968).

129. Thomas Aquinas, *Summa Theologiae* 1.80.3.4; 1.43.6.7; *De Veritate: The Disputed Questions of Truth* (Chicago: Henry Regnery, 1953), 22.2.1. See Karl Rahner, "The Experience of God Today," *Theological Investigations* (New York: Crossroad, 1982), 11.154.

130. M. D. Chenu, *Nature, Man and Society in the Twelfth Century,* 83; Frederick Copleston, *Aquinas* (Baltimore: Penguin Books, 1955), 110; for this theme, see Arthur Lovejoy, *The Great Chain of Being* (Cambridge: Harvard University Press, 1936).

131. Thomas Aquinas, *Summa Contra Gentiles* (Notre Dame, Ind.: University of Notre Dame Press, 1975), 3.40.4.

132. Thomas Aquinas, *Summa Theologiae* 2–2.4.8.2.

133. Ibid., 1.12.13.1.

134. Maimonides, in *Guide of the Perplexed,* cited in Gershom Scholem, *Major Trends in Jewish Mysticism,* 11.

135. Thomas Aquinas, *Summa Theologiae* 1.1.3; see also, *De Potentia* (London: Burns, Oates and Washbourne, 1932), 7.5.14.

136. Thomas Aquinas, *Summa Theologiae* 1.1.9.3.

137. Gershom Scholem, *Major Trends in Jewish Mysticism,* 4; Moshe Idel, *Kabbala* (New Haven: Yale University Press, 1988), 70–72; see also Mary Carruthers, *The Book of Memory,* 165–66.

138. Bernard McGinn, *Meister Eckhart: Teacher and Preacher* (New York: Paulist Press, 1986); Frank Tobin, *Meister Eckhart: Thought and Language* (Philadelphia: University of Pennsylvania Press, 1986).

139. Thomas Merton, *Conjectures of a Guilty Bystander* (Garden City: Doubleday, 1966), 53–54.

140. John Caputo, *The Mystical Element in Heidegger's Thought* (Athens: University of Ohio Press, 1978); Reiner Schürmann, *Meister Eckhart: Mystic and Philosopher* (Bloomington: Indiana University Press, 1978).

141. Thomas Aquinas, *De Veritate* 8.3.

142. Thomas Aquinas, *Summa Theologiae* 1.79.10.3; 1.85.1.4; 1–2.12.1.

NOTES TO CHAPTER 4

1. Ernest Cassirer, *The Individual and the Cosmos in Renaissance Philosophy* (New York: Barnes and Noble, 1963), 10; Amos Funkenstein, *Theology and*

Scientific Imagination from the Middle Ages to the Seventeenth Century (Princeton: Princeton University Press, 1986), 66.

2. Geoffrey Parrinder, *Mysticism in World Religions* (New York: Oxford University Press, 1946), 149.

3. *The Cloud of Unknowing*, ed. James Walsh (New York: Paulist Press, 1981).

4. Johan Huizinga, *The Waning of the Middle Ages* (Garden City: Doubleday, 1954), 224.

5. Ibid., 221.

6. Frank Tobin, *Meister Eckhart*, 122–24, 158.

7. John Caputo, *The Mystical Element in Heidegger's Thought*, 274.

8. Frank Tobin, *Meister Eckhart*, 86.

9. Bruce Kimball, *Orators and Philosophers* (New York: Teachers College Press, 1986), 77–78.

10. James Hillman, *Revisioning Psychology* (New York: Harper and Row, 1975), 195–96; Ernest Cassirer, *The Individual and the Cosmos in Renaissance Philosophy*, 143.

11. Giovanni Pico della Mirandola, *On the Dignity of Man* (Indianapolis: Bobbs-Merrill, 1965).

12. Many authors, including Cusanus and Ficino, assume that this "will to be whatever he wishes to be" is a Christian ideal; some authors mix the ideal with Cicero and Greek myth, as in Juan Luis Vives, *The Fable of Man* (Madrid: M. Aguilar, 1947), and Gianozzo Manetti, *On the Dignity and Excellence of Man* (Padova: Antenore, 1975).

13. Marjorie O'Rourke Boyle, *Erasmus on Language and Method in Theology* (Toronto: University of Toronto Press, 1977).

14. Ibid., 83.

15. Martin Luther, "The Bondage of the Will," in *Discourse on Free Will*, ed. Ernst Winter (New York: Frederick Ungar, 1961).

16. Marjorie Boyle, *Erasmus on Language and Method in Theology*, 21.

17. Kathy Eden, *Hermeneutics and the Rhetorical Tradition*, 72–73; Alfred North Whitehead, *Process of Reality* (New York: Free Press, 1978),160.

18. Erik Erikson, *Young Man Luther* (New York: W. W. Norton, 1958).

19. Elizabeth Eisenstein, *The Printing Press as an Agent of Change* (Cambridge: Cambridge University Press, 1977), 314, 374, 436.

20. John Dillenberger, *Protestant Thought and Natural Science* (Notre Dame, Ind.: University of Notre Dame Press, 1988), 31.

21. Martin Luther, "Treatise on Good Works," in *Luther's Works* (Philadelphia: Fortress Press, 1955), 44.139.

22. *Sermons of Martin Luther* (Grand Rapids: Baker Book House, 1980), 319; "Commentary on John's Gospel," in *Works*, 22.155; in "The Babylonian Captivity of the Church," in *Three Treatises* (Philadelphia: Fortress Press, 1970), 381: "proved revelation."

23. Martin Luther, "Commentary on Psalms," in *Works*, 14.37.

24. Martin Luther, "The Babylonian Captivity of the Church," 128.

25. Martin Luther, "Commentary on Gospel of John," in *Works,* 24.366.

26. Martin Luther, "Commentary on Galatians" (1535), in *Works*, 26.73; similarly in "Commentary on John's Gospel," in *Works*, 24.371 (quote in text).

27. Martin Luther, "Commentary on Psalms," in *Works*, 14.30.

28. Martin Luther, "Commentary on Galatians" (1535), in *Works*, 27.24; "Commentary on Galatians" (1519), in *Works*, 27.171 (quote in text).

29. Martin Luther, "Commentary on John's Gospel," in *Works*, 24.367.

30. Martin Luther, "Commentary on Genesis," in *Works*, 3.150.

31. Ibid., 3.275.

32. Martin Luther, "Commentary on Galatians" (1535), in *Works,* 27.90.

33. Martin Luther, "Commentary on John's Gospel," in *Works*, 24.368.

34. Martin Luther, "Commentary on Genesis,"in *Works,* 4.45; see William Placher, *The Domestication of Transcendence* (Louisville: Westminster/John Knox Press, 1996), 49.

35. Martin Luther, "Bondage of the Will," in *Works*, 23.129; also: "I call both the law and the gospel the words of God," 121.

36. Martin Luther, "Commentary on Galatians" (1535), in *Works*, 27.101; "Commentary on Genesis," in *Works*, 3.120.

37. Martin Luther, "Commentary on John's Gospel," in *Works,* 24.402; in *Werke* (Weimar: H. Bohlau, 1883), 26.93: "Christliche Offenbarung and Predigt."

38. Martin Luther, "Commenary on Galatians" (1535), in *Works*, 26.72.

39. Jaroslav Pelikan, *Vindication of Tradition* (New Haven: Yale University Press, 1984), 65.

40. Jaroslav Pelikan, *Obedient Rebels* (New York: Harper and Row, 1964), 93.

41. Eric Gritsch, *Martin Luther: God's Court Jester* (Philadelphia: Fortress Press, 1983), 105.

42. James Atkinson, *Martin Luther* (Atlanta: John Knox Press, 1968), 243.

43. Norman Cohn, *The Pursuit of the Millennium*, 235–50.

44. Martin Luther, "Commentary on Genesis," in *Works,* 6.481, 488–89.

45. Martin Luther, "An Open Letter to the Christian Nobility of the German Nation concerning the Reform of the Christian Estate," in *Three Treatises*, 54.

46. Heiko Oberman, *The Roots of Anti-Semitism in the Age of Renaissance and Reformation* (Philadelphia: Fortress Press, 1984), 117–19.

47. Heiko Oberman, *Roots*, 105, 320; on "sharp mercy," Eric Gritsch, *Martin Luther,* 140.

48. Edmundo O'Gorman, *The Invention of America* (Bloomington: Univesity of Indiana Press, 1961); Gabriel Moran, "Religious Education toward America," *Religious Education* 72 (Sept./Oct., 1977): 473–83.

49. For Thomas Aquinas, religion is a virtue, part of justice; *Summa Theologiae,* IIa, IIae, 81.4.

50. Quoted in Peter Harrison, *'Religion' and the Religions in the English Enlightenment* (Cambridge: Cambridge University, 1990), 13.

51. Ernest Cassirer, *The Individual and the Cosmos in Renaissance Philosophy,* 71–72.

52. Wilfred Cantwell Smith, *The Meaning and End of Religion* (New York: New American Library, 1964), 39.

53. Karl Barth, *The Theology of John Calvin* (Grand Rapids: William B. Eerdmans, 1995), 114; also Michael Walzer, *Revolution of the Saints* (Cambridge: Harvard University Press, 1965), 26.

54. John Calvin, *Institutes of the Christian Religion* (Philadelphia: Presbyterian Board of Christian Education, 1936), 1.1.47.

55. Karl Barth, *The Theology of John Calvin,* 162, 165.

56. John Calvin, "Commentary on Romans," in *Works* (Edinburgh: Calvin Translation Society, 1849), 12.71.

57. John Calvin, *Institutes of the Christian Religion* 1.6.1.

58. Ibid., 1.7.1.

59. Ibid., 1.1.9.

60. Ibid., 1.1.7.

61. Karl Barth, *The Theology of John Calvin,* 167.

62. John Calvin, *Institutes of the Christian Religion* 1.7.1.

63. Jonathan Smith, "Religion, Religions, Religious," in *Critical Terms for Religious Studies,* ed. Mark Taylor (Chicago: University of Chicago Press, 1998), 275; Peter Harrison, *'Religion' and the Religions in the English Enlightenment,* 39.

64. John Bossy, *Christianity in the West* (New York: Oxford University Press, 1985), 170.

65. Wilfred Cantwell Smith, *The Meaning and End of Religion,* 41.

66. Peter Harrison, *'Religion' and the Religions in the English Enlightenment,* 185 n. 19, for a list of these books; Jonathan Smith, "Religion, Religions, Religious," 269–84.

67. Colin Gunton (*A Brief Theology of Revelation* [Edinburgh: T&T Clark, 1995]) begins the book by asking, "Why are theologians embarrassed by the concept of revealed religion?" Gunton assumes that "revealed religion" is equivalent to "religions of revelation." He does not consider the possibility that theologians have good reason to be embarrassed by "revealed religion."

68. Peter Byrne, *Natural Religion and the Nature of Religion: The Legacy of Deism* (New York: Routledge, 1989), 1, 2.

69. In *Summa Theologiae* 2.2.94.1, Aquinas uses *"physicam theologiam"* referring to the rational as opposed to mythical and civic theology of the Greeks. Aquinas cites Augustine in *The City of God* 18.14 for this use. The first use of "theologia naturalis" that may have relevance to the seventeenth-century is Raymond of Sebond in the mid-fifteenth century: Michael Buckley, *At the Origins of Modern Atheism* (New Haven: Yale University Press, 1987), 69. Note also that Byrne's attributing of "special revelation" to Aquinas is also an anachronism.

70. Edward Herbert, *De Religione Laici,* ed. Harold Hutcheson (New Haven: Yale University Press, 1944), 99.

71 Ibid., 129; see also Edward Herbert, *De Veritate* (Bristol: Arrowsmith, 1937), 303, 308.

72. Edward Herbert, *A Dialogue between a Pupil and his Teacher* (London, 1768), 56.

73. Edward Herbert, *De Religione Laici,* 129; several versions of these articles are found in *De Veritate,* 123, 89, 105–7.

74. Edward Herbert, *De Religione Gentilium* (London, 1705), 31; *A Dialogue between a Pupil and his Teacher,* 57.

75. James Deotis Roberts, *From Puritanism to Platonism in Seventeenth-Century England* (The Hague: Martinus Nijhoff, 1968), 116.

76. Benjamin Whichcote, *Aphorisms,* ed. W. R. Inge (London, 1930), 109.

77. Benjamin Whichcote, *Works* (Aberdeen, 1751), 4.287–89.

78. Benjamin Whichcote, *Works,* 3.50–52.

79. Ralph Cudworth, *The True Intellectual System of the Universe,* 3 vols. (London: Thomas Tegg, 1845).

80. John Dryden, *Religio Laici* (London: Jacob Tonson, 1682), preface.

81. For citations from Robert Boyle's "Usefulness of Natural Philosophy," see David Noble, *The Religion of Technology* (New York: Knopf, 1998), 64.

82. The *Corpus Hermeticum* was translated in 1460 by Marsilio Ficino. It was thought to be the writings of the Egyptian sage Hermes Trismegistus. It was probably written in the later years of the Roman Empire as it shows a Neoplatonic influence. The document was the basis of much of Renaissance magic and later Neoplatonist writing.

83. Quoted in Steven Shapin, *The Scientific Revolution* (Chicago: University of Chicago Press, 1996), 33.

84. Alfred North Whitehead, *Science and the Modern World* (New York: Free Press, 1967), 76: "The clergy were in principle rationalists, whereas the men of science were content with a simple faith in the order of nature."

85. Basil Mitchell, *Morality, Religious and Secular* (Oxford: Clarendon Press, 1980), 85.

86. See Hannah Arendt, *Human Condition* (Chicago: University of Chicago Press, 1958), 260; Ernest Cassirer, *The Individual and the Cosmos in Renaissance Philosophy,* 55; John Dillenberger, *Protestant Thought and Natural Science* (Notre Dame, Ind.: University of Notre Dame Press, 1988), 88.

87. The church granted permission in 1741 for the publication of Galileo's complete works. The whole case was finally reviewed by the church in a statement by Pope John Paul II on Oct. 31, 1992; see William Drees, *Religion, Science and Naturalism* (Cambridge: Cambridge University Press, 1996), 62.

88. Lewis Mumford, *The Myth of the Machine: The Pentagon of Power* (New York: Harcourt, Brace and World, 1970), 57. It is strange that Pope John Paul II (*On the Relationship between Faith and Reason* [Washington: U. S. Catholic Conference, 1998], 52) enthusiastically cites Galileo as saying the same thing as the Second Vatican Council. Galileo, Aristotle, and Pascal are the only secular authors to appear in the pope's 132 footnotes.

89. Quoted in Peter Harrison, *'Religion' and the Religions in the English Enlightenment,* 148; on Leibniz and his universal language, see Stephen Toulmin, *Cosmopolis* (New York: Macmillan, 1990), 100.

90. Margaret Wertheim, *Pythagoras's Trousers: The Ascent of Mathematical Man* (New York: Random House, 1995), 91.

91. Francis Bacon, *The New Organon and Related Writings* (Indianapolis: Bobbs-Merrill, 1960), book I, 62; *Advancement of Learning*, book II, 78.

92. Francis Bacon, *The New Organon,* book I, 88.

93. Francis Bacon, "The Great Instauration," in *The New Organon and Related Writings*, 14–16; in the preface to this work, Bacon refers to the "apocalypse or true vision of the footsteps of the Creator imprinted on his creatures."

94. For discussion of this theme, see Susan Moller, *Women in Western Political Tradition* (Princeton: Princeton University Press, 1979); Genevieve Lloyd, *The Man of Reason: Male and Female in Western Philosophy* (Minneapolis: University of Minnesota Press, 1984), 11–15; William Leiss, *Domination of Nature* (New York: Braziller, 1972).

95. Michael Buckley, *At the Origins of Modern Atheism*, 131; Margaret Wertheim, *Pythagoras's Trousers*, 21.

96. Michael Buckley, *At the Origins of Modern Atheism*, 139.

97. Alexander Pope, "Epitaph on Newton," *Poetry,* ed. L. Untermeyer (New York: Harcourt, Brace, 1934), 430.

98. Basil Willey, *The Eighteenth Century: Studies in the Idea of Nature in the Thought of the Period* (Boston: Beacon Press, 1961), 139.

99. Margaret Wertheim, *Pythagoras's Trousers*, 124; John Dillenberger, *Protestant Thought and Natural Science*, 125.

100. John Locke, *An Essay Concerning Human Understanding* (New York: Everyman's Library, 1961), 4.19.14.

101. Ibid., 4.18.2

102. See Stephen Williams, *Revelation and Reconciliation* (Cambridge: Cambridge University Press, 1995), 27–36.

103. John Locke, *An Essay Concerning Human Understanding,* 2.9.3.

104. John Locke, *The Reasonableness of Christianity* (Stanford: Stanford University Press, 1958), par. 243.

105. John Locke, *The Second Treatise on Civil Government* (New York: Prometheus, 1986), 30.

106. John Locke, *An Essay Concerning Human Understanding,* 4.3.6; 4.10.10.

107. Immanuel Kant, *What Is Enlightenment?* (New York: Liberal Arts Press, 1959), 83–89.

108. Basil Willey, *The Eighteenth Century*, 3.

109. Samuel Clark, *A Discourse Concerning the Unchangeable Obligations of Natural Religion and the Truth and Certainty of the Christian Revelation* (London, 1738).

110. John Toland, *Christianity Not Mysterious* (New York: Garland Press, 1978), "Letter to Serena," fifth letter.

111. Matthew Tindal, *Christianity as Old as Creation* (New York: Garland Press, 1978), 31.

112. Joseph Butler, *Analogy of Religion, Natural and Revealed to the Constitution and Course of Nature* (New York: Nelson and Phillips, 1875), 194–95.

113. Ibid., 273.

114. Arthur Lovejoy, *The Great Chain of Being*, 289.

115. Ibid., 224.

116. Most notably in the eighteenth century is David Hume, *Dialogues Concerning Natural Religion* (New York: Routledge, 1991).

117. Denis Diderot, *Diderot's Early Philosophical Works* (Chicago: Open Court, 1976), 31–32.

118. Diderot: "It is . . . very important not to mistake hemlock for parsley; but to believe or not believe in God is not important at all." Quoted in Michael Buckley, *At the Origins of Modern Atheism*, 225.

119. Michael Buckley, *At the Origins of Modern Atheism*, 225.

120. Paul d'Holbach, *The System of Nature* (New York: Garland Press, 1984), 1.22.

121. Ibid., 2.218.

122. Quoted in Michael Buckley, *At The Origins of Modern Atheism*, 254.

123. Paul d"Holbach, *The System of Nature,* 1.11.

124. Musonius, quoted in Wayne Meeks, *The Moral World of the First Christians* (Philadelphia: Westminster Press, 1986), 48.

125. For a contemporary example of this problem, see Jane Jacobs, *The Nature of Economies* (New York: Modern Library, 2000), ix: "Human beings exist wholly within nature as part of natural order in every respect."

126. Robert Wokler, *Rousseau* (New York: Oxford University Press, 1998), 10.

127. Karl Barth, *Protestant Thought in the Nineteenth Century* (London: SCM Press, 1972), 233.

128. Hannah Arendt, *The Human Condition* (Chicago: University of Chicago Press, 1958).

129. Jean-Jacques Rousseau, *The Confessions* (London: Penguin Books, 1954), 2.43.

130. Jean-Jacques Rousseau, *Emile or On Education* (New York: Basic Books, 1967), 307.

131. Ibid., 303.

132. Jean-Jacques Rousseau, *The Social Contract* (New York: Hafner, 1947), book 4, part 3.

133. Quoted in Ernest Becker, *The Heavenly City of the Eighteenth-Century Philosophers*, 46.

134. Maurice Cranston, *The Noble Savage* (Chicago: University of Chicago Press, 1991), 358.

135. Jean-Jacques Rousseau, *Discourse on Inequality* (New York: Penguin Books, 1984), preface.

136. Jean-Jacques Rousseau, *Emile*, 194.

137. Burke's book is *Letter to a Member of the National Assembly*; see also Louis Mercier, *Rousseau Considered as One of the First Authors of the Revolution*, 1791.

138. Robespierre, quoted in James Miller, *Rousseau: Dreamer of Democracy* (New Haven: Yale University Press, 1984), 132; Bernard Yack, *The Longing for Total Revolution* (Princeton: Princeton University Press, 1985), 83.

139. Alfred North Whitehead, *Science and the Modern World.*

140. Henry May, *The Enlightenment in America* (New York: Oxford University Press, 1976), 99; also Garry Wills, *Inventing America* (Garden City: Doubleday, 1978).

<hr>

NOTES TO CHAPTER 5

1. Georg Hegel, *Lectures on the Philosophy of Religion* (Berkeley: University of California Press, 1984); Immanuel Kant, *Religion within the Limits of Reason Alone* (New York: Harper Torch, 1960); Friedrich Schleiermacher, *Christian Faith* (New York: Harper Torch, 1963).

2. Henry May, *The Enlightenment in America* (New York: Oxford University Press, 1976).

3. Hans-Georg Gadamer, *Truth and Method,* 2nd ed. (New York: Crossroad, 1989), 239.

4. Heinrich Heine, *Religion and Philosophy in Germany* (Boston: Beacon Press, 1959).

5. Karl Barth, quoted in Gabriel Daly, "Revelation in the Theology of the Roman Catholic Church," *Divine Revelation,* ed. Paul Avis (Grand Rapids: Eerdmans, 1997), 26.

6. Friedrich Nietzsche, *Beyond Good and Evil,* 231.

7. Immanuel Kant, *Religion within the Limits of Reason Alone,* 143.

8. Christian Wolff, *Preliminary Discourse on Philosophy in General* (Indianapolis: Bobbs-Merrill, 1963).

9. Quoted in Wayne Booth, *Modern Dogma and the Rhetoric of Assent* (Chicago: University of Chicago Press, 1974), 149.

10. Immanuel Kant, *The Critique of Pure Reason,* 2nd ed. (Buffalo: Prometheus Books, 1990), preface.

11. Immanuel Kant, *Religion within the Limits of Reason Alone,* 131.

12. Ibid., 98–99.

13. Ibid., 162.

14. Ibid., 122.

15. Ibid., 78.

16. Ibid., 102.

17. Ibid., 90.

18. Immanuel Kant, *The Critique of Practical Reason* (New York: Longmans, 1909), 126.

19. Immanuel Kant, *The Critique of Judgment* (Indianapolis: Hackett, 1987), 410; *Religion within the Limits of Reason Alone,* 125.

20. Immanuel Kant, *Religion within the Limits of Reason Alone,* 126.

21. Ibid., 135.

22. Ibid., 11.

23. Friedrich Schleiermacher, *On Religion* (Cambridge: Cambridge University Press, 1988); *Christian Faith: Brief Outline of the Study of Theology;* Edward

Farley, *Practical Theology,* ed. Don Browning (New York: Harper and Row, 1983), 25.

24. Friedrich Schleiermacher, *Soliloquies* (Chicago: Open Court, 1926).

25. Friedrich Schleiermacher, *On Religion,* fifth sermon; *Christian Faith,* 60–62.

26. Friedrich Schleiermacher, *Christian Faith,* 50.

27. Ibid.

28. Ibid., 14.

29. Ibid.

30. Ibid., 50.

31. Ibid., 51.

32. Ibid., 17.

33. Friedrich Schleiermacher, *Soliloquies,* 17.

34. Lewis Hanke, *Do the Americas Have a Common History?* (New York: Knopf, 1964), 267.

35. Timothy Smith, *Revivalism and Social Reform in Mid-Nineteenth-Century America* (New York: Abingdon Press, 1975), 230, 235.

36. Alain Finkielkraut, *Defeat of the Mind* (New York: Columbia University Press, 1995), 18.

37. *Presbyterian Quarterly* 2 (1853): 416; Ernest Lee Tuveson, *Redeemer Nation* (Chicago: University of Chicago Press, 1968), 76.

38. Arthur Lovejoy, *The Great Chain of Being,* 143; Mary Midgley, *Evolution as Religion* (New York: Methuen, 1985).

39. For apocalyptic religion in nineteenth-century Europe, see Eugen Weber, *Apocalypses* (Cambridge: Harvard University Press, 1999), 119–46; Ernest Sandeen, *The Roots of Fundamentalism* (Chicago: University of Chicago Press, 1970), 42: "America in the early nineteenth century was drunk on the millennium."

40. James Moore, *The Post-Darwinian Controversies: A Study of the Protestant Struggle to Come to Terms with Darwin in Great Britain and America* (Cambridge: Cambridge University Press, 1979).

41. Jon Roberts, *Darwinism and the Divine in America: Protestant Intellectuals and Organic Evolution 1859–1920* (Madison: University of Wisconsin, 1988).

42. Ibid., 162.

43. Ibid., 159.

44. George Marsden, *Fundamentalism and American Culture* (New York: Oxford University Press, 1980), 18.

45. Henry Ward Beecher, *Evolution and Religion* (New York: Chester E. Newman, 1885), 44–55.

46. Henry Ward Beecher, *Yale Lectures in Preaching* (New York: J. B. Ford, 1872), 76–84.

47. Henry Ward Beecher in *God's New Israel,* ed. Conrad Cherry (Englewood Cliffs: Prentice Hall, 1971), 213.

48. William Lawrence, cited in *God's New Israel,* 250.

49. Arthur McGiffert, "The Kingdom of God," cited in George Marsden, *Fundamentalism and American Culture*, 50.

50. H. Richard Niebuhr, *The Kingdom of God in America* (New York: Harper Torch, 1959), 193.

51. Leon Festinger, *When Prophecy Fails*, 13–23.

52. *Scofield Reference Bible* (New York: Oxford University Press, 1909), 5.

53. James Carpenter, *Revive Us Again: The Reawakening of American Fundamentalism* (New York: Oxford University Press, 1998), 247–49.

54. George Marsden, *Fundamentalism and American Culture*, 56.

55. Ibid., 60; see also Reuben Torrey, *The Return of the Lord Jesus Christ* (Los Angeles: Bible Institute of Los Angeles, 1913).

56. George Marsden, *Fundamentalism and American Culture*, 56.

57. Karl Barth, who is sometimes associated with fundamentalism, is in agreement with this criticism of fundamentalism as eliminating from the Bible "the form in which it confronts us." In *Against the Stream*, 233, Barth writes, "It is a remarkable contradiction that the very people who make the most extravagant claims for the Bible are thereby being fundamentally unfaithful to it."

58. Vincent Crapanzano, *Serving the Word: Literalism in America from the Pulpit to the Bench* (New York: New Press, 2000).

59. Ibid.

60. Dwight Moody, "The Return of Our Lord," in William McLoughlin, *American Evangelicals 1800–1900* (New York: Harper Torch, 1968), 184–85.

61. Bernard Weisberger, *They Gathered at the River* (Boston: Little, Brown, 1958), 211.

62. Timothy Weber, *Living in the Shadow of the Second Coming* (Chicago: University of Chicago Press, 1987).

63. Henry Emerson Fosdick, "Shall the Fundamentalists Win?" *Christian Century* (June 8, 1922): 22–29; some of the books published after 1917 include: Shailer Matthews, *Will Christ Come Again?* (Chicago: American Institute of Sacred Literature, 1917); George Eckman, *When Christ Comes Again* (New York: Abingdon Press, 1917); James Snowden, *The Coming of the Lord: Will It Be Premillennial?* (New York: Macmillan, 1919); George Prestin Mains, *Premillennialism: Non-Scriptural, Non-Historic, Non-Scientific, Non-Philosophical* (New York: Macmillan, 1920).

64. Edward Larson, *Summer for the Gods: The Scopes Trial and America's Continuing Debate over Science and Religion* (Cambridge: Harvard University Press, 1999).

65. Richard Hofstadter, *Anti-Intellectualism in American Life* (New York: Vintage Books, 1962), 127.

66. Joel Carpenter, *Revive Us Again: The Reawakening of American Fundamentalism*.

67. Martin Heidegger, *Being and Time* (Albany: State University of New York Press, 1996), 190 (sec. 43).

68. Julian Young, *Heidegger, Philosophy and Nazism* (Cambridge: Cambridge University Press, 1997); Hugo Ott, *Heidegger: A Political Life* (New York: Basic Books, 1993).

69. Michael Murray, *Heidegger and Modern Philosophy* (New Haven: Yale University Press, 1978), 294–95.

70. William Richardson, "Heidegger and God—and Professor Jonas," *Thought* 40 (Spring, 1965): 39: "The worst that can be said out of fairness to his philosophy in the context of the Nazi experience is not that his philosophy compelled capitulation but that it was unable to prevent it."

71. Martin Heidegger, *Being and Time*, 131–33 (sec. 30).

72. Ibid., 134–44. (sec. 31–32).

73. Ibid., 49–62 (sec. 12–14).

74. Martin Heidegger, "Letter on Humanism," in *Basic Writings* (New York: Harper and Row, 1977), 230, 245.

75. Martin Heidegger, *Being and Time*, 219–46 (sec. 46–53).

76. Ibid., 236–46 (sec. 52–53); idem, "Language," in *Poetry, Language and Thought* (New York: Harper and Row, 1971).

77. Martin Heidegger, "Conversations on a Country Path," in *Discourse on Thinking* (New York: Harper, 1969), 62.

78. Martin Heidegger, *Principle of Reason* (Bloomington: Indiana University Press, 1991), 96; idem, *Introduction to Metaphysics* (New Haven: Yale University Press, 2000), 69; see Raymond Tallis, *Enemies of Reason* (New York: St. Martin's Press, 1997), 253.

79. Hans Jonas, *The Phenomenon of Life* (New York: Dell, 1966), 248.

80. Martin Heidegger, "Conversations on a Country Path," 62; the interview is in *Der Spiegel* (May 31, 1976).

81. Martin Heidegger, *Being and Time,* 113 (sec. 26): "Dasein in itself is essentially being-with"; for criticism of his *mitseinandersein*, see Zygmunt Bauman, *Postmodern Ethics* (Oxford: Blackwell, 1993), 220.

82. Martin Heidegger, "Letter on Humanism," 209.

83. On his meaning of pre-understanding, see Rudolf Bultmann, "The Historicity of Man and Faith," in *Existence and Faith,* ed. Schubert Ogden (Cleveland: Meridian Books, 1960), 99–100. For criticism of what he presupposes, see Hans-Georg Gadamer, *Truth and Method* (1989), 295–96.

84. Rudolf Bultmann, "The Concept of Revelation in the New Testament," in *Existence and Faith,* ed. Schubert Ogden, 59.

85. Ibid., 88.

86. Rudolf Bultmann, *History and Eschatology: The Presence of Eternity* (New York: Harper Torch, 1957), 152: "Jesus Christ is the eschatological event."

87. Rudolf Bultmann, *Theology of the New Testament* (London: SCM Press, 1955), 2.175.

88. Rudolf Bultmann, *History and Eschatology,* 78–79.

89. Ibid., 79, 78.

90. Rudolf Bultmann, *Jesus Christ and Mythology* (New York: Charles Scribner's Sons, 1958), 76.

91. Rudolf Bultmann, *History and Eschatology,* 151–55; for criticism, see Ernst Bloch, *Atheism in Christianity* (New York: Herder and Herder, 1972), 40;

Herbert McCabe, *What Is Ethics All About?* (Washington: Corpus Books, 1969), 142.

92. Gabriel Daly, "Revelation in the Theology of the Roman Catholic Church," 28.

93. Karl Rahner, *Theology of Death* (New York: Herder and Herder, 1961).

94. Nicholas Lash, *Easter in Ordinary* (Charlottesville: University of Virginia Press, 1988), 165.

95. Karl Rahner, *Belief Today* (New York: Sheed and Ward, 1967), 111; idem, *Foundations of Christian Faith* (New York: Seabury Press, 1978), 14.

96. Karl Rahner, *Freedom and Man* (New York: Herder and Herder, 1965), 217; "Revelation" in *Sacramentum Mundi* (New York: Herder and Herder, 1968), 5.349.

97. George Lindbeck, *The Nature of Doctrine* (Philadelphia: Westminster/ John Knox, 1984), 62: "The notion of an anonymous Christianity present in the depths of other religions is from this [linguistic-cultural] perspective nonsense, and a theory of the salvation of non-Christians built upon it seems thoroughly unreal."

98. Karl Rahner, "Christianity and Non-Christian Religions," *Theological Investigations* (Baltimore: Helicon, 1966), 5.115–34; see also Paul Knitter, *No Other Name* (Maryknoll, N.Y.: Orbis Books, 1985), 128.

99. Karl Rahner, "Thoughts on the Possibility of Belief," *Theological Investigations,* 5.7.

100. Karl Rahner, *Hearers of the Word* (New York: Herder and Herder, 1969).

101. Karl Rahner, "What is a Dogmatic Statement?" *Theological Investigations*, 5.61.

102. Karl Rahner, "Revelation," in *Sacramentum Mundi*, 5.355.

103. Karl Rahner, "The Resurrection of the Body," *Theological Investigations* (Baltimore : Helicon, 1963), 2.213.

104. Martin Buber, *Eclipse of God* (New York: Harper's, 1957), 75–76, for Buber's criticism of Heidegger's comments on the Hebrew prophets.

105. Martin Buber, *I and Thou* (New York: Charles Scribner's Sons, 1958).

106. Ibid.

107. See his comment on his cat in *I and Thou*, 146.

108. Martin Buber, *Hasidism* (New York: Philosophical Library, 1948), 65.

109. Martin Buber, *I and Thou*, 94.

110. Ibid., 63.

111. Martin Buber, *Eclipse of God*, 50.

112. Martin Buber, "The Man of Today and the Jewish Bible," in *On the Bible: Eighteen Studies*, ed. N. N. Glatzer (New York: Schocken Books, 1968), 8.

113. Gabriel Moran, *Scripture and Tradition* (New York: Herder and Herder, 1963).

114. "The Man of Today and the Jewish Bible," 6.

115. Ibid., 8.

116. Ibid.

117. Martin Buber, *Israel and the World* (New York: Schocken Books, 1948),

101: "Suddenly we feel a touch as of a hand. It reaches down to us, it wishes to be grasped—and yet what incredible courage is needed to take the hand, to let it draw us up out of the darkness! This is redemption."

118. Barbara Ellen Galli, *Franz Rosenzweig and Judah Halevi* (Montreal: McGill University Press), 1995.

119. Franz Rosenzweig, *The Star of Redemption*, 379.

120. Critics note that for Judah ha-Levi Christianity is subordinate to Judaism, acting as a preparation for the Messiah among the gentiles; for Rosenzweig, the two are alternate paths. See *The Star of Redemption* (Notre Dame, Ind.: University of Notre Dame, 1985), 395–415; Maurice Bowler, "Rosenzweig on Judaism and Christianity—The Two Covenant Theory," *Judaism* 12 (1973): 475–81. On Islam and revelation, see *Star of Redemption*, 164–66.

121. Franz Rosenzweig, *Kleinere Schriften* (Berlin: Schocken Books, 1937), cited in Bernard Martin, *Great Twentieth-Century Jewish Thinkers* (New York: Macmillan, 1970), 123.

122. "Letter to Martin Buber," in Bernard Martin, *Great Twentieth-Century Jewish Thinkers*, 158; Bernhard Casper, "Franz Rosenzweig's Criticism of Buber's I-Thou," in *Martin Buber: A Centenary Volume,* ed. Haim Gordon and Jonathan Bloch (New York: Ktav, 1984), 139–54.

123. Ibid.

124. Franz Rosenzweig, *Star of Redemption*, 186, 182.

125. "Letter to Martin Buber," 158.

126. Franz Rosenzweig, *On Jewish Learning* (New York: Schocken Books, 1965), 111.

127. *Franz Rosenzweig's "New Thinking,"* ed. Alan Undoff and Barbara Galli (Syracuse, N.Y.: Syracuse University Press, 1999), 99.

128. Richard Cohen, *Elevations: The Height of the Good in Rosenzweig and Levinas* (Chicago: University of Chicago Press, 1994), 36.

129. Franz Rosenzweig and Eugen Rosenstock-Huessy, *Judaism despite Christianity* (Birmingham: University of Alabama Press, 1969), 119–20; the term is used first in his letter to Rudolf Ehrenberg (Nov. 18, 1917) in *Franz Rosenzweig's "New Thinking,"* 46.

130. Franz Rosenzweig, *Star of Redemption*, 405.

131. See especially the work of Jürgen Moltmann, *Theology of Hope* (London: SCM Press, 1967); idem, *The Experiment Hope* (Philadelphia: Fortress Press, 1975).

132. Alan Undoff and Barbara Galli, *Franz Rosenzweig's "New Thinking,"* 93; Abraham Heschel, *The Earth Is the Lord's* (New York: Harper Torch, 1966), 72: "According to the Kabbalah, the redemption is not an event that will take place all at once at the end of days nor something that concerns the Jewish people alone. It is a continual process, taking place at every moment."

133. Franz Rosenzweig, *The Star of Redemption*, 415.

134. In Nahum Glatzer, *Franz Rosenzweig: His Life and Thought* (Philadelphia: Jewish Publication Society, 1953), 346: letter to Rosenstock-Huessy.

NOTES TO CHAPTER 6

1. On the "practical," see Donald Schon, *The Reflective Practitioner* (New York: Basic Books, 1983).

2. Abraham Heschel, *Man's Quest for God* (New York: Charles Scribner's Sons, 1954), 106.

3. Martin Buber, *Between Man and Man* (New York: Macmillan, 1965), 69: "In answering I am given into the power of his grace, but I cannot measure heaven's share in it."

4. Arthur Atkins, *Merit and Responsibility: A Study in Greek Values* (New York: Oxford University Press, 1960), 3; Marion Smiley, *Moral Responsibility and the Boundaries of Community* (Chicago: University of Chicago Press, 1992), 33–57.

5. W. Cantwell Smith, "Responsibility," in *Modernity and Responsibility*, ed. Eugene Combs (Toronto: University of Toronto Press, 1983), 79.

6. René Descartes, *The Philosophical Writings of Descartes* (Cambridge: Cambridge University Press, 1991), 3.99–100, 302–4, 365–66; John Cottingham, "'A Brute to the Brutes?' Descartes' Treatment of Animals," *Philosophy* 53 (1978): 551–59.

7. E. P. Evans, *The Criminal Prosecution and Capital Punishment of Animals* (London: Faber and Faber, 1906).

8. Vicki Hearne, *Adam's Task: Calling Animals by Name* (New York: Knopf, 1986).

9. See the helpful reflections on this point in Alasdair MacIntyre, *Dependent Rational Animals* (Chicago: Open Court, 1999).

10. William Bennett, *The Book of Virtues* (New York: Simon and Schuster, 1994).

11. Martin Heidegger, *The Principle of Reason* (Bloomington: University of Indiana Press, 1991), 96; see also "Language" in *Poetry, Language and Thought* (New York: Harper and Row, 1971), 209.

12. Martin Buber, *I and Thou* (New York: Charles Scribner's Sons, 1958), 115.

13. Martin Buber, "Education," in *Between Man and Man* (New York: Macmillan, 1965), 92: "We practice responsibility for that realm of life allotted and entrusted to us for which we are able to respond, that is, for which we have a relation of deeds which may count—in all our inadequacy—as a proper response."

14. Edward Wilson, *On Human Nature* (Cambridge: Harvard University Press, 1978); G. Stent, *Morality as a Biological Phenomenon* (Berkeley: University of California Press, 1978); for a spirited criticism of today's Darwinism, see Marilynne Robinson, *The Death of Adam* (Boston: Houghton Mifflin, 1998), 28–75.

15. William Schweiker, *Responsibility and Christian Ethics* (Cambridge: Cambridge University Press, 1995), 146–47.

16. *Compact Edition of the Oxford English Dictionary*, 2.2514.

17. Friedrich Nietzsche, *The Birth of Tragedy* and *The Genealogy of Morals* (Garden City: Anchor Books, 1956), 190.

18. Ibid.

19. Friedrich Nietzsche, *Beyond Good and Evil* (Hammondsworth: Penguin Books, 1973), 45.

20. Ibid., 28.

21. See Friedrich Nietzsche, *Will to Power* (New York: Vintage Books, 1968); Hannah Arendt, *The Life of the Mind: Part II: Willing* (New York: Harcourt, Brace, Jovanovich, 1972), 172.

22. Paul Tillich, *The Protestant Era* (Chicago: University of Chicago Press, 1966), 188.

23. Gabriel Marcel, *Philosophy of Existentialism* (New York: Citadel, 1961), 99.

24. Annie Dillard, *Pilgrim at Tinker Creek* (New York: Harper and Row, 1974), 270.

25. Hayim Donin, *To Be a Jew* (New York: Basic Books, 1972), 35: "The overall reason given by the Torah for demanding of the Jew that he follow all its laws and regulations is that Israel become holy."

26. Abraham Heschel, *The Earth Is the Lord's: The Sabbath* (New York: Harper Torch, 1966), 75.

27. Plotinus, *The Enneads* (London: Faber and Faber, 1969); John Rist, *Plotinus: The Road to Reality* (Cambridge: Cambridge University Press, 1967); R. Blaine Harris, ed., *Neoplatonism and Indian Thought* (Norfolk: International Society for Neoplatonic Studies, 1982).

28. Pinchas Lapide, *Jewish Monotheism and Christian Trinitarian Doctrine* (Philadelphia: Fortress Press, 1981), 65.

29. Albert Schweitzer, *Ethics and Civilization* (London: A & C Black, 1923).

30. Aldo Leopold, *A Sand County Almanac* (New York: Oxford University Press, 1989).

31. James Nash, *Loving Nature: Ecological Integrity and Christian Responsibility* (Nashville: Abingdon Press, 1991).

32. L. Thomas, "Human Nature, Love and Morality: The Possibility of Altruism," *Sociobiology and Epistemology*, ed. J. Fetzer (Boston: D. Reidel, 1985); Frans de Waal, *Good Natured: The Origins of Right and Wrong in Humans and Other Animals* (Cambridge: Harvard University Press, 1996).

33. E. O. Wilson, *On Human Nature* (Cambridge: Harvard University Press, 1976).

34. James Watson, *A Passion for DNA* (Cold Spring Harbor, N.Y.: Cold Spring Harbor Laboratory Press, 2000).

35. Richard Dawkins, *The Selfish Gene* (New York: Oxford University Press, 1989).

36. Basil Mitchell, *Morality, Religious and Secular* (Oxford: Clarendon Press, 1980), 127.

37. Dietrich Bonhoeffer, *Ethics* (New York: Macmillan, 1965), 259; Frank Kermode, *Genesis of Secrecy* (Cambridge: Harvard University Press, 1979), 38.

38. Frederick Douglass, *Narrative of the Life of Frederick Douglass* (Cambridge: Harvard University Press, 1967).

39. Amatai Etzioni, *The Spirit of Community* (New York: Crown, 1993), 251–67; Dallin Oaks, "Rights and Responsibility," *The Responsive Community* 1 (Winter, 1990–91): 40.

40. Johannes Morsink, *The Universal Declaration of Human Rights: Origin, Drafting and Intent* (Philadelphia: University of Pennsylvania Press, 1999).

41. Yael Danieli and others, *The Universal Declaration of Human Rights: Fifty Years and Beyond* (New York: Baywood, 1999); on the notion of basic rights, see Henry Shue, *Basic Rights*, 2nd ed. (Princeton: Princeton University Press, 1996).

42. J. G. F. Powell, ed., *Cicero the Philosopher* (Oxford: Oxford University Press, 1995); Thomas Aquinas, *Summa Theologiae*, 2–2. 94.2; John Finnis, *Aquinas: Moral, Political and Legal Theory* (Oxford: Oxford University Press, 1998); Alan Donagan, *The Theory of Morality* (Chicago: University of Chicago, 1977), 1–31.

43. Telford Taylor, *The Anatomy of the Nuremberg Trials* (New York: Knopf, 1992); Martha Minow, *Between Vengeance and Forgiveness* (Boston: Beacon Press, 1999), 29–51.

44. Larry Arnhart, *Darwinian Natural Right: The Biological Ethics of Human Nature* (Albany: State University of New York Press, 1998).

45. Max Weber, "Politics as a Vocation," *On Being Responsible*, ed. James Gustafson and James Laney (New York: Harper and Row, 1968).

46. Ibid., 301.

47. Michael Joseph Smith, *Realist Thought from Weber to Kissinger* (Baton Rouge: Louisiana State University Press, 1986), 53.

48. Ibid., 51.

49. W. A. Visser't Hooft, *The Ten Formative Years 1938–48* (Geneva: World Council of Churches, 1948); *The Evanston Report* (New York: Harper and Brothers, 1955); J. H. Oldham, "A Responsible Society," in *Man's Disorder, God's Design* (New York: Harper, 1948), 3.120–54.

50. José Miguez, *Doing Theology in a Revolutionary Situation* (Philadelphia: Fortress Press, 1975), 29; Ernest Lefever, *Amsterdam to Nairobi* (Washington: Ethics and Public Policy, 1979).

51. H. Richard Niebuhr, *The Responsible Self* (New York: Harper and Row, 1978); *The Meaning of Revelation* (New York: Macmillan, 1962).

52. Agnes Heller, "What Is and What Is Not Practical Reason," in *Universalism vs. Communitarianism*, ed. David Rasmussen (Cambridge: MIT Press, 1990), 166: "The ominous 'Am I my brother's keeper'? is the paragon of the wrong response (for it means the refusal to take responsibility)."

53. Richard Cohen, *Elevations: The Height of the Good in Rosenzweig and Levinas*, 295; Heidegger (*Being and Time,* 114–15 [sec. 26]) addresses this question under the rubric of care; he warns against "leaping in" to take over someone else's concerns, treating a person as a thing. On this one theoretical point, I think Heidegger is more persuasive than Levinas.

54. Eugene Levinas, *Otherwise than Being* (Boston: Kluwer Academic, 1991), 10.

55. Ibid., 84, 87–88; also, *Nine Talmudic Readings* (Bloomington: Indiana University Press, 1990), 85.

56. Dietrich Bonhoeffer, *Ethics*, 233; Paul Feyerband, *Farewell to Reason* (London: Verson, 1971), 155: "If I have a friend, I'll wish to know much about him but my curiosity will be limited by my respect for his privacy."

57. Dietrich Bonhoeffer, *Ethics*, 235.

58. Hans Jonas, *Phenomenon of Life*, 93.

59. Ira Byock, *Dying Well* (New York: Riverhead, 1997); Daniel Callahan, *The Troubled Dream: Living with Mortality* (New York: Simon and Schuster, 1993).

60. Anthony Giddens, *The Transformation of Intimacy* (Stanford: Stanford University Press, 1992), 107–8.

61. Mary Midgley, *The Ethical Primate* (New York: Routledge, 1994), 82: "We are free—not if we do something unpredictable but—if our act is our own."

62. *New York Times* (August 24, 2000): A8.

63. Elisabeth Kubler-Ross, *On Death and Dying* (New York: Macmillan, 1969).

64. Ibid., 40.

65. Dietrich Bonhoeffer, *Ethics*, 226–27.

66. Max Scheler, *On the Eternal in Man* (Hamden, Conn.: Archon Books, 1972), 246–55.

67. Gabriel Moran, *Grammar of Responsibility* (New York: Crossroad, 1996), 113–22.

68. S. N. Eisenstadt, ed., *Max Weber on Charism and Institutional Building* (Chicago: University of Chicago Press, 1968), 155; Hans Jonas, *The Imperative of Responsibility* (Chicago: University of Chicago Press, 1984), 1.

69. Elizabeth Wolgast, *Ethics of an Artificial Person* (Stanford: Stanford University Press, 1992), 9–10.

70. Hannah Arendt, *The Life of the Mind.* Vol I: *Thinking* (New York: Harcourt, Brace, Jovanovich, 1978), 5.

71. Friedrich von Hügel, *The Mystical Element of Religion* (New York: E. P. Dutton, 1923), 1.43.

72. Thomas Aquinas, *Sentences* 2.10.2.1: "The simple necessity of will does not contradict freedom."

73. Michael Polanyi, *Personal Knowledge* (New York: Harper Torch, 1964), 309; Dennis Dennett, *Elbow Room* (Cambridge: MIT Press, 1984), 157.

74. P. W. Duff, *Personality in Roman Private Law* (Cambridge: Cambridge University Press, 1938).

75. Lyall Watson, *Dark Nature: A Natural History of Evil* (London: Hodder and Stoughton, 1995), 264–65.

76. James Coleman, *The Asymmetrical Society* (Syracuse: Syracuse University Press, 1982), 84.

77. Peter French, *Responsibility Matters* (Lawrenceville: University of Kansas Press, 1992), 143.

78. Martin Heidegger, *Being and Time,* 319 (sec. 68); Franz Rosenzweig, *Star of Redemption,* 227–42.

79. "Whoever has the opportunity to protest the misdeeds of his city and does not do so shares in the misdeeds of his city, and whoever has the opportunity to protest the misdeeds of the world and does not do so shares in the misdeeds of the world." *Shabbat* 54b, in *The Talmud* (New York: Paulist Press, 1989), 88.

80. J. R. Lucas, *Responsibility* (Oxford: Clarendon Press, 1993), 77.

81. Nicholas Tavuchis, *Mea Culpa: A Sociology of Apology and Reconciliation* (Stanford: Stanford University Press, 1991), 95.

82. Peter French, *Responsibility Matters,* 145.

83. Educational literature regularly overextends the schoolteacher's responsibility to a responsibility for the student's life and learning; Alan Tom, *Teaching as a Moral Craft* (London: Longman, 1984), 80: "By accepting this obligation to foster desirable outcomes, the teacher assumes responsibility for the student." Carl Rogers, *Freedom to Learn for the 80s* (Columbus, Oh.: Merrill, 1983), 137: "I am simply going to speak personally and raise the question that I would ask myself if I were given responsibility for the learning of a group of children."

84. On the ambiguity of the term "child" and the consequent confusion about children's rights, see Michael Freeman and P. Veerman, eds., *The Ideologies of Children's Rights* (Dordrecht: Martin Nijhof, 1992); Lawrence Houlgate, "Children, Paternalism and Rights to Liberty," in *Having Children,* ed. Onora O'Neil and William Ruddick (Oxford: Oxford University Press, 1979).

85. Edmund Morgan, *The Puritan Family* (New York: Harper Torch, 1966), 91; Bernard Wishy, *The Child and the Republic* (Philadelphia: University of Pennsylvania Press, 1968); Mary Cable, *The Little Darlings* (New York: Scribner's, 1975).

NOTES TO CHAPTER 7

1. Lewis Thomas, *The Medusa and the Snail* (New York: Viking, 1979); Ben Shahn, *The Shape of Content* (New York: Vintage, 1957).

2. Alan Rosenberg and Evelyn Silverman, "The Issue of the Holocaust as a Unique Event," in *Genocide in Our Time,* ed. Michael Dobkowski and Isidore Wallimann (Ann Arbor: University of Michigan Press, 1992); Walter Laquer, *The Terrible Secret* (Boston: Little, Brown, 1981); Lucy Dawidowicz, *The Holocaust and the Historians* (Cambridge: Harvard University Press, 1981); Michael Berenbaum, "The Uniqueness and Universality of the Holocaust," in *Religious and Philosophical Implications,* ed. John Roth and Michael Berenbaum (New York: Paragon House, 1989); Philip Lopate, "Resistance to the Holocaust," *Tikkun* (May-June, 1989). The issue surfaced strongly in discussion of Jonah Goldhagen's *Hitler's Willing Executioners* (New York: Knopf, 1996); see Norman Finkelstein and Ruth Bettina Birn, *A Nation on Trial* (New York: Metropolitan Books, 1998).

3. In Peter Novick, *The Holocaust in American Life* (Boston: Houghton Mifflin, 1999), the author gives a thorough and balanced history of the place of the Holocaust in the recent history of the United States, but he cannot comprehend what the term unique means in the discussion. He calls the claim of uniqueness "offensive," "fatuous," "vacuous," "distasteful."

4. For a summary, see Gabriel Moran, *Uniqueness: Problem or Paradox in Jewish and Christian Traditions* (Maryknoll, N.Y.: Orbis Books, 1992), 25–40.

5. *Gates of Prayer: The New Union Prayer Book* (New York: Central Conference of American Rabbis, 1977).

6. Franz Rosenzweig, *Judaism Despite Christianity* (Birmingham: University of Alabama Press, 1969).

7. Martin Buber, *Israel and the World* (New York: Schocken Books, 1948), 168–69.

8. Calvin Goldscheider and Alan Zuckerman, *The Transformation of the Jews* (Chicago: University of Chicago Press, 1984), 4.

9. David Hartmann, *A Living Covenant* (New York: Free Press, 1985); Marc Ellis, *Beyond Innocence and Redemption* (New York: Harper, 1990),150: "The conflict in Israel and Palestine also challenges the Jewish People to move beyond a particularity that emphasizes uniqueness in order to justify exclusivity."

10. Paula Fredriksen, *From Jesus to Christ* (New Haven: Yale University Press, 1989), 214–15.

11. The comparison to pregnancy is common: William Zinser, *On Writing Well* (New York: Harper and Row, 1980), 42: "Any oaf can rule that . . . being 'rather unique' is no more possible than being rather pregnant."

12. Annie Dillard, *For the Time Being* (New York: Knopf, 1999), 58: "That mass killings and genocides recur on earth does not mean they are similar. Each instance of human, moral evil, and each victim's personal death, possesses its unique history and form." Dillard is right that each death is "unique," but she is surely wrong to say that genocides are not "similar." If there were not similarities, the word "genocide" would not exist. Like so many writers, she misses the paradox of uniqueness. The case is unique; therefore, it is similar to all the others.

13. Emil Fackenheim, *What Is Judaism?*, 24.

14. Paul Tillich, *Systematic Theology* (Chicago: University of Chicago Press, 1951), 1.138.

15. David Novak, *Jewish–Christian Dialogue: A Jewish Justification* (New York: Oxford University Press, 1989), 53.

16. Mircea Eliade, *Images and Symbols* (Princeton: Princeton University Press, 1991), 172; Guilford Dudley, *Religion on Trial: Mircea Eliade and His Critics* (Philadelphia: Temple University Press, 1977), 96.

17. Steven Katz, *Mysticism and Religious Traditions* (New York: Oxford University Press, 1983), 26.

18. Perle Epstein, *Kabbalah* (Garden City: Doubleday, 1978), 55: "When I open the book *Zohar*, I behold the whole universe" (Baal Shem Tov).

19. Yosef Yerushalmi, *Zakhor: Jewish History and Jewish Memory* (Seattle: University of Washington Press, 1982), 42.

20. George Mendenhall, "Covenant," in *Interpreter's Dictionary of the Bible* (New York: Abingdon Press, 1962); Howard Greenstein, *Judaism: An Eternal Covenant* (Philadelphia: Fortress Press, 1983).

21. The Septuagint chose the unusual word *diathēkē* to translate Hebrew *bĕrît*; Dennis McCarthy, *Old Testament Covenant* (Richmond: John Knox, 1972), 1; Delbert Hillers, *Covenant: The History of a Biblical Idea* (Baltimore: Johns Hopkins University Press, 1969), 181.

22. Krister Stendahl, *Paul among Jews and Gentiles*; E. P. Sanders, *Paul, the Law and the Jewish People* (Philadelphia: Fortress Press, 1983).

23. Franz Rosenzweig, *Star of Redemption*, 413–17; Maurice Bowler, "Rosenzweig on Judaism and Christianity—The Two Covenant Theory," in *Judaism* 22 (1973): 475–81.

24. David Novak, *Jewish-Christian Dialogue*, 108.

25. Franz Rosenzweig, *Star of Redemption*, 116–18, 164–66, 215–17.

26. Annemarie Schimmel, *Deciphering the Signs of God* (Albany: State University of New York Press, 1994), 252–53.

27. Ronald Clements, *Abraham and David* (Naperville: Allenson, 1967), 83; John Bright, *Covenant and Promise* (Philadelphia: Westminster Press, 1976), 39.

28. *Sanhedrin* 56a–56b, in *The Talmud*, 209; Frank Crüsemann, *The Torah* (Philadelphia: Fortress Press, 1996), 4; Maimonides, *Mishneh Torah*, XIV, 5, 9, 1.

29. John Bright, *Covenant and Promise*, 128; Delbert Hillers, *Covenant*, 54.

30. Gerd Theissen, *Sociology of Early Palestinian Christianity* (Philadelphia: Fortress Press, 1978), 78–79.

31. Norbert Lohfink, *The Christian Meaning of the Old Testament* (Milwaukee: Bruce, 1968), 46.

32. Andrew Greeley, *The Bible and Us* (New York: Warner Books, 1990), 281: "The only reasonable resolution of the Messiah argument is the conclusion that in some Catholic sense of the word Jesus was a (the) Messiah but in no Jewish sense of the word"; Gerd Theissen, *Sociology of Early Palestinian Christianity*, 108: "The Jesus movement was, however, the first to incorporate the failure of a messianic expectation into a religious belief."

33. Aloysius Pieris, "The Buddha and the Christ," in *The Myth of Christian Uniqueness* (Maryknoll, N.Y.: Orbis Books, 1987), 171; H. Richard Niebuhr, *The Meaning of Revelation* (New York: Macmillan, 1941), 55–56: "Such uniqueness is a characteristic of all events in time and the unique Jesus does not differ in this respect from the unique Socrates and the unique Hitler."

34. James Charlesworth, *Jesus within Judaism* (Garden City: Doubleday, 1989), 45.

35. Geza Vermes, *Jesus the Jew* (Philadelphia: Fortress Press, 1981), 225.

36. Donald Hagner, *The Jewish Relevance of Jesus* (Grand Rapids: Zondervan, 1984), 171–90; on the seven kinds of Pharisees, see *Yerushalmi* 14b, in *The Talmud*, 81.

37. John Howard Yoder, *Politics of Jesus* (Grand Rapids: Eerdmans, 1972).

38. George Lindbeck, *The Nature of Religious Doctrine* (Philadelphia: Westminster Press, 1984).

39. Karl Barth, *Church Dogmatics*, I, 1: "By the thing it calls revelation the Bible always means a unique event, one occurring in that place and at that time." Barth's use of "unique," however, has some flexibility: "Holy Scripture is the record of a unique hearing of a unique call and a unique obedience to a unique command." That use could be more personally inclusive but his main use is tied to a past event.

40. Oscar Cullmann, *Christ and Time* (Philadelphia: Westminster Press, 1964), 121–74; for the most pointed criticism of Cullmann's book, see Rudolf Bultmann, "History of Salvation and History," in *Existence and Faith*, 226–40.

41. Oscar Cullmann, *Christ and Time*, 84.

42. Wolfhart Pannenberg, *Revelation as History*, 144; Oscar Cullmann, *Christ and Time*, 120–21.

43. Paul Kirsch, *We Christians and Jews* (Philadelphia: Fortress Press, 1975), 36–37.

44. Pinchas Lapide, "Is Jesus a Bond or a Barrier?" in *Journal of Ecumenical Studies* 14 (Summer, 1977): 482.

45. In recent times, see the ambitious attempt of Pierre Teilhard de Chardin, *The Future of Man* (New York: Harper and Row, 1964); and idem, *Divine Milieu* (New York: Harper, 1960).

46. Jacob Neusner, *The Incarnation of God: The Character of Divinity in Formative Judaism* (Philadelphia: Fortress Press, 1988), 7: "I understand that the use of the term 'incarnation' may trouble those who regard it as particular ('unique') to Christianity. Theologians invoke the principle of the absolute uniqueness of Christianity. . . . Christians accustomed to regarding the union of divinity and humanity in the person of Jesus Christ, God incarnate, as unique, will address their complaints not to me but to the definition of incarnation I have taken from the most current and standard encyclopedia I could find."

47. *Sanhedrin* 4:5 and 8:4, in *The Talmud*, 15; a similar text is in the Qur'an 5:35: "And if any one saved a life it would be as if he saved the life of the whole people."

48. Karl Rahner, *Foundations of Christian Faith*, 254.

49. Catherine Keller, *Apocalypse Then and Now*, 176.

50. In the past, Protestants claimed that they can encounter God's word directly without the intermediacy of the priest. Catholics claimed that they encounter God directly in the sacraments without the Bible being an intermediary. These days the differences are muted, but it is not evident that thinking about intermediaries has been clarified.

51. Karl Rahner, "Thoughts on the Possibility of Belief," 15.

52. Victor Frankl, *Man's Search for Meaning* (New York: Washington Square, 1985), 99.

53. Konrad Lorenz, *On Aggression* (New York: Harcourt, Brace and World, 1966).

54. Hannah Arendt, *The Human Condition*, 157–58; James Gustafson, *Ethics from a Theocentric Perspective* (Chicago: University of Chicago Press, 1981), 83.

55. M. D. Chenu, *Nature, Man and Society in the Twelfth Century*, 81.

56. Roger Sorrell, *Saint Francis of Assisi and Nature* (New York: Oxford University Press, 1989), 8: For Francis of Assisi, the Bible "asserts the belief in a divine creation, organized according to a plan that is hierarchical and unchanging, with all parts having their established positions and dependent on divine will and action. This was the most fundamental basis for Francis's conception of the natural world."

57. Samuel Beckett, *Endgame* (New York: Grove Press, 1958). Hamm says: "We do what we can." Clov's reply: "We shouldn't."

58. Eric Freyfogle, *Justice and the Earth* (New York: Free Press, 1993), 72, 76; Arthur Lovejoy (*The Great Chain of Being*, 199) describes the eighteenth century's picture of "unique man": "He thus has, after all, a kind of uniqueness in nature, but it is an unhappy uniqueness. He is, in a sense in which no other link in the chain is, a strange hybrid monster."

59. Peter Medawar, "The Uniqueness of the Individual," *The Uniqueness of the Individual* (London: Methuen, 1957), 143–85.

60. Ibid., 185.

61. Carl Degler, *In Search of Human Nature: The Decline and Revival of Darwinism in American Social Thought* (New York: Oxford University Press, 1991), 347: "Even culture, that characteristic once thought to be unique to human nature, can now be seen as having its origin, however rudimentary, in our animal ancestors."

62. John Hick, *Death and Eternal Life* (New York: Harper & Row, 1980), 55.

63. Leo Tolstoy, *A Confession: The Gospel in Brief: What I Believe* (New York: Oxford University Press, 1958), 55.

64. Elisabeth Kubler-Ross, *On Death and Dying*, 276.

65. Karl Rahner, *The Theology of Death*.

66. Caroline Walker Bynum, *The Resurrection of the Body in Western Christianity 200–1136* (New York: Columbia University Press, 1994).

67. Karl Rahner, *Foundations of Christian Faith*, 269; Neil Gillman, *The Death of Death* (Woodstock, VT: Jewish Lights, 1997).

68. Gerard Sloyan, *Jesus in Focus* (Mystic, Conn.: Twenty-Third Publications, 1983), 146.

69. Rowan Williams, *Resurrection* (New York: Pilgrim Press, 1986); Herbert McCabe, *What Is Ethics All About?* (Washington: Corpus, 1969), 142.

70. Northrop Frye, *The Educational Imagination* (Bloomington: Indiana University Press, 1964), 64, writes in referring to *Macbeth*: "If you wish to know the history of eleventh-century Scotland, look elsewhere; if you wish to know what it means to gain a kingdom and lose one's soul, look here."

71. Johann Wolfgang von Goethe, *Maxims and Reflections*, in Walter Kaufmann, *From Shakespeare to Existentialism* (Garden City: Anchor Books, 1959), 54.

72. Steven Toulmin, *Cosmopolis: The Hidden Agenda of Modernity* (New York: Macmillan, 1990), 100.

73. Mary Midgley, *Beast and Man* (New York: Meridian Books, 1980), 306.

74. Franz Rosenzweig, *The Star of Redemption*, 164.

75. Emil Fackenheim, *To Mend the World: Foundations of Future Jewish Thought* (New York: Schocken Books, 1982), 39: "Judaism is 'universalistic' for it teaches that the righteous of all nations enter the Kingdom of Heaven. Christianity is 'particularistic' for it bars from the Kingdom all unsaved non-Christians, no matter how great their righteousness."

76. Jaroslav Pelikan, *Jesus through the Centuries* (New Haven: Yale University Press, 1985), 19: "The very issue of universality which has been taken to be the distinction between the message of Paul and Jewish particularism, was for Paul what made it necessary that Jesus be a Jew."

77. See the reflection on this point with reference to Spinoza and Rosezweig in Emil Fackenheim, *To Mend the World* (New York: Schocken, 1982), 80–81.

78. Paul Knitter, *No Other Name*, 36.

NOTES ON CHAPTER 8

1. Karl Barth, *The Theology of John Calvin*, 158.

2. For a good example of this sequence, see *The Tibetan Book of Living and Dying* (San Francisco: Harper, 1992).

3. Immanuel Kant, *What Is Enlightenment?*

4. For a summary of this literature, see Alan Tom, *Teaching as a Moral Craft*, 15–26.

5. Aristotle, *Physics* 202b; and John Dewey, *How We Think* (New York: D.C. Heath, 1934), 34–35.

6. David Elkind, *Children and Adolescents* (New York: Oxford University Press, 1970), 99.

7. Peter Elbow, *Embracing Contraries* (New York: Oxford University Press, 1986), 70.

8. Kenneth Eble, *A Perfect Education* (New York: Macmillan, 1966), 15.

9. Karl Barth, *Church Dogmatics*, 3.299.

10. Franz Rosenzweig, *The Star of Redemption*, 199–204.

11. David Hartmann, *A Living Covenant: The Innovative Spirit in Traditional Judaism*, 6.

12. *Shabbat* 31a, in *Our Masters Taught*, ed. Jakob Petuchowski (New York: Crossroad, 1982), 32.

13. *Aboth* 6:6, in *The Living Talmud* (Chicago: University of Chicago Press, 1957), 230.

14. Abraham Heschel, *The Insecurity of Freedom* (Philadelphia: Jewish Publication Society of America, 1966), 237.

15. Krister Stendahl, *Paul among the Jews and Gentiles*, 17–18.

16. Jaroslav Pelikan, *Jesus through the Centuries*, 1.

17. John Cobb, *Christ in a Pluralistic Age* (Philadelphia: Westminster Press, 1983), 126.

18. Werner Jaeger, *Early Christianity and Greek Paideia*, 60–86. Jaeger notes (p. 24) that the Septuagint had used *paideia* where the Hebrew meant a chastisement of the sinner that brings about a change of mind.

19. Plato, *Laws* 897b.

20. Clement of Alexandria, *Pedagogue* 1.12 (PG 8:369).

21. Clement of Alexandria, *Stromata* 1.8 (PG 8:736).

22. Ibid., 2.6 (PG 8:964).

   Ibid., 1.1 (PG 8:688).

   Ibid., 1.5 (PG 8:720).

   Ibid., 1.6 (PG 8:728).

   Augustine, *De disciplina christiana* 14 (CCSL 42:223).

   Ibid., 4:12 (CCSL 32:135); Cicero, *The Orator* 21, 69.

   . Augustine, *Retractions* 1:12 (CCSL 57:36); idem, *The Teacher* (Indi-
 .lis: Hackett Publications, 1995), espe. 14.46.20 (CCSL 29:202).

29. This passage in vv. 8 to 12 was directed toward an inner circle of Jesus' disciples. He criticizes the titles of *rabbi, abba,* and *didaskalos,* honorific titles of the time.

30. Augustine, *The Teacher* 1.1 (CCSL 29;157).

31. Ibid., 14.45.5 (CCSL 29:202).

32. Maria Montessori, *The Absorbent Mind* (New York: Holt, Rinehart and Winston, 1967).

33. Carl Rogers, *Freedom to Learn* (Columbus, Oh.: Merrill, 1969); Steven Pinker, *The Language Instinct* (New York: Morrow, 1994), 39.

34. Augustine, *The City of God* 10.14 (CCSL 47:288).

35. Johann Comenius, *The Great Didactic* (New York: Russell and Russell, 1967); Jean-Jacques Rousseau, *Emile.*

36. Conor Cruise O'Brien, *On the Eve of the Millennium* (New York: Ananse, 1995).

37. Thomas Aquinas, *De Veritate* 11.

38. Ibid., 11.1.8.

39. Thomas Aquinas, *Summa Theologiae* 1.2.4; 1.2.6. ad 3; 1.2.9.10.

40. Ibid., 1.80.3.4; 1.43.6.7.

41. Thomas Aquinas, *De Veritate* 22.2. ad 1.

42. Mary Carruthers, *The Book of Memory,* 30, 186.

43. David Burrell, *Aquinas: God and Man* (Notre Dame, Ind.: University of Notre Dame Press, 1979).

44. Augustine, *De doctrina christiana* 1.1 (CCSL 32:6).

45. Josef Pieper, "The Philosophical Act," in *Leisure the Basis of Culture* (New York: Mentor Books, 1952), 108f.

46. Horace Bushnell, *Christian Nurture* (Grand Rapids: Baker Book House, 1979); George Albert Coe, *A Social Theory of Religious Education* (New York: Scribner's, 1928); for Dewey's reflections on revelation, John Dewey, "Christianity and Democracy," in *The Early Works,* vol. 4 (Carbondale: Southern Illinois University Press, 1971), 3–10.

47. Martin Buber, *The Eclipse of God,* 44.

48. Martin Buber, *I and Thou,* 57.

49. Martin Buber, *Two Types of Faith* (New York: Harper, 1961), 57.

50. Martin Buber, *I and Thou,* 63.

51. Ibid., 166.

52. Martin Buber, *The Eclipse of God*, 39.

53. Martin Buber, *Hasidism*, 191.

54. Martin Buber, *The Eclipse of God*, 36.

55. Martin Buber, "The Man of Today and the Jewish Bible," 9.

56. Martin Buber, "Education," in *Between Man and Man*, 89.

57. Martin Buber, "The Question to the Singular One," in *Between Man and Man*, 45.

58. Martin Buber, "Education," in *Between Man and Man*, 88.

59. Martin Buber, *The Eclipse of God*, 95.

60. C. H. Dodd, *Gospel and Law* (New York: Columbia University Press), 1–24.

61. Margo Culley and Catherine Portuges, *Gendered Subjects: The Dynamics of Feminist Teaching* (Boston: Routledge and Kegan Paul, 1985).

62. Gotthold Lessing, "The Education of the Human Race," in *Lessing's Theological Writings*, ed. Henry Chadwick (London: Adams and Charles Black, 1956), 82–83.

63. Brian Vickers, *In Defense of Rhetoric* (Oxford: Clarendon Press, 1988); Takis Poulakis, ed., *Rethinking the History of Rhetoric* (Boulder, Colo.: Westview, 1993); James Kinneavy, *Greek Rhetorical Origins of Christian Faith* (New York: Oxford University Press, 1987).

64. Paul Ricoeur, *Essays on Biblical Interpretation* (Philadelphia: Fortress Press, 1980), 102; David Kelsey, *The Uses of Scripture in Recent Theology* (Philadelphia: Westminster Press, 1975), 39.

65. John Dominic Crossan, *The Dark Interval* (Chicago: Argus Press, 1975), 121–22.

66. Hastings Rashdall, *The Universities of Europe in the Middle Ages*.

67. Alasdair McIntyre, *Three Versions of Moral Enquiry* (Notre Dame, Ind.: University of Notre Dame, 1990), 33, 233.

68. M. D. Chenu, *Nature, Man and Society in the Twelfth Century*, 252.

69. Robert Wilken, *John Chrysostom and the Jews* (Berkeley: University of California Press, 1983), 106: John Chrysostom complains, "What greater disgrace than to walk from the pulpit with blank silence."

70. Wayne Meeks, *The Moral World of the First Christians* (Philadelphia: Westminster Press, 1986), 125.

71. P. E. Kretzmann, *Luther on Education in the Christian Home and School* (Burlington: Lutheran Literary Board, 1940).

72. Dietrich Bonhoeffer, *Ethics*, 283.

73. Bronislaw Malinowski coined the term "phatic communion" for this "yes" or "uh-huh," a kind of speech in which ties are created by the mere exchange of words; see Bronislaw Malinowski, "The Problem of Meaning in Primitive Language," in C. K. Ogden and I. A. Richards, *The Meaning of Meaning* (New York: Harcourt, Brace, Jovanovich, 1989), 296–336.

74. Josef Pieper, *Four Cardinal Virtues* (New York: Harcourt, Brace and World, 1965), 105; Abraham Heschel, *Who Is Man?* (Stanford: Stanford University Press, 1965), 80.

75. G. K. Chesterton, *St. Francis of Assisi* (Garden City: Image Books, 1957), 78.

76. Dietrich Bonhoeffer, *Ethics*, 292.

77. Hannah Arendt, *The Human Condition*, 241.

78. Two examples are the request by the pilot who dropped the atomic bomb on Nagasaki to apologize to the city in 1985 and the apology of the United Church of Canada to the native peoples of Canada. Both apologies were acknowledged and not accepted. See Nicholas Tavuchis, *Mea Culpa: A Sociology of Apology and Reconciliation* (Stanford: Stanford University Press, 1991), 110–111, 150.

79. Martha Minow, *Between Vengeance and Forgiveness* (Boston: Beacon Press, 1999), 52–90; Desmond Tutu, *No Future without Forgiveness* (New York: Doubleday, 1999).

80. P. C. Rosenblat, *Grief and Mourning in Cross Cultural Perspective* (New Haven: Human Relations Area Files, 1976).

81. Thomas Aquinas, *Catena Aurea: A Commentary on the Four Gospels* (Southampton, Eng.: St. Austin Press, 1997), 49.

82. Geoffrey Gorer, *Death, Grief and Mourning* (Garden City: Doubleday, 1965).

83. John Hick, *Death and Eternal Life,* 253.

84. Plato (*Republic* 394–98) worried over this feature of representation

85. Examples would include Samuel Beckett, *Endgame*; Tom Stoppard, *The Real Inspector Hound* (New York: Grove Press, 1968).

86. Wayne Booth, *The Company We Keep* (Berkeley: University of California Press, 1988), 252.

87. Mary Carruthers, *Book of Memory*, 24–25.

88. Plato, *Laws* 537e.

89. Josef Pieper, *Guide to Thomas Aquinas* (New York: Pantheon, 1962), 83.

90. Cicero, *The Orator* 62–64; Philippa Smith "How Not to Write Philosophy: Did Cicero Get It Right?" in *Cicero the Philosopher,* ed. J. G. F. Powell (New York: Oxford University Press, 1995), 308.

91. Alfred Crosby, *The Measure of Reality: Quantification and Western Society 1200–1600* (New York: Cambridge University Press, 1996), 59.

92. *'Erubhin* 13b, in Jacob Petuchowski, *Our Masters Taught*, 41.

93. *Yerushalmi Sanhedrin* 4:2, in *The Talmud*, 11: To Moses' plea that the Lord reveal the final truth, the Lord replies: "There are no pre-existent final truths in doctrine or law; the truth is the considered judgment of the majority of authoritative interpreters in every generation."

94. Lionel Blue, *To Heaven with Scribes and Pharisees* (New York: Oxford University Press, 1976), 86.

95. Thomas Aquinas, *The Literal Exposition on Job*, ed. Anthony Damico (Atlanta: Scholars Press, 1989), 112; Josef Pieper, *Guide to Thomas Aquinas,* 117.

96. Theodore Sizer, *Horace's Compromise* (Boston: Houghton Mifflin, 1992), 126–28.

97. John Stuart Mill, *On Liberty* (New York: Norton, 1975), 36.

Index

Luther, Martin, 78–83, 88, 94, 123, 200; attitude toward Islam, 83; attitude toward Judaism, 83; casual use of "revelation," 78; conflict with Erasmus, 77, 212; on the discovery of America, 83; main uses of revelation, 79–81; prefaces to the book of Revelation, 82; recovery of Christian sources, 78; and *sola scriptura,* 82; on the "word of God," 78–79

Mackintosh, C. H., 112
Maimonides, 70, 73
Malinowski, Bronislaw, 262 n. 73
Mandela, Nelson, 209
Marx, Karl, 101
Marxism, 66
mathematics, 92
May, Henry, 101
McCosh, James, 111
McGinn, Bernard, 227 n. 20, 236 n. 103
Meaning of Revelation, The (Niebuhr), 146
Medawar, Peter, 184
mediation, 180–81
Meditations (Descartes), 77
Meister Eckhart, 62, 74, 76, 81
Mencken, H. L., 115
Mersenne, Marin, 92
Merton, Thomas, 74
Messiah, 49, 179; relationship to the term Christ, 179
metaphors: in Aquinas, 73; of eating, 41, 74; of going up to God, 60–61; in Meister Eckhart, 76; of vision, 24–26, 31, 68
Methodius of Patara, 64
Midgley, Mary, 186
Mill, John Stuart, 214, 229 n. 21

millenarian/millennialist movements, 46–47, 56, 82, 161, 232 n. 2
Millerites, 112
modernity, 102, 162
monasteries: and preservation of ancient texts, 62; reading at meals, 74
Montessori, Maria, 197
Moody, Dwight, 114
moral, the, as aspect of the practical, 133
Mormons, 112
Mumford, Lewis, 91–92
Muntzer, Thomas, 82
"my brother's keeper," 147
Mystical Theology (Pseudo–Dionysius), 75
mysticism: challenge to scholastic reason, 76; flowering of, 75–76; Jewish, 27, 169. *See also* Neoplatonism
mystery: meaning of, 37; paradox of, 38; Paul's use of, 38

natural law, 145
neo-orthodoxy, 167, 168
Neoplatonism, 62–63, 88, 141; as alternative to mathematics, 90
Newton, Isaac, 90–91, 93–94, 96, 97, 98; proof of God's existence, 94
Niebuhr, H. Richard, 111–12, 146
Nietzsche, Friedrich, 39–40, 103, 118; concept of the human as a "responsible animal," 139
North Africa, as the "Bible belt of Christianity," 55
Novick, Peter, 256 n. 3
Nuremberg trials, 145

Old Testament, 22, 23; as traditional term, 44, 228 n. 9